Dreaming Identities

CULTURAL STUDIES

Series Editors
Janice Radway, Duke University
Richard Johnson, University of Birmingham

DREAMING IDENTITIES

IDENTITIES

Class, Gender, and Generation in 1980s Hollywood Movies

Elizabeth G. Traube

Westview Press

Boulder • San Francisco • Oxford

Cultural Studies

Copyright © 1992 by Westview Press, Inc.

Published in 1992 in the United States of America by Westview Press, Inc., 5500 Central Avenue, Boulder, Colorado 80301-2847, and in the United Kingdom by Westview Press, 36 Lonsdale Road, Summertown, Oxford OX2 7EW

Library of Congress Cataloging-in-Publication Data
Traube, Elizabeth G.
  Dreaming identities : class, gender, and generation in 1980s
Hollywood movies / Elizabeth G. Traube.
    p. cm. — (Cultural studies)
  Includes bibliographical references and index.
  ISBN 0-8133-1313-9 — ISBN 0-8133-1314-7 (pbk.)
  1. Sex role in motion pictures.   2. Patriarchy (Psychology)—
United States—History—20th century.   3. Middle classes—United
States—Attitudes.   4. Femininity (Psychology)—United States—
History—20th century.   5. Feminism and motion pictures.
6. Motion picture audiences.   I. Title.   II. Series.
PN1995.9.S47T73   1992
791.43′655′09048—dc20   92-7248
                                                                           CIP

Printed and bound in the United States of America

The paper used in this publication meets the requirements
of the American National Standard for Permanence of Paper
for Printed Library Materials Z39.48-1984.

10   9   8   7   6   5   4   3   2   1

Contents

5 Who Will Do the Caring? Domestic Men and Independent Women in the Movies

Acknowledgments

THE ESSAYS COLLECTED in this volume were written over the last seven years. Over the course of that period, what began as a critical response to a particular movie developed into a new research interest in contemporary American mass culture, which I continue to pursue. The interdisciplinary atmosphere promoted at the Wesleyan Center for the Humanities made this reorientation possible. Faculty fellowships at the Center provided time for research, and three of the essays were originally written for and presented at events sponsored by the Center. Moreover, the Center brought to Wesleyan diverse scholars involved in cultural studies, including Carl Freedman, Neil Lazarus, Michael Denning, Gyan Prakash, Nancy Armstrong, Fred Pfeil, Janice Radway, Judith Goldstein, Michael Sprinker, Susan Willis, and Leonard Tennenhouse, and I have benefited greatly from their expertise. For all this and more, I am grateful to Richard Vann and Richard Ohmann, who served as directors of the Center during the 1980s.

The Center also provided a context in which a group of Wesleyan faculty members met to discuss and design a program in cultural studies, in the process generating a spirit of collective endeavor that still endures. I thank all who participated in the study group over the years, especially Hazel Carby, Alex Dupuy, Akos Östör, Richard Slotkin, Richard Stamelman, and Khachig Tölölyan.

To Sally Banes and Noël Carroll, who were also members of the study group, I owe a very special debt. We watched movies together, argued over interpretations, discussed theories, and exchanged manuscripts. As the only person in cinema studies who was closely involved in my work, Noël provided encouragement of special value to me, and I have drawn extensively on his writings in developing my ideas. Sally was in all respects the most generous reader I could ever hope to find, and these essays owe much to her critical insights.

Special thanks are due to three other people. Without Moishe Postone, I would never have undertaken this project, and although he may have seen only one of the movies discussed in these essays, he has enriched my understanding of all of them. Bruce Greenwald encouraged me, as only he can do, through his critical appreciation and his appreciative criticism. To my mind, Karen Bock coauthored the final chapter in this volume; the writing is mine, but my thought developed in the course of our collective reception of popular movies and television shows to the point where I can no longer clearly separate her ideas from my own.

Many other friends have contributed in various ways, by reading manuscripts, discussing movies, and by taking a general interest in my work. In particular, I thank Marilyn Arthur, Vincent Crapanzano, Alice Himelstein, Gail Kligman, David Konstan, Ellen Rooney, and Elisabeth Young-Bruehl.

For editorial advice offered prior to first publication of several of the chapters, I thank Julia LeSage, Tony Pippolo, Michael Fischer, George Marcus, Arjun Appadurai, and Carol Breckenridge.

At the Wesleyan Center for the Humanities, I drew on the professional skills and generosity of Pat Camden and Jackie Rich. I am also grateful to Joanne Palmer and Valborg Proudman for their assistance at various stages in the preparation of this volume.

My editor at Westview, Gordon Massman, has proved as efficient as he was enterprising and enthusiastic. I owe special thanks to Richard Johnson for his detailed and immensely helpful comments on the manuscript.

I have benefited as much from Victoria Traube's intelligent, well-reasoned skepticism as from her industry contacts. While we participate in different stages of the cultural circuit, I think our common involvement in mass entertainment has helped to bring us closer. I thank my mother, Mildred Traube, who puts up with my lectures on the movies and with much more besides. I dedicate this book to my father, Shepard Traube, who once feared that I would become an actress, was delighted when I went into anthropology, and surely never expected me to become a critic of the movies. He would probably have said of these essays that I take Hollywood's products more seriously than he did, but I know that he would have been proud.

Elizabeth G. Traube

Credits

EARLIER VERSIONS of four of the chapters in this book were published in the following journals. Permission to reprint them is gratefully acknowledged.

Chapter 1   *Jumpcut* 30 (1985): 12–14.

Chapter 2   *Persistence of Vision* 3, no. 4 (1988): 71–94.

Chapter 3   *Cultural Anthropology* 4, no. 3 (1989): 273–300. Reproduced by permission of the American Anthropological Association. Not for sale or further reproduction.

Chapter 4   *Public Culture* 3, no. 2 (1991): 1–28.

Permission to reprint excerpts from the following songs is also gratefully acknowledged.

p. 44   "It's a Long Road," from the motion picture *First Blood*. Lyrics by Hal Shaper; music by Jerry Goldsmith. Copyright © 1982 by Anabasis Music/Elcajo Music; administered worldwide by Anabasis Music. All rights reserved. Used by permission.

p. 48   "Brothers in the Night," from the motion picture *Uncommon Valor*. By Ray Kennedy, David Ritz, and Kevin Dukes. Copyright © 1983, 1984 by Famous Music Corporation and Ensign Music Corporation. Used by permission.

p. 55   "Peace in Our Life," from the motion picture *Rambo: First Blood, Part Two*. Lyrics by Frank Stallone; music by Frank Stallone, Peter Schless, and Jerry Goldsmith. Copyright © 1985 by Anabasis Music/Carolco Music/Elcajo Music/Val Songs Music/Lincoln Pond Music. All rights administered by Anabasis Music and Carolco Music. All rights reserved. Used by permission.

Introduction

WRITING A BOOK about the movies was the last thing on my mind. I just wanted to have some fun. It was a Saturday night in Chicago during spring 1984, and I went with two friends to a midnight showing of *Indiana Jones and the Temple of Doom* (hereafter referred to as *Indiana Jones*), which had just been released.

I had enjoyed *Raiders of the Lost Ark* tremendously and was looking forward to the "prequel." My friends, I suspect, went along largely to humor me, but we were all in high spirits, anticipating a good time. A few hours later we were huddled in a neighborhood bar, our expectations thwarted. We stayed until dawn, trying to dispel the intense displeasure that the movie had aroused in us. Critical analysis offered a means to that end, a substitute for the entertainment we had gone looking for but had not found. From our frustration and the discussion it precipitated grew the article that appears as Chapter 1 in this volume.

At the time, my friends and I took it for granted that our negative responses to the movie were conditioned by our lives outside the movie theater. To use terms that I learned only later on, as social spectators we had found the spectator positions constructed in the text so uncomfortable that we could occupy them only fitfully, if at all. This viewpoint would not have struck us as controversial, for we were not film critics and knew nothing of the debates that had characterized that field since the mid-1970s.

Although we were disturbed by the movie and remained preoccupied with it for several weeks (to the bemusement of our colleagues), it was not because we attributed special powers to mass entertainment cinema. "Cinematic apparatus" was not a term in our theoretical vocabulary, and we never thought movies had unconditional capacities to control the subjectivity of their audiences. We did assume that there were

1

ideological messages embedded in the movie that had aroused our indignation and that these messages tended to be left unarticulated by mainstream critics and ordinary viewers alike, who receive Hollywood's products as "entertainment."[1] What concerned us, however, was not beliefs the movie might be imposing on audiences but the sociohistorical moment in which audiences appeared to be receptive to its ideological appeal. In short, we suspected or, to be more precise, we feared that George Lucas and Steven Spielberg's latest blockbuster had something to tell us about America in the Reagan era.

Our intellectual backgrounds no doubt disposed us to relate movies to larger contexts. An anthropologist by training, I habitually refer cultural narratives to other social practices and to the ideological matrices out of which meaningful practices are generated. Moishe Postone, one of my two companions and the coauthor of the chapter on *Indiana Jones and the Temple of Doom,* is a social theorist whose main project at that time was a reinterpretation of Karl Marx's *Capital.* We were used to treating ideological discourses as dimensions of wider social struggles, and it was Moishe's insight into how struggle inscribed itself within the movie that organized our analysis.

Since our essay first appeared, a good deal has been written about the ideological project embodied in Lucas and Spielberg's Star Wars and Indiana Jones movies (Rubey 1978; Ryan and Kellner 1988; Biskind 1990). Critics have shown how the two trilogies affirm regressive, backward-looking values at multiple levels, while packaging their nostalgic message for consumption by a high-tech, middle-class audience; and they have suggested, as did we, that in celebrating a represented return to innocence, the movies anticipated and reinforced the rightward turn in American political culture.[2] What we foregrounded in our interpretation of *Indiana Jones* was the movie's own inadvertent resistance to its regressive trajectory. By "reading against the grain," as I have since learned to call the interpretive practice, we detected the traces of an alternative narrative that, we argued, could have subverted the dominant narrative of return to an idealized earlier state.[3]

In the dominant narrative, order entails the subordination of women to men and of colonized races to their colonial rulers, and these relationships are coded as homologous. But while the movie uses the device of reviving an earlier genre to conceal its lighthearted racism from itself, it seemed to us to have considerable difficulty in resolving the patriarchal component of its plot.

On the one hand, an underlying fear of female sexuality rises so close to the surface of the narrative that it threatens to overwhelm the romantic subplot. As Peter Biskind (1990: 132) has since observed, it is difficult to avoid concluding that in the temple scene Indy's unconscious wish is to see the heroine die. According to our interpretation, on the other hand, the same segment also reveals and conceals an opposite desire, which is to be reunited with the nurturing woman in a relationship of mutual recognition. Although this utopian wish finds only indirect representation, it survives the forces that repress it, manifesting itself in the form of a momentary disturbance in the unfolding of the dominant narrative.

It is, of course, for the reader to decide if our interpretation is convincing. What I want to pursue here are its theoretical bases and implications. For us, the tensions that we detected within the movie pointed toward contradictory tendencies in the larger society. These, I concede, we evoked rather than explored, for we had not undertaken in that article to integrate film criticism with the interpretation of political culture. We simply wanted to suggest that if the Reagan administration and its New Right allies proposed to restore an idealized past, when authority was securely vested in white, male, middle-class Americans, there were multiple sites of resistance to this conservative ideology that were recognized to different degrees in Hollywood movies. Lucas and Spielberg had set out to create a new mythology for the disaffected 1960s generation to which they belonged. As their project unfolded, it steadily lost such countercultural content as it had initially contained and became increasingly, albeit unintentionally, complicit with the rehabilitation of patriarchal authority underway within the state (Biskind 1990). At the same time, if only through the violence with which it had to be repressed in the trilogies, a contending vision struggled for expression, a vision of a world free of gender domination, a world in which fear of otherness would be transcended.

In the studies that I conducted over the following years, which are now brought together in this book, I continued to look for that other vision. Most of the time I found myself commenting on its absence, tracing the multiple ways in which Hollywood movies made during the 1980s confounded rebellion with submission, resistance with incorporation, equality with privilege, the collective with the individual interest. Nevertheless, I also caught glimpses of an emergent ideal, partially blocked by the movies themselves, yet also present in them as a utopian possibility that viewers can abstract and hold in their imagination.

*   *   *

Readers familiar with contemporary debates about mass culture may recognize the characteristic formulation of what has become known as a "cultural studies" approach. And indeed, as I began to focus my research on mass market Hollywood movies, it was to cultural studies that I increasingly turned. By Chapter 3 that turn is explicit, and I articulate a version of the theoretical model that continues to guide my research. In this model, mass culture appears as a "contested terrain," to use the now-fashionable phrase, a site where producers and receivers of cultural commodities engage from different positions and with unequal resources in a multifaceted struggle over meaning. In emphasizing contestation and struggle, cultural studies positions itself between the two poles of a debate over mass culture that it seeks to transcend. At one pole of that debate mass culture is viewed as the property of its producers, the elites who control what have come to be known as the culture industries. In this viewpoint, developed by the cultural critics of the Frankfurt School and also represented in the Althusserian-Lacanian paradigm as applied to film studies, mass culture appears as an instrument for ideological manipulation, a form of social control through which false or inauthentic beliefs are reinforced and inculcated in audiences. At the other pole, where the reference is usually to "popular culture," the object of study is viewed as the property of receiving audiences and taken as a faithful expression of collective beliefs and values. From this populist, audience-centered perspective, what is involved is a new mythology, a unifying belief system that may be produced by media professionals in highly concentrated industrial centers but belongs, nevertheless, to the people who receive it.

The critical move in cultural studies is to replace these symmetrically opposed and partial viewpoints with a model that comprehends the different moments or stages of cultural processes, what Richard Johnson describes in a well-known, state-of-the-art essay as a "circuit of the production, circulation and consumption of cultural products" (1986–1987: 46). Once mass culture is viewed from the perspective of a total circuit, neither its producers nor its receivers appear as its sole possessors. Thus, as Johnson argues, the producers of cultural commodities must draw upon ongoing social experience for raw materials, selectively borrowing elements of meaning from lived cultures, reworking them, and incorporating them into commercial cultural products. Such products, however, are raw materials for their receivers, "who make their own *re*-appropriations of the elements first borrowed from their lived culture and forms of subjectivity" (1986–1987: 52).

One consequence of the circuit model is that, while the distinction between cultural commodities and lived cultures takes on enhanced analytical importance, it does not represent distinct, rigidly bounded domains. Michael Denning has made this point forcefully in an important article entitled "The End of Mass Culture" (1990). As precise as his title is polemical, Denning's argument aims to reconstitute the object of knowledge. Commenting on Stuart Hall's "Notes on Deconstructing 'the Popular'" and Frederic Jameson's "Reification and Utopia in Mass Culture," both from 1979, Denning observes that these theorists do not abolish the antinomy between control and expression, the ideological and the utopian, the manipulative commercial product and the authentic cultural creation but rather relocate it within mass culture itself. What this implies in Denning's formulation is not that all cultural commodities necessarily contain subversive moments but that "mass culture" no longer names the "other" to more "authentic" forms of cultural expression. Instead it designates the historically unfolding dialectic between the culture produced in commodity form by the culture industries (and the state apparatuses) and the diverse social groups, differentiated by class, race, gender, and generation, that receive such commodities and reappropriate them into their own cultural productions.

Reception is always an event. It unfolds in time and place, and it involves concrete persons—actual audiences whose responses to cultural commodities are mediated by their particular sociohistorical circumstances and by the interpretive resources that they bring to their viewing experiences. But cultural commodities, especially media representations, also lead what Johnson (1986-1987: 51) calls a "separated existence" as texts, suspended between the original conditions of their production and the ever-changing moments when they are actually consumed or received. Apprehended as texts, media representations can be interrogated for their formal properties. Text-based studies informed by the circuit model of culture analyze textual pressures or constraints on receiving audiences, the "conditions and possibilities of reading," as Christine Gledhill (1988: 74) calls them, which can be abstracted from particular narrative forms and genres.

Contrary to some reception theorists (Fiske 1991), I do not believe that the social "relevance" that audiences may read into a text is independent of its structural organization.[4] Although actual processes of text reception are not unilaterally controlled by textual structures, they are never entirely autonomous of them. Indeed, one type of experience that spectators bring to any viewing involves their prior encounters with other texts, through which they acquire a practical mastery in following textual cues.[5] By this account the capacity of a text to "position" its audiences is neither absolute nor insignificant but is realized only through the cultural competencies that audiences possess.

To recognize the active role of audiences in constructing textual meanings is not to ignore or deny the influences exerted by texts.

Cultural studies relies on a model of social spectators who actively and variably respond on the basis of prior experiences to cues structured into texts. By contrast, the dominant paradigm in film studies assumes a fundamentally passive spectator whose "positioning" entails subjection to the text's inherent powers.

This latter paradigm, which I will refer to as Althusserian-Lacanian, emerged in France among theorists enthralled with the productivity of semiotic systems. During the 1970s it came to dominate film studies in both Britain and the United States through the medium of such journals as *Screen* and *Camera Obscura*. Its dominance is breaking up in the early 1990s, partly as a result of counterarguments coming from other modes of film criticism and from cultural studies. Central to the debate are what critics see as the inattention to history in the dominant paradigm, especially in its psychoanalytic version, which tends to treat the symbolic as the only dimension of power. Marxist as well as psychoanalytic versions of the paradigm share a reluctance to distinguish the textual from the social spectator, which justifies a neglect of reception studies and promotes a general overvaluation of the ideological effects of film. Indeed, as Noël Carroll has observed in his book *Mystifying Movies* (1988: 88), if contemporary Althusserian-Lacanian film theory were to be believed, Hollywood movies are almost solely responsible for the positioning of capitalist subjects. Their ideological potency, moreover, is supposed to derive from certain formal features of what contemporary film theorists call classical realist cinema.

A central argument, advanced in different versions by Stephen Heath (1981), John Ellis (1981), Christian Metz (1982), and other film theorists, is that linguistic categories derived from Emile Benveniste (1971) can be transferred to the classical Hollywood cinema and used to unmask its ideological effects. The primary distinction in Benveniste's linguistic theory is between the utterance (*l'énoncé*) and the enunciation (*l'énonciation*). The utterance is a finished string of discourse, a combination of elements into a whole of varying length. Enunciation is the process of creating an utterance, which includes a speaker, a listener, a worldly referent, a context or situation, as well as the linguistic means that the speaker puts to use. A secondary distinction has to do with whether or to what degree a given utterance bears the marks of its enunciation, by including or excluding reference to the speaker and/or the context, for instance. On this basis, Benveniste distinguishes two modes of enunciation. In what he calls "discourse," the enunciative act is inscribed in the utterance—for example, by the use of first and second person pronouns or other shifters. By contrast, "history" or "story" (the French *histoire* conveys both senses) makes no overt reference to its production. Its authorless appearance is said to create the impression that events are narrating themselves without the intervention of a speaker.

In adapting these categories, film theorists reinflected the concept of the historic mode by identifying classic realist film as a discourse that does not merely omit but conceals or effaces the marks of its enunciation. In other words, realist films falsely present themselves as *histoire,* narration without a speaker, when in actuality, they are discursive and are authored by the camera's "look" or "gaze." Viewers, the argument continues, are encouraged to take the apparently authorless realist film as reality narrating itself without ideological bias. Moreover, viewers are induced to identify themselves with the absent or disguised enunciator, which is to say they assume the look of the camera. From the deceptive transparency of realist films and the covert positioning of the viewer by the camera is said to derive much of the classical cinema's ideological effect.

Carroll (1988) questions the philosophical assumptions of contemporary film theory and finds the model of the cinematic apparatus implausible in numerous respects. The model, he argues, misrepresents the experience of spectators, and it fails to account for important principles of narration in fiction films. Actual movie audiences, he contends, do not believe that films are authorless representations and that reality is somehow narrating itself, nor do they identify uniformly with the camera.[6] Moreover, with respect to the mode of cinematic narration, many realist films are overtly discursive as opposed to historic, making use of fictional narrators who address the audience or even alluding to their actual production by occasionally baring their own devices. Films also vary in what David Bordwell (1985: 59–61) calls their communicativeness, the range of knowledge about the narrated events that they make available to the audience. As Carroll (1988: 159–160) observes, it is difficult to square the claim that spectators identify with the absent enunciator with the film's ability to withhold knowledge from us regarding the story.[7]

Whereas Carroll's philosophical critique is developed from the viewpoint of an alternative model of cinematic narration and film viewing, criticism emanating from cultural studies is grounded in the circuit model of cultural production. From this viewpoint what is protested is the tendency of the dominant paradigm to abstract cultural commodities from their sociohistorical contexts of production and reception. Much of the recent debate has focused on questions raised by feminist psychoanalytic film criticism concerning female spectatorship and the representation of women in the classic narrative cinema.

Over the course of the 1970s, feminist film criticism swung sharply toward the "ideological" pole in the mass culture debate and assumed an attitude of uncompromising hostility toward "patriarchal Hollywood." At the time this turn took place, the "utopian" pole of the debate was occupied by sociologically oriented studies of the "images of women" in popular films, of which the most influential remains Molly Haskell's *From Reverence to Rape,* first published in 1975.[8] While studies of this latter type were not uncritical, the operating assumption was that the representation of women in Hollywood films had changed over time, under the influence of social forces, and the authors looked for more "positive" images among the "negative" ones that predominated. By a "positive" image, sociologically minded feminist critics intended strong, active, independent heroines, who reflected progressive social tendencies and could serve as role models for female spectators.

Such considerations were rather magisterially swept aside by the Lacanian paradigm that ruled feminist film criticism for a decade. In the version of the cinematic apparatus model that Lacanian feminists developed, the manipulative "look" of the camera, or "the gaze," as it became known, is understood to be gendered. More specifically, the charge levied against the classic narrative cinema is that the gaze it privileges is male, and the female spectator who takes pleasure in its products is accused of participating in her own subjugation.

The strongest formulation of this critique is Laura Mulvey's much discussed essay, "Visual Pleasure and Narrative Cinema," which first appeared in 1975. Mulvey's thesis is that Hollywood films reproduce and perpetuate male domination through their visual codes. Men, she argues, are the active bearers of the gaze in Hollywood films, and women are its passive objects, an asymmetry that is supposedly constructed through the agency of the camera and reinforced by the respective narrative functions of male and female characters. Men drive the cinematic narrative forward, usually along an oedipal trajectory, confronting and overcoming assorted obstacles. From time to time they pause for a moment (and the action pauses with them) in order to contemplate the spectacle that is woman. According to Mulvey, the camera's "gaze" encourages male and female spectators alike to look with the man in the film as he looks at the woman.

To account for the joys of looking (her self-defined problem in the article), Mulvey turns to psychoanalysis, which has a theory of visual pleasure.[9] Through a somewhat tortuous Lacanian logic, she argues that since contemplation of the female form inevitably arouses castration anxiety in men, cinematic images of women threaten to undermine the very pleasure they are supposed to provide. But castration anxiety can be managed through fetishism and voyeurism, and Mulvey posits cinematic strategies that correspond to these perverse psychic strategies. To reduce the psychic threat posed by female icons, films either transform the women they represent into beautiful fetish objects, disavowing the threat by denying women's lack, or alternatively, they denigrate women and subject them to voyeuristic controls, thereby enabling the male spectator to take a sadistic pleasure in their contemplation.

The implications of this argument for female spectators are grim. On the one hand, what women represent in films are the psychosexual anxieties of men; women are projections of the male unconscious, alternately idealized as passive objects (fetishism) or sadistically disparaged (voyeurism). On the other hand, since the tyrannical camera compels female spectators to view female characters from these male perspectives, women are limited to the masochistic pleasure of watching their own objectification or denigration. The end result, according to Mulvey, is that in enjoying Hollywood films, women are positioning themselves as obedient patriarchal subjects, and she proposed an avant-garde feminist countercinema as an instrument of subversion.[10]

Although Mulvey modified her position slightly in subsequent essays (1977, 1981), she remained committed to her model of patriarchal Hollywood, and it has proved both influential and controversial. During the 1980s, the field of feminist psychoanalytic film criticism split into those who defended and extended the model and those who sought to modify it in important ways. This latter group, in which I would include Teresa de Lauretis (1984), Linda Williams (1987 [1984]), and Tania Modleski (1988a), took up the problem of the female spectator, rejecting Mulvey's claim that Hollywood films are either exclusively or unambiguously in the service of male viewing pleasure and arguing that female spectatorship is a more complex process than Mulvey's model allowed. Hollywood, in their critiques, no longer appears as monolithically patriarchal. Repression of female subjectivity is the dominant tendency of mainstream cultural production, according to these critics, but it could also be resisted from within cultural products themselves.

The focus of these critics was not the historically situated viewing audience but the spectator positions constructed in cinematic texts. Through close and persuasive readings of particular Hollywood films, they argued that classic realist works could offer distinct positions for female viewers and give expression to "a specifically female desire" (Modleski 1988a: 2). Concentration on genres designed for female audiences played a key role in precipitating these reassessments. Thus Williams (1987 [1984]) offered her interpretation of a maternal melodrama as an intervention in the theoretical debate, and Modleski (1984) had conducted a study of popular romances before attempting to recuperate Hitchcock's films for feminist theory.

Two interrelated claims characterize these rethinkings. First, the existence of a "female look" is posited as a central narrative feature of particular films and a distinctive source of pleasure for female spectators. In *Stella Dallas* (1937), according to Williams, there is an appeal to a "female reading competence" that has roots in pre-oedipal experience. Drawing on Nancy Chodorow's (1978) work in feminist object relations psychoanalysis, Williams traces the viewing practices of female spectators to the role of the mother-daughter bond in subject formation. Girls, in Chodorow's model, sustain the early identification with the mother, which boys are required to repudiate, and thus their entry into the oedipal triangle is relatively continuous with the pre-oedipal stage. In Williams's reading of the theory, this asymmetry seems to work to the advantage of women, enabling them to take pleasure in emotional connectedness with other women, as well as in relationships with men.[11] *Stella Dallas,* she continues, makes use of this socially inculcated capacity for attunement by instructing female spectators to identify with the multiple spectator positions inscribed in the text. As a result, Williams argues, spectators are caught in a textually structured contradiction. While the film asks them to accept its patriarchal resolution—Stella's maternal sacrifice of herself to her daughter's happiness—it simultaneously encourages them to experience that sacrifice as fundamentally unjust.

From this interpretation follows a second claim, which is that mainstream films can reveal the tensions for women of existence under patriarchy. That argument is further developed by Modleski, who extends it beyond films addressed specifically to women and challenges Mulvey's model of the sadistic male spectator. In *The Women Who Knew Too Much* (1988a), Modleski argues that the apparently misogynistic films of Alfred Hitchcock are driven by a profound ambivalence toward femininity. Although she does not mention feminist object relations theory, she effectively pursues the other side of Chodorow's model, the problematic implications for men and women alike of a masculinity based on repudiating and repressing identification with the mother.

Not all psychoanalytic feminists accepted these rethinkings of gendered film spectatorship. E. Ann Kaplan, whose own interpretation of *Stella Dallas* was implicitly at issue in Williams's essay, responded with strong reaffirmations of the unadulterated, phallic power of the cinematic "gaze."[12] In *Women and Film: Both Sides of the Camera* (1983), Kaplan had laid out a strict Lacanian model of patriarchal subject positioning. Hollywood films, in her view, are instruments of control, operating systematically to repress any pre-oedipal or "nonsymbolic" aspects of femininity that might pose a threat to the phallocentric order. Rejecting the new concern with "the female spectator," Kaplan denied that films could be viewed differently by men and women, and she defined the task for feminist film criticism as the analysis of "patriarchal myths (that) function to position women as silent, absent, and marginal" (1983: 34). In this model neither "the patriarchal cinema" nor patriarchy itself has a historical dimension. In Kaplan's Lacanian discourse the oedipal repression of female sexuality and reproduction of phallic power is a transhistorical process that endlessly repeats itself in Hollywood films.

At this stage of the debate, however, both sides relied exclusively on psychoanalytic models of cinematic pleasure. While the respective models had different implications for film spectatorship, a common assumption was that texts could be analyzed independently of their historical contexts of viewing. What varied was that for Kaplan textual meaning was univocal, whereas Williams, Modleski, and others found multiple and contradictory interpretive possibilities structured into the texts they studied. Unlike Kaplan, moreover, they assumed that reading competence varied between women and men, thus calling attention to spectatorial activity as well as textual constraints. However, variation was defined solely in terms of sexual difference as a product of the gendered asymmetry in oedipal socialization, not as conditioned by any other social experiences. It was as if all that men and women brought with them into a movie theater, or what they regressed to, as the Lacanian model would have it, were their earliest psychosexual fears and desires.

The next move—from my perspective, a critical one—suggests the influence of cultural studies on feminist film criticism. Stated briefly, the move was to supplement attention to the textual spectator, the subject positions constructed in a text, with a new concern for the social spectator, the actual audiences who attend particular films at specific historical moments. What is restored to film criticism with this refocusing is the social world in which films are produced and received, the world outside and prior to the movie theater, which penetrates cultural products at two moments in their circuit.

In part, this marks a return to the much disparaged project of the "images of women" approach, which was to connect particular cinematic tendencies to wider social currents. What facilitated the temporary displacement of sociological by psychoanalytic film criticism was a problematic tendency in the former to construct this relationship in oversimplified terms, to see film as a reflection rather than a mediation of its social context. To Lacanian feminists caught up in analyzing the textual production of meaning, any attempt to address the sociohistorical referents of cinematically represented events then came to appear as evidence of "reflectionism," that shameful index of semiological naïveté.[13]

Fortunately the denial of the social did not go unchallenged. Unfortunately, however, feminist interest in film spectatorship as a social activity has sometimes been accompanied by a refusal to consider its psychosexual dimensions. A blanket hostility to psychoanalytic explanation characterizes certain 1980s approaches to cultural analysis, as if to reciprocate for the Lacanian indifference to history and condescension toward sociological method.[14] Yet there is a nonreductive way of connecting psychic regimes to sociohistorical processes. In this viewpoint, desire takes its meanings from the multiple social forces that pattern it, which extend beyond the family to other social relations of power and subordination. As Lynne Segal argues: "[W]hat we need to explore is how meanings—especially the significance accorded to the phallus—intersect with the historically specific and changing power relations between women and men within the wider social structures and practices that produce them" (1990: 92). To my mind the most productive positions are those, like Segal's, that avoid polarizing the psychic and the social dimensions of cultural production, so as to confront instead the project of their integration.

Within feminist film criticism both Linda Williams and Christine Gledhill have made interventions that I find particularly helpful. In her contribution to the volume *Female Spectators* (1988, edited by E. Deirdre Pribram), Williams first contrasts sociological and psychoanalytic approaches to the representation of women in film. Observing that the first tradition has looked for the *reflection* of sociohistorical conditions in cinematic images of women, while the other has approached film as an instrument for the *repression* of women, Williams proposes to "look instead at the way . . . film reflects *and* represses the contradictions of its historical moment" (1988: 21). The move to transcend the methodological opposition is reminiscent of cultural studies, as is the analysis in which Williams relates the ideological complexity of Michael Curtiz's *Mildred Pierce,* originally released in 1945, to the contradictory historical situation of its female viewers.[15]

What the film seeks to repress, she argues, is not the transhistorical threat of the feminine but historically particular tensions in gender and class relations that the war had unleashed. For its female audiences Mildred's economic independence reflected their own lived experiences of relative autonomy and achievement during a war that is only indirectly represented in the film. Initially, Williams suggests, absence of direct reference to the war makes possible a stronger expression of the exhilarating aspects of women's new power than would have been acceptable to the dominant ideology of national unity in everyday life. But if the film covertly reflects a pleasurable sense of empowerment that more overt representations of "home-front matriarchy" denied, it also requires "a much more massive *repression* of that power" (1988: 24). To the 1945 woman viewer the perverse character assigned to Mildred's power in the plot prepares the way for the film's attempt to manage the anxieties that it arouses. In Williams's analysis these are not universal psychic anxieties but concerns about women's position under patriarchy that arose at a historically specific moment, when certain unprecedented opportunities that had been made available to women were about to be closed off. Says Williams:

> Thus the lesson of *Mildred Pierce* is neither the eternal repression of the feminine nor its realistic reflection, but very specific, and historically changing, forms of repression and reflection that operate hand in hand. [It] is to say that current feminist hindsight can often get in the way of seeing the real ideological conflicts experienced by the historical viewer and managed by the text. (1988: 28)

Like Williams, in this volume I view Hollywood films from the perspective of a particular historical moment and specific ideological conflicts that it produced for women and men. As she does, I try to identify the distinctive ways in which socially lived concerns are absorbed into and managed in mass-cultural texts. Another particularizing, contextualizing strategy that I pursue is articulated by Christine Gledhill, also in *Female Spectators,* and involves identifying the diverse social audiences to whom films appeal.

Gledhill has consistently and cogently criticized Lacanian feminist film theory, or "cine-psychoanalysis," as she calls it. In "Developments in Feminist Film Criticism," a slightly revised version of a 1978 article that appeared in the 1984 volume *Re-Vision* (edited by Mary Ann Doane, Patricia Mellencamp, and Linda Williams), she warned of the danger for feminist criticism in defining its object solely in terms of the cinematic production of meaning. If the critic avoided a vulgar reflectionism by this means, she also ran the risk of losing the ability to connect cinematic representations of women to femininity as a socially lived experience, defined by an array of social practices. With this caveat Gledhill rejected the Lacanian privileging of language as the unique site for the production of identities, arguing that multiple historical, social, and economic forces not only produce women but differentiate them along lines of race and class. From this perspective feminist film theory has two problems: to account for how sexual difference intersects with other differences, and to explore how systems of representation such as film interact with other power relations in social life.[16]

Gledhill pursues her critique of cine-psych in "Pleasurable Negotiations," her contribution to *Female Spectators*. Even more strongly than Williams, she insists on the distinction between the feminine spectator, constructed by the text, and the female audience, constructed and differentiated by sociohistorical categories of class, race, gender, and generation. "The question now confronting feminist theory," she continues, "is how to conceive their relationship" (1988: 67).

Gledhill's proposal is that we reconceptualize the relationship of media texts to receiving audiences as a process of "negotiation," which she defines as a process of struggle between competing frames of reference, motivation, and experience. What underpins this model is not the monolithic and irresistible "dominant ideology" of Althusserian-Lacanian theory, ruthlessly interpolating subjects into a symbolic order, but the concept of "hegemony" developed by Antonio Gramsci (1973, 1985) and now central to cultural studies. What is predicated of ideology in a hegemony model is that it must be continually reproduced, which is to say internalized in some degree by subjects whose consciousness it never exhausts, who may resist or contest it in various ways. In Gledhill's terms, hegemonic ideologies are "not simply imposed . . . but are subject to continuous (re)negotiation" (1988: 8).

Gledhill goes on to argue with other cultural studies theorists that negotiation or struggle can be apprehended at each stage in the circuit of cultural forms, from production to reception. Her own focus is on the analysis of "textual negotiations," the multiple and contending possibilities of meaning embedded in a text as these might appear to particular social subjects. As I understand her, what Gledhill is proposing is a mode of textual criticism designed to complement ethnographic studies of text reception. To determine "the political *effects* of textual ideologies," she concedes, requires ethnographic inquiry into the actual uses made of cultural forms by particular receivers, on the model of Janice Radway's (1984) pioneering study of romance readers. But texts, Gledhill continues, "are not open to any and every interpretation," as I also argue in this volume. For the textual critic committed to a circuit model, the task is to tack between specific textual practices and their potential, socially located receivers, "suggesting what [texts] are capable of generating for different social audiences" (1988: 74).

A recent and ambitious text-based study with a sociohistorical dimension is Jackie Byars's *All That Hollywood Allows* (1991), an analysis of representations of gender in Hollywood melodramas of the 1950s.

Drawing on cultural studies as an alternative to cine-psych, Byars offers a series of intriguing interpretations of 1950s melodramas. Her strategy is to isolate tensions, contradictions, and ambiguities in classical films—to point out, for instance, how often the narrative resolutions fail to close off the questions generated in the plots. Contextualized in a portrait of the 1950s as a period of struggle, when many women were quietly resisting the cult of domesticity and returning to the work force, these readings explore how struggle unfolds at the level of the text. In opposition to the cine-psychoanalytic critique of patriarchal Hollywood, Byars argues for what she calls a "recuperative" approach that "enables us to hear the strong, feminine, resisting voices even within mainstream cultural artifacts" (1991: 20).

All That Hollywood Allows is an extremely interesting book. Byars critically reviews debates within feminist film theory, and she offers suggestive readings of the oppositional meanings conveyed in mainstream cultural forms. Yet I am reluctant to identify cultural studies too closely with the "recuperation" of "resisting voices," on the one hand, and I would have liked more analysis of the class dimensions of those voices, on the other. To take the second point, both class and race figure in Byars's analyses largely as signifiers, ways in which different versions of femininity are distinguished in the films.[17] In other words, they operate as textual categories, called upon to supplement the interpretation of particular films, not as sociohistorical categories by which audiences are constructed. That working-class people and minorities are often used as symbols of the past in Hollywood movies is certainly true, but to comment on such symbolism is not constitutive of "a class analysis," as Byars suggests.

Moreover, while it may be comforting to think that cultural studies can keep itself busy retrieving the subversive moments embedded in popular cultural forms, I would argue that cultural studies has as much or more to tell us about how oppositional meanings from lived culture are absorbed, defused, and contained within dominant forms—in short, about how hegemonies are continually renegotiated. Not recuperation but the circuit model is the hallmark of cultural studies. Consequently, I am uncomfortable with Byars's (1991: 137) suggestion that most films (those that reinforce dominant ideologies) are adequately explained by cine-psych, whereas a "significant minority" (those that offer resistance) need to be handled in other ways.

Finally, I simply note that Byars and I put the same psychoanalytic theory to different uses. Independently of developments in feminist film theory, of which I was at first unaware, I began to draw on object relations psychoanalysis. Unlike both Byars and Williams, however, I do not use the theory to identify a "female gaze" in films that center on communities of women. Nor is the thrust of the theory, as I understand it, to offer "a positive reassessment of female development" (Byars 1991: 142), although I would agree that it asks us to revalue activities that have traditionally been regarded as woman's domain. But perhaps because my understanding owes more to Jessica Benjamin in *The Bonds of Love* (1988) than to Nancy Chodorow or Carol Gilligan, I take the object relations model of gender development as a critique of male and female socialization alike, a model of how gender polarity damages males and females in symmetric ways. What concerns me with respect to Hollywood films is how often over the 1980s they appealed to regressive desires for a protective paternalism by condensing feminine or feminized power with early psychosexual fears of the engulfing mother.

*   *   *

What I have just presented is an outsider's account of feminist film theory. Retrospectively I can identify approaches more or less consistent with my own; Gledhill's work, in particular, informs the final chapter in this volume. But my project took shape independently of the debates over cine-psych, and it led me initially into other areas of research.

Especially in the first chapters, I give less attention to specifically cinematic techniques of narration than to the provenance of the stories that films tell. What initially drew me to the movies analyzed in Chapters 2 and 3 was their status as reworkings of central cultural myths. *Rambo: First Blood, Part Two* (hereafter referred to as *Rambo*) and the other movies about rescuing men missing in action in Vietnam reproduce the myth of the frontier, a literary mythology that developed over the colonial and early national periods in America. *The Secret of My Success,* a 1987 comedy that first caught my attention with its hyperfestive plot resolution, presents itself as a version of the American success myth, which dates back to the same periods and claims Benjamin Franklin and Horatio Alger among its makers.

These closely related literary mythologies have long and well-documented histories, and it was to those that I turned. In the case of the frontier mythology, my task was greatly facilitated by Richard Slotkin's (1973, 1986) masterful analyses of its sociohistorical development, from the colonial captivity narratives through the proliferating versions of the Indian-fighter myth that mediated the U.S. history of industrialization. While there is no comparable synthetic study of American success mythology, a diverse, wide-ranging literature maps the historical transformations of what has come to be known as the American Dream.

Produced by historians, sociologists, and literary critics, this literature explores the interactions between stories of mobility through individual effort and the formation of the American middle classes.[18]

Both these narrative genres have shaped gender as well as class identities over extended periods of time. Frontier heroes who test themselves against the savage and success heroes out to change their fortunes through adventure have provided models of manly determination for generations of male readers. If there are broad, generic continuities among the historical tokens of these narrative types, there are also ideologically significant shifts in their construction within and between historical periods. Variations in the qualities assigned to coexisting heroes may indicate class-specific versions of manhood, as Michael Denning (1987: 167–184) has demonstrated with reference to the working-class readership of nineteenth-century dime novels. Changes in generic protagonists over time are symptomatic of the pressures of new sociohistorical conditions on received cultural forms and may be signs of larger cultural transformations.

In both cases, as Slotkin (1986: 26–32) argues, a mediating role is played by the mythmakers, the producers of commercial culture, who incorporate their own orientations to their audiences and to changing circumstances into their cultural productions. But if generic shifts and variations are not direct reflections of historical situations, they nevertheless suggest a way of connecting contemporary mass-cultural texts to the lives of their receivers. For the question that can be asked of a text from the perspective of its generic antecedents is this: Why should this particular instantiation of a cultural myth either appeal or fail to appeal to audiences at this particular historical moment? Or to phrase the question in terms of the genres that became my focus: What versions of manhood are incarnated in the Indian fighters and self-made men who populate contemporary mass-cultural fictions, and how are they related to their sociohistorical conditions of production and reception?

The cultural narratives that were reworked in 1980s movies also figured prominently in political rhetoric throughout the Reagan era. Conservative politicians used the resonant language of myth to assimilate the lived present to a storied past. Domestically the New Right attack on the welfare state was based on the old tale of rags to riches, which constructs success and failure as indices of individual moral character. If the poor appeared in this discourse as domestic savages, victims of their own supposed lack of moral restraint, the frontier myth was invoked to construct assorted foreign nations as savage opposites of an America restored to its civilizing mission.[19]

Such polarities are partial realizations of a narrative scheme that situates the idealized self between the extremes of savage chaos and overcivilized order.[20] Opposed from below by the savage Other, the self's productive disposition also sets it against authoritarian decadence, variously located in feudal Europe or the corrupt Metropolis, mythical societies where privileged classes enjoy wealth without labor. New Right discourse made this conventionalized antagonism between working people and idle elites into a major theme, shaping a style of right-wing populism designed to appeal to popular resentment of bureaucratic authority. In the role of the decadent aristocracy, Reagan and his New Right allies cast an assortment of liberal intellectuals, politicians, and Washington bureaucrats—putative nonproducers who became known in conservative discourse as the New Class.[21]

Gender categories are an important dimension of the myths that were mobilized, and they played a key role in conservative political ideology during the 1980s. Most obviously, of course, Americans were exhorted to stand tall against savage foes, like the frontier heroes of old, but the martial enactments of manhood attempted during the Reagan presidency were not overwhelming successes. They were supplemented by discursive practices that opposed a frontier spirit of entrepreneurial masculinity to the decadent femininity of a Metropolitan privileged class.[22] Moreover, right-wing populism extended its attack on the feminized liberal elites of its imagination to those who had supposedly joined their ranks through unfair advantage. Fundamental to the conservative critique of affirmative action is the idea that rising by any means other than individual effort is a feminine mode of success, which is practiced, accordingly, by women and minorities but repudiated by real men.

Susan Jeffords treats such political rhetoric as part of a general "remasculinization of American culture" that serves as an instrument for the "regeneration of the interests, values, and projects of patriarchy" (1989: xi). In Jeffords's analysis a critical site for regenerating masculinity is the representation of Vietnam. Literary works and Hollywood movies about Vietnam veterans, she argues, are masculine reactions against recent changes in gender relations. Their true subject is neither the war itself nor imperialist U.S. policies but the renewed battle of the masculine to reconsolidate its control over the feminine. From this perspective, wars, whether actual or represented (and it is not entirely clear what the difference would be in Jeffords's model), are essentially "forums" for the reaffirmation and reconstitution of masculine identities. Moreover, Jeffords elaborates, this regenerated masculinity defines itself as an autonomous, self-sufficient principle, denying its dependency on women by absorbing conventionally feminine capacities.

There is much of interest in Jeffords's work, and her analysis of the Vietnam films has many features in common with my own. Nevertheless, our approaches to the analysis of gender are fundamentally different. Jeffords uses what, following R. W. Connell (1987: 54–61), I take to be a "categorical theory," which treats gender in terms of internally undifferentiated categories of masculinity and femininity, related to each other by power and conflict of interest. "Masculinity," in Jeffords's analysis, is a symbolic construct that contributes to patriarchal social arrangements, a "mechanism for the operation of patriarchy" (1989: 181). What this view ignores are "the social arrangements that give a particular kind of masculinity a hegemonic position in sexual politics and that marginalize others" (Connell 1987: 58).

Like Jeffords, I view mass culture in the 1980s as one site for a process of remasculinization. However, where Jeffords suggests that the masculine was reconstituted in a unitary form, with equal appeal to men as a group, I look for connections between competing versions of manhood and specific audiences of men, differentiated by class, race, and generation. Even where the same mass-cultural texts appeal across social lines, male audiences are likely to negotiate them and incorporate them into their fantasy lives in different ways, conditioned by their particular social positions. Moreover, the mass-mediated masculinity produced during the 1980s was internally divided. "A diversity of 'masculinities' jostle to present themselves as the acceptable face of the new male order," Lynne Segal (1990: 293) observes of the past decade. To lump these together as "the masculine" in battle against "the feminine" is to obscure the interplay between class and gender identities in mass-cultural fantasies. Any given form of masculinity is not only defined in relation to its feminine opposite but also stands in hierarchical relationships to other masculinities. These hierarchies within the major gender categories are never static. In Connell's (1987: 131) model, when some one version of masculinity becomes hegemonic, it marginalizes others, which then provide the basis for still other versions that celebrate the qualities excluded from the dominant ideal. As an example Connell mentions the romantic, "'wild' masculinities" that emerged in the nineteenth century as reactions against the rationalization of society. These developed in several directions, generating bohemian homosexual subcultures resistant to bourgeois respectability, as well as the aggressive, violent masculinities that were mobilized in European fascisms, especially in the movement stage.[23]

What Jeffords interprets as "a renewed sense of American masculinity" (1989: 169) is a specific, mass-mediated version of aggressive masculinity, incarnated in characters immediately descended from the antibureaucratic vigilante heroes of earlier Hollywood movies, more distantly related to the martial men of Fascist ideologies by a common antagonism to the perceived abstractness of late capitalist society. By far the best known version of this particular phenomenon is *Rambo,* which I also analyze as a fantasy of remasculinization, or more precisely, rebarbarianization. Jeffords's mistake, as I see it, is to ignore the class basis for the ideological appeal of this particular "wild" masculinity and to assimilate all the male heroes of the 1980s to a single type.

Rambo plays most directly, if not exclusively, on blue- and white-collar working-class resentments of managerial controls, displaced onto the (Carter) government, woven together with a messianic version of the New Right critique of liberalism and secular humanism, and freighted with psychosexual fears of persecution and abandonment. The result is a fantasy considerably more imaginative than anything New Right ideologues produced but appealing to a broadly similar audience of discontented, resentful social groups, primarily from the older working and middle classes, who provided the core for right-wing populism. Like New Right attacks on the liberal reforms of the past decades, such movies were constructed to arouse fears of change, flux, transition; and they offered as the solution a return to an idealized past when men were men. During the 1980s, moreover, Hollywood joined New Right leaders in directing socially rooted discontents against independent, upwardly mobile women. Movies as well as political discourse attacked uncontrolled, ambitious women as the cause of a moral crisis that, given its definition, called for a strong, authoritarian patriarch.

In these chapters, however, I argue that Hollywood versions of patriarchy varied in socially significant ways, both internally and in relation to the conservative discourses that certain movies absorbed. Nor was the ideology produced in political sites homogeneous, for that matter. Reagan himself only intermittently wore a sternly patriarchal face, usually when he was taking something away from the poor, and how widely an authoritarian image contributed to his popularity is arguable. It is well known that many of his supporters did not share his opposition to abortion, and polls suggest that voting for Reagan did not necessarily mean acceptance of his other New Right policies. Leaving electoral politics aside, I would simply note that the pleasures Reagan provided appear to have been multitiered. For example, when the president evoked the character of Rambo in his speeches, audiences were presented with an implicit choice: They could identify the speaker with the hero-redeemer who defends traditional values against corrupt elites, or alternatively they could admire his consummate skill in using popular culture to construct his own media image.

Ability to manipulate images happens to be precisely what Rambo lacks, and it is condemned in the movie as a form of the negative principle of the abstract. But 1980s movies popularized another type of hero who does not share Rambo's deficiency. On the contrary, he is a master of disguises, a skilled manipulator of appearances, a new form of an older trickster figure who succeeds through verbal cunning rather than hard work and self-denial. The new hero does not lack expertise. He is a highly skilled professional, a master at whatever he does, be it catching crooks, saving corporations, or outwitting adult authorities. But the distinctive style of his performance, at once flawlessly efficient and boyishly rebellious, eventually wins him approval from a higher authority who shares his playful, pleasure-seeking disposition. The fantasy here, analyzed in Chapters 3 and 4, is of outwitting bureaucracy on its own terms, converting the very traits it requires into a liberatory force. Such fantasies, I argue, could be viewed from various positions, which I try to differentiate. But these fantasies were produced by and primarily for a particular class, the professional-managerial class (PMC), and more specifically, for the generation designated by Fred Pfeil (1985) as "the baby-boom professional-managerial class."

Also described as the "new middle class" and the "professional middle class," this particular class or class fraction is situated "between labor and capital," in the Ehrenreichs' (1977) definition, with uncertain boundaries below and above. It comprises a diverse assortment of "salaried mental workers," ranging from schoolteachers and nurses at the lower end (whose income and status put them closer to labor) to wealthy, influential executives at the upper end (who may participate in the ruling corporate elite). Barbara Ehrenreich points out that status for the PMC, unlike both the corporate elites and the old entrepreneurial middle class, "is based on education, rather than on the ownership of capital or property" (1989: 12). Such symbolic capital, Ehrenreich goes on, is peculiarly evanescent; although the wealth that purchases education is transmissible, skill and knowledge themselves, or the credentials of their possession, "must be renewed in each individual through fresh effort and commitment" (1989: 15).

Although a minority of the PMC are self-employed professionals, most are dependent on large, bureaucratic organizations, and their history as a class is bound up in the bureaucratization of American society that began in the mid-1800s. That process also produced a white-collar working class, originally and still overwhelmingly female, which assists in the performance of "mental work." Unlike white-collar workers, however, professionals and managers ordinarily perform work that involves considerable autonomy and requires special skills, including skill in managing others. Often, moreover, professional and managerial occupations take on a guildlike quality, by virtue of the lengthy process of credentialization. Managed white-collar workers in highly rationalized jobs and self-directing professional-managerial elites with vocational pride in their work thus experience bureaucracy from very different positions.

A distinctive work orientation contributes to an ethos that partly constitutes these heterogeneous "middle strata" as a class (Pfeil 1985: 272). Career success depends equally on mastering the rules and conventions of bureaucratic organizations and on an ability to assert and control one's self-image in a way that commands recognition from peers and superiors.[24] As Barbara Ehrenreich argues, reproduction of this work orientation is no small task and places distinctive demands on child raising. Middle-class parents, Ehrenreich observes, face a dilemma conditioned by the contradictory qualities required for success: "On the one hand, they must encourage their children to be innovative and to 'express themselves,' for these traits are usually valued in the professions. But the child will never gain entry to a profession in the first place without developing a quite different set of traits, centered on self-discipline and control" (1989: 84).

When it comes to encouraging self-expression, middle-class parents have a powerful if unstable ally in the consumer culture of late capitalism, which tirelessly promotes indulgence as a means of individualization. At no time were those calls more insistent than in the mid-1980s, at the height of the Reagan era. But the middle classes cannot consume, Ehrenreich also suggests, without stirring up their characteristic anxiety: "a fear of inner weakness, of growing soft, of failing to strive, of losing discipline and will" (1989: 15). For some, at least, that worst fear seemed to have been realized in the 1960s generation, especially as their image was relayed by the mass media.

Over the course of the 1980s, sections of the professional middle class drifted rightward and joined the new conservative bloc. Hollywood moviemakers reinforced and in some cases anticipated the rightward turn. Mark Crispin Miller (1986, 1990) and Peter Biskind (1990) have convincingly periodized the 1980s as an "epoch of revision" in Hollywood, when both the aesthetic experimentation and the relatively critical messages that had characterized mainstream moviemaking during the 1970s were systematically repudiated or revised out. Comedy made a striking recovery over this revisionist period, even invading such genres as the male-oriented action adventure, and the shift is symptomatic of the general reorientation. For festivity became a preferred form of resolution in the 1980s, both in movies and in the feel-good patriotism that celebrated the nation's newly recovered pride. Miller (1990: 230–246) traces what he calls "the new happy ending" across the multiple genres in which it appears, noting how 1980s movies repeatedly dissolve the (pseudo) oppositions they set up, promising that there is room for all within the corporate order.

Like Miller and Biskind, I focus on the managing of antiauthoritarian tendencies in movies whose seemingly rebellious, independent heroes contract symptomatic bargains with paternalistic figures of authority. As do they, I take the primary audience for these fantasies to be the youth, young adults, and aging baby-boomers of the professional-managerial class, whom movies and politicians alike welcomed back into the fold. Nor should we forget that moviemakers are themselves professionals and may incorporate their own class experience into their products. If 1980s movies are dominated by ambivalent fantasies of reconciliation with authority, we should keep in mind the growing dependence of production on the new media monopolies that have absorbed the major studios.[25]

What I think distinguishes my analyses is their increasingly close attention to both the class and gender identities of movie audiences. In Chapters 3, 4, and 5 I argue that the most successful appeals to middle-class audiences in mid-1980s movies blended a Reagan-era fantasy of unrestricted desire with a particular version of the promise of "remasculinization." In brief, whereas many 1970s movies reflect darkly on the dehumanizing powers of bureaucratic organizations, these organizations reemerge in 1980s fictions as sites for enacting a manhood of a certain type.[26] Whatever other attributes he is assigned, this new man is a master of appearances, a "transforming hero" who skillfully manipulates and controls his public face.

In Chapters 3 and 4 I describe this style of masculinity as "postmodern," a term that has the disadvantage of conveying more to some readers than may be intended.[27] I use it in the sense defined by Fred Pfeil (1985) as the aesthetic of a particular class generation, the baby-boom PMC. While the cultural forms that I analyze are at the low (mass culture) "pole" of the spectrum Pfeil constructs, in content and occasionally in form they convey at least some of the features he cites as constitutive of the postmodern. In particular, the films endorse, not without ambivalence, a thematic of deindividualization, manifested in the recurrent fantasy of inventing or staging one's own identity, and related, I also argue, to a distinctive class orientation to work.

If the concept of the postmodern can reach too far, as when it seems to subsume all aspects of cultural production and personhood under late capitalism, Judith Stacey points out that it also shares with other *post-* words a capacity to evoke notions of contestation, ambivalence, and uncertainty. Stacey herself uses "the postmodern family" to signal contemporary arrangements that she sees as "diverse, fluid, and unresolved" (1990: 17), and she extends the same characterization to gender identities. This volume as a whole and Chapters 4 and 5 in particular address the incorporation into 1980s movies of ongoing, lived struggles over masculinity and femininity. Focusing primarily on texts rather than their receivers, I do not attribute to the movies any particular effects on subjectively held gender ideologies. Rather, my project is to try to map the resources that are provided in 1980s movies for reinventing gender identities in daily life.

Overall the results are not encouraging from a feminist perspective. Hollywood movies during the Reagan era organized desire along traditionally asymmetric lines, encouraging men to pursue an inflated version of the American Dream from which women continued to be excluded. Moreover, female desire took on an increasingly threatening character as the cinematic era unfolded. In movies that overtly endorse different social values and sensibilities, the figure of a demonized independent woman justifies the reassertion of patriarchal controls. More than misogynistic, such fantasies are pointedly antifeminist, and the chapter on "Transforming Heroes" (Chapter 4) connects the demonization of independent women in movies to the authoritarian political culture of the Reagan era. However, I also observe in that chapter that as masculinities vary, so too do antifeminisms, and this insight is developed in the final chapter in this volume, "Who Will Do the Caring?" This is by far the longest of the chapters and, I think, the most attentive to audiences and to ideology production in different domains. The subject is the representation of the family in everyday social practice, New Right political discourse, psychoanalytic theory, and 1980s movies. Rather than summarize the argument, I want to pursue one claim, which is that the sensitive new male of 1980s mass culture is a contested figure.

What Jeffords had detected in the self-sufficient men of Vietnam representation is an instance of a wider tendency to convert traditionally feminine attributes into an additional index of masculine superiority, thus reconfiguring gender polarity rather than transcending it. Paul Smith makes a similar point in a trenchant critique of 1980s action movies, observing that "A touch of sensitivity or vulnerability brings another arm, a further resiliency to masculinity's dominatory arsenal" (1989: 40). With their casually attuned heroes, movies like *Lethal*

Weapon and *Heartbreak Ridge* offer male audiences an ideal of sensitivity, only to instruct them to discard it. Far from encouraging men to respond to the actual demands being made on them by women, Smith argues, the plots are constructed to suggest that what women really want are violent macho men.

But sensitive, feminized men also appear in female-oriented genres such as. family melodrama and romantic comedy in the form of the caring father, the domestic man who takes on (or takes over) nurturant responsibilities. Many feminists have attacked this type, not without cause. Most 1980s movies construct good, nurturing fathers as substitutes for bad, overambitious mothers, and such constructions have strong antifeminist implications. Nevertheless, even plots in which men outdo women as mothers do not always distort beyond all recognition the social discourses about gender that provide their raw materials. Moreover, 1980s movies occasionally took a more utopian turn, imagining new men who were not required to teach women the old lessons, but joined them instead in collaborative projects.

Without question the dominant tendency in mass-cultural fictions is to limit and contain new possibilities—in this case, to pattern changing gender relations on the model of the old patriarchal polarities of masculine and feminine. Still, the new possibilities that are absorbed into received cultural forms continue to stretch the forms, sometimes in unexpected ways. And in the very process of reconstructing images of male hegemony out of increasingly recalcitrant materials, movies recognize to some degree what Judith Stacey describes as the "contested, ambivalent and undecided character of contemporary gender and kinship arrangements" (1990: 17).

Neither the practical relations between men and women nor cultural concepts of gender remained static during the 1980s. The very intensity of the right's ongoing "pro-family campaign" is proof of that. If the traditional family needs such passionate defenders, it is because it is indeed under attack, or rather, the old form of family life based on gender domination is no longer taken for granted. Inequalities between the sexes persist, as do polarized images of masculinity and femininity. "Yet," Lynne Segal reminds us, "neither our images of men and women nor sexual inequalities themselves persist everywhere equally and unbroken" (1990: 308). If Hollywood movies of the 1980s tend overall to reconstruct patriarchal symbols of men and women, the very fragmentation of images and the experimental aura of some of the new composites provides a potential resource, albeit a limited and highly compromised one, for reinventing gender identities.

My intention, however, is not to recuperate the Hollywood cinema of the 1980s. On the contrary, it seems to me important to recognize that a great part of the energy for cultural production during the Reagan era went into reversing critical tendencies and rehabilitating images of masculine authority. What I want to reiterate is that cinematic returns of the father varied in socially significant ways that notions of resurgent patriarchy or patriarchal Hollywood obscure. In the chapters that follow, I try to keep the class dimensions of gender politics in view. To this end, I focus on the competing versions of masculinity and femininity constructed in the movies and, more and more closely as the sequence of chapters unfolds, on the social sources of their appeal to particular audiences.

The class audience that figures most prominently in this volume is the professional middle class, to which I myself belong, as do the producers of mass culture. Inasmuch as the culture this class produces and consumes implies something about its political inclinations, the results of this study are at best ambiguous. On the one hand, my analyses suggest that the resentful authoritarianism of New Right ideology, which found its way into movies such as *Rambo,* was not aimed primarily at professional-middle-class audiences. On the other hand, there is surely a move to contain oppositional impulses in the 1980s fantasy of unlimited (male) desire fulfilled within the paternalistic corporation. Nevertheless, as Fred Pfeil (1985: 292) observes, many "postmodern" Hollywood movies have their utopian moments, however brief and highly distorted these may be, fictional alliances across lines of class, race, and gender that articulate the "dream of . . . an unprecedented collectivity," which I also found expressed in the carnivalesque resolution to *The Secret of My Success.*

The larger point made by Pfeil and by Barbara Ehrenreich (1989) is that the political direction of the professional middle class remains a choice to be made. Under Reaganism, there appears to have been a swing from left to right, from equality to privilege, from the dream of collectivity to the pursuit of self-interest, and its reversal requires something more than new movies. To precipitate "the next great shift," as Ehrenreich (1989:256–257) calls it, will take new alliances between the professional middle class and the working classes; and it will take new agendas that reconnect the struggle for gender equality to the struggle for social justice. Such alliances, the matrix for a renewal of mass culture, would also expand the possibilities of reading our current forms. In the context of a more progressive political culture, I like to think that we might negotiate new pleasures from *The Secret of My Success* or perhaps even *Ferris Bueller's Day Off*. At the least, it would become easier to disengage the rebellious desire that drives these movies from the cycle in which heroes who so merrily commit symbolic patricide are required to identify themselves with paternal authority.

1

The Return of the Repressed: Lucas and Spielberg's Temple of Doom

MOISHE POSTONE & ELIZABETH G. TRAUBE

EORGE LUCAS and Steven Spielberg have emerged in recent years as masters of Hollywood entertainment cinema. They specialize in slick, technically sophisticated science fiction and adventure films that are modeled on the popular culture of the 1930s and 1940s and that promise a way to recover the innocent pleasures of childhood movie viewing. Yet Lucas and Spielberg's high-tech, traditionalist mythology is not innocent, and this is nowhere so apparent as in their latest blockbuster, *Indiana Jones and the Temple of Doom.*

Although much of the critical debate on this film revolved around its entertainment value and its suitability for children, some critics observed that the film projects a world view. For instance, David Denby noted that "it is clear that Lucas and Spielberg do not intend any 'commentary' on the pop junk of their youth. On the contrary, they have simply found the world they want to live in" (*New York Magazine,* June 4, 1984). Denby, however, did not proceed to examine the parameters of that world. J. Hoberman went further and scathingly characterized the film's assumption as racist and sexist (*The Village Voice,* June 5, 1984). Yet he stopped short of examining the process by which those ideologies are produced and transmitted in the film. Our purpose in this chapter is to examine that process of ideology production in *Indiana Jones.*

Serious analysis of "entertainment" films encounters widespread resistance in the United States today. Such a stance is itself ideological, for it obscures the political significance of mass entertainment and hinders processes of social and cultural self-reflection. By turning to the popular culture of the 1930s and 1940s, Lucas and Spielberg are expressing and helping to shape a widespread American yearning, ascendant since the mid-1970s and embodied in the Reagan presidency. It is a longing to return to earlier, presumably simpler, times, a longing provoked by an increasingly complex world in which the very basis of U.S. self-understanding—the upward political, social, and economic trajectory of the United States relative to the rest of the world—began to crumble. The resultant cultural disorientation has led to a desire to escape the complexities of the present, reinforced by a reluctance to understand social problems in social terms that is deeply embedded in American popular consciousness. This desire to avoid life's complexities is a basic motif in the Lucas/Spielberg films. Hollywood's young superbards take no delight in any heroism that operates within society or in mastering life's ordinary and extraordinary trials. Rather, they celebrate a desire to flee from all such complications and disguise their avoidance of society as manly adventure.

It is not simply the desire to escape into the past, however, that marks *Indiana Jones*; it is also the content of that return. Under cover of a playful nostalgia for earlier exotic adventure films, comics, and movie serials, Lucas and Spielberg have magnified and given new power to two major themes of earlier mass culture, namely, imperialist domination and patriarchal domination. These themes are drawn together in *Indiana Jones* through what appear to be loosely connected plot lines: the adventure story and the love story. Both plot lines unfold to structurally similar resolutions in which a lighthearted reaffirmation of old-fashioned sexism and racism appears as the necessary alternative to the forces of darkness.

Not only the film's ideological project but also its latent mode of operation need to be analyzed, for it is by arousing and playing upon deeply rooted fears that the film solicits our acquiescence to the "rightness" of the order depicted in the resolution. The adventure story and the love story are integrated by projecting onto a cultural Other a fantasy of female sexuality as an evil, destructive, archaic power of death. The subordination of this power then becomes the precondition of civilization.

The opening episode in a Shanghai nightclub in 1935 brings together the archaeologist-adventurer Indiana Jones, a showgirl and singer named Willie Scott, and Jones's sidekick, Short Round. The latter is a Chinese orphan boy, rescued by Jones from a life of small-time urban crime, who worships his surrogate father and at first treats Willie as a potential rival. Following a rapid series of adventures, the three of them end up in an impoverished village somewhere in northern India. The villagers are starving, and their dignified headman links his people's plight to the "power of dark night," which has once more arisen in the palace of Pankot. This evil power is embodied in the nefarious Thugs, historically a group of professional assassins. The Thugs have stolen the magic stone of the village, the *Shivalinga,* which is a phallic-shaped ritual object representing the god Shiva. The loss of this stone has brought famine upon the village and, to complete the attack on the life-principle, the villagers' children have been kidnapped and enslaved in the palace. Jones agrees to recover the ritual stone for the villagers. He and his companions proceed to the palace, where foul shrines and vampire bats foreshadow sinister activities. This premonition is swiftly fulfilled at a repulsive banquet attended by various Hindu dignitaries and a visiting British colonial officer.

That same night, immediately after an interrupted sexual encounter with Willie, Jones discovers a secret passageway that leads to a chamber deep below the palace. There they watch the evil priest perform a human sacrifice to the goddess Kali, who represents the destructive manifestations of the Mother Goddess and consort to Shiva. After the sacrifice, Jones seizes the villagers' stone and discovers the abducted village children, who are toiling in the palace mines. But Jones and his companions are captured. He is forced to drink the "blood of Kali," which robs him of his soul and enslaves him to the goddess. As a test of his loyalty, Jones is ordered to sacrifice Willie, but in the very nick of time Short Round breaks the evil spell by burning Jones with a flaming torch. Restored to himself, Jones rescues Willie from the pit of lava over which she is dangling, liberates the children, and leads his companions out of the mines. The final victory over the Thugs takes place high up on a bridge.

The film has the narrative structure of a quest romance, in this case, a journey to hell and back again, a move from light into darkness, followed by a return to light. The story as a whole thus consists of a bracket around a central part, which is the quest proper. Rhythm and tone together reflect and express the sequential structure of the narrative. As many reviewers have noted, the energetic, action-packed pace and playful humor of the framing sequences contrast sharply with the increasingly oppressive, constricted atmosphere and total absence of comic relief that characterize the film's central sequence. For many reviewers, the film "goes wrong" when it abandons its breakneck, cunningly crafted pacing and loses its sense of humor. Where it is that the film goes remains to be seen.

It is not difficult to detect the film's overt ideological implications. Like one of its models, *Gunga Din, Indiana Jones* is a cinematic variant on the theme of the "white man's burden." The film seeks to represent imperialism as a civilizing, socially progressive force and so to legitimize Western domination of others. Its strategy is to identify oppression with the indigenous system of rule; for if the suffering of indigenous peoples is the product of their own institutions, then those institutions may be rightfully supplanted. Hence the film does not present a blanket condemnation of Indian otherness but rather divides that otherness into two categories that correspond to an oppressed peasantry and an oppressive, exploitative ruling class.

At the same time, the film constructs imperialist and indigenous forms of domination as polar opposites, thereby denying the possibility that these forms might have anything in common. One way in which it effects this split is by using the gender categories of male and female to express the difference between the "legitimate" Western rulers and their "illegitimate" Indian counterparts. This strategy implicitly weds the film's political content to its psychosexual content, and it powerfully reinforces the depiction of the white man as the paternalistic defender of justice against oppression and of the civilized order against primordial female chaos.

The film's gender model of political domination places the villagers in the position of children, dependent on the paternal West for protection. Within this framework, the villagers are sympathetically represented, and indeed, a sign of Jones's status is his interest in their affairs. Jones treats the simple, downtrodden villagers with great courtesy. He is portrayed here as an enlightened man, with a healthy, relativistic respect for alternative cultural traditions. He lectures Willie (and indirectly the audience) for recoiling from the unappetizing guest-food, which is all that the starving villagers have to offer. He provides a model of manly conduct for Short Round, who politely accepts the food. In these scenes Jones acts as all-knowing scientist, ego ideal for little boys, and champion of helpless villagers, all rolled into one. The paternalistic relation of the white scientist to his object of research underscores the more general paternalism of Jones's relation to his needy charges.

The Indian aristocrats, however, are represented as radically alien and monstrously evil. Lucas and Spielberg seek to show how what appears beautiful and gracefully opulent is really hideous and depraved. This tactic partly accounts for the film's loss of pace. Many films use a convention of maintaining a tension between the enemy's refined exterior and his or her true inner nature, thereby increasing a suspenseful sense of foreboding. Lucas and Spielberg only briefly acknowledge that convention. The maharaja's minister who greets Jones and company as they enter the palace seems a cultivated, knowledgeable, Oxford-educated man. Before the assembled guests and dignitaries are seated at the luxuriously appointed table, we get a quick glimpse of an indigenous courtly culture, practically the last aesthetically pleasing images that the film offers us. There are musicians, dancers, and singers, not to mention Willie herself, who appears bedecked in Indian finery, so radiant that Jones verbally acknowledges her attractiveness for the first time. What is emphasized in this scene is the seductive, alluring, sensual character of Indian court culture with its beauty, charm, and graceful opulence. But these images of the seductive, alluring Other are hastily and permanently reversed in the banquet scene. At the table, Jones, the child maharaja, his minister, and a visiting British colonel discuss the palace's political history. It had been a center of the murderous Thugee cult, which was later suppressed by the British. Jones is assured that despite what the villagers may have told him, the cult no longer exists. Yet in counterpoint to all this talk, we have before us the visual evidence that the bad past has indeed returned. We are bombarded by culinary images of snakes, live eels, beetles, eyeball soup, and monkey brains on the half-skull. Lucas and Spielberg evidently enjoy playing with their food, but the game is not innocent. It evokes our disgust, not only for the feast but also for the lascivious pleasure with which the Indians consume the loathsome food. The banquet scene does not so much reveal to us the depravity *behind* exotic sensuality as it impresses upon us that sensuality *is* depraved.

Although the scene may have been designed to be grossly humorous, that "humor" serves to displace the viewer's attention from the content of the conversation to the vile feast. It had been a conversation that provided at least shreds of material for an historical understanding of the present conflict as a moment in a political struggle. That sort of understanding is implicitly negated by the scene's emphasis on the culinary representation of Otherness. This displacement suggests that the bad past that has returned is not to be understood through discourse and is not interpretable in sociohistorical terms. Rather the badness is inherent in the very nature of the Other, a nature that is graphically embodied in the food the Other consumes. Such a depiction implies that historical circumstances are ultimately irrelevant to an understanding of the world. The film presents culturally different forms of resistance and rebellion as if they were not socially rooted, intelligible responses to concrete forms of exploitation and injustice. Instead, consistent with a strong tendency in the United States today, the film seeks to explain the world in terms of the Other's evil nature rather than in historical terms.

The film subsequently treats depraved sensuality as the sign of the evil emanating from Kali. The bloodthirsty Mother Goddess is depicted as lusting after human flesh and being worshiped by adoring throngs of entranced, arm-waving, dehumanized followers. We see the living heart torn from a sacrificial victim who, mysteriously still alive, is then lowered into a whirling pool of lava, accompanied by a crescendo of drumbeats and chants. What we suspected at the dinner scene is confirmed by the scene of human sacrifice. Indian aristocratic culture is not merely decadent but savagely regressive. And within the Western tradition, an unmistakable sign of that regression is the triumph of the female principle over the male: Shiva, the Lord, has been laid low by the Mother, at whose feet the *linga* now sits.

The scene that unfolds within the Temple of Doom is a lavish amalgamation of countless Hollywood renditions of sinister primitive cults. But this film unmasks the enemy's true nature in a specific way. From sensual depravity it moves to depicting savage evil, and then it reveals how savagery is manipulated by a brutally oppressive class. The cult leaders have not only impoverished the villages, but they also exploit child labor. The abducted children must toil endlessly in the mines in search of two sacred stones that were hidden from the British. What the children's evil masters hope to obtain from this labor is not natural riches but pure power, as the missing stones will supposedly enable the forces of Kali to dominate the world.

The narrative construction of the Indian rulers evokes in the viewer a strong desire for their destruction. As the rulers' evil nature is revealed in ever more hideous terms, expectations arise to see such absolute evil absolutely eradicated. This longed-for resolution, moreover, would serve social justice by saving the peasants from the tyranny of their lords. Yet the film's representation of that tyranny inadvertently calls attention to another mechanism of ideology production. The images of children laboring in the mines indicate that the film not only represents the Indian ruling classes as negatively alien and other but also projects onto them attributes of the Western ruling classes. Forced child labor on a massive scale has far more to do with nineteenth-century capitalism domestically and twentieth-century capitalism abroad than with traditional India. Moreover, there is indeed a form of production where the real goal is not the things produced but the abstract social power they embody. Yet that form, the production of surplus value, is not to be found in the mysterious darkness of other cultures but in the light of our own. The film transposes a critique of the capitalist ruling class onto the Indian ruling classes and fuses the critique with a depiction of the cultural alien's depravity and evil. Its project is to deflect onto the Other frustration and anger that are domestically engendered. Such projection has an ideological intent: to legitimate imperialism as apparently progressive, a channel of action and a civilizing mission for the white man who cannot change things at home.

As exploitative rulers, the Indians bear a mystified resemblance to the Western ruling classes. The film, however, goes to great lengths to associate the Indian enemy with femaleness, which is fleetingly depicted as seductive opulence and then, in greater detail, as sensual depravity and primordial chaos. Constituted in opposition to a savage, corrupt, female evil, imperialism appears as a civilizing, purifying, male force. Jones and the British function in the film as bestowers of law, order, and reason upon a helpless peasantry, who are as childlike in their dependency on Western paternalism as in their vulnerability to the evil Mother's forces.

Altogether absent from these representations is any mention of the darker side of imperialist domination. Yet whatever "gifts of civilization" colonial rulers may have bestowed, the motivating force behind imperialist expansion was to exploit colonized societies of their labor, material products, and needs. On such matters, the film remains significantly silent.

But then, the film would hardly represent Western exploitation, since the film is itself a form of exploitation. Its vivid portrayal of the Other as a violent and dangerous enemy constitutes a violent and dangerous act. Such a portrayal both reflects and produces conceptions of the world "out there" as the place of evil.

Specific characteristics of the film's self-validating condemnation of the Other point toward a psychosexual dimension of ideological processes. Not unlike many British colonial officers, to judge by their reports, the film seems fixated on the sensual depravity of the feminized Indian rulers, whereas it presents the contrasting masculinity of the Western "civilizers" in a sublimated form. Jones and the British reject perverse sensual pleasure and seek gratification in the moral exercise of power. The psychosexual dynamics here emerge more clearly in the context of the love story. In many of the older exotic adventure films, the "love interest" is manifestly subsidiary and peripheral to the adventure story. *Indiana Jones* brings the latent structure of adventure-romance very close to its surface and so discloses the psychosexual desires and fears that lie at the very core of the genre.

Other reviewers have called attention to the film's sexist characterization of the heroine. Willie is portrayed as a brainless, whining, incompetent gold digger, a dumb blond who contrasts sharply with the spunky heroine of *Raiders of the Lost Ark*. In our reading, however, the film inadvertently reveals its sexist portrayal of the woman as superficial, a defense against a deeply rooted fear of female sexuality. We have already noted that the temple episode breaks in rhythm and tone with the surrounding sequences and elicits a pervasive sense of horror. That horror, we argue below, is structurally conditioned; its force derives from the thinly masked nature of the quest as a flight from sexuality that becomes a fantasized encounter with primeval femaleness.

This trajectory is implied at the very beginning of the film, in an apparently trivial exchange. When Willie first hears that Jones is an archaeologist, she says, "Archaeologists—I thought they were funny little men searching for their Mommies." "That's 'mummies'," Jones snaps and thinks that he has corrected her. Shortly thereafter, he is poisoned, and the vial with the antidote winds up in Willie's bosom. Jones, understandably enough, has no time to waste in supplication, and when Willie delays in handing over the precious antidote, he takes it from her by force. Mistaking his state of desperation for passion, she protests that she's not that kind of girl. The scene is playful, yet it sets up the tension between male and female that organizes the entire film. Underlying that tension is a deep ambivalence toward the female. Either the woman appears to the man, as she does in this scene, as a desirable, life-giving figure who, however, must be forcibly subjugated; or, embodied in Kali, she manifests herself as a deadly threat.

This threat informs the love story, with its stereotyped progression from initial antagonism to desire. Jones and Willie do not openly acknowledge their mutual attraction until they have come into the palace, where Willie (whom we first saw emerging from a paper dragon's mouth) is metamorphosed back into an exotic seductress. After the banquet scene, Jones parts company with Short Round and solicitously offers Willie an apple, from which he takes the first bite. Predictably, this initiates a sexual encounter, which subsequently founders over the issue of control. She insists that her aphrodisiac charms will make him forget all other women; he demurs, characterizing himself as a scientific investigator of female sexuality who will not prejudge the results of his research. The outcome is that their mutual desire goes unsatisfied, and he returns to his bedroom. She has a temper tantrum, whereas he discharges his frustrated arousal by other means—by engaging in a struggle to the death with an enormous Thug who suddenly appears out of nowhere. Upon disposing of his assailant, Jones rushes into

Willie's chamber, apparently to see if any Thugs are molesting her. She betrays the limitations of her nature, or better, her limitation to her nature, in assuming that he has returned to consummate their sexual relationship. Reality and fantasy are here reversed. Willie's assumption that Jones has returned to continue where they had left off is made to appear silly. She fails to comprehend that his desire has been subordinated to the "reality principle," that is, the struggle with the Thugs, who are under every bed. Jones now has more important business than sex. His search of the room leads him to a voluptuous female statue; when he touches its breasts, a hidden passageway opens. Willie looks on, puzzled and exasperated, and tries to draw his attention to her own breasts.

Within the sequential logic of the plot, what follows is a direct consequence of Jones's having avoided sex with Willie. After all, had he chosen her breasts over the statue's, the passageway would never have opened. At another level, however, what ensues is a fantasy realization of that sexual encounter, expressed as a nightmarish anxiety dream. The fantasy moves from the erotic to the antierotic, from distorted desire to the utter negation of desire. Ultimately, this fantasy realization of sex vindicates the avoidance of sexuality.

Consider first what awaits them in this passageway that opens wide upon his touching the stone breasts. Inside it is not only moist and dank but teeming with hideous life—millions of insects, creeping and crawling, many-legged things of all shapes and sizes. There is no adventuresome rhythm to this episode. The viewer is not excited or thrilled but almost unbearably disgusted and repelled by the imagery. Lucas and Spielberg follow this scene with an alternative fantasy of the dangers that lurk in dark enclosed places. Jones and Short Round get trapped in a chamber that promptly starts to close in upon them. Huge spikes emerge from the floor and ceiling, creating the effect of terrible, ravenous jaws, a graphic variant of the motif of the "toothed vagina."

Disturbing as these images may be, they remain within the bounds of fear of female eroticism. But the passage further inward is also a passage backward, a regression from the woman as seductress to Kali, the primordial mother in whom life and death are merged. Deep below the earth, between the legs of the hideous idol, is a pool of lava with a vortex that opens and closes to receive and consume its victims. To return to the womb of Kali is to meet one's death; the "Mommy" has indeed become the "mummy."

When Jones is captured and forced to drink the black blood of Kali, there is a symmetric inversion of his earlier relationship to a female breast (that is, Willie's). Now the breast is not the object but rather the agent of violence, and the liquid that the man is forced to swallow is not an antidote but a poison. *This* poison subjugates men to the female, and *its* cure is phallic. The dry fire of Short Round's torch, the surrogate son's love of the father, frees Jones from Kali's spell and averts the threat of her wet fire. Gradually now the film reacquires its upbeat, masculine rhythm of adventure and conquest. The return journey has begun, out from darkness and up into the light, where proper order is rapidly restored. The evil priest and his followers are defeated by Jones and the British, with a little help from the phallic power of Shiva's *linga*. The stone and the children are restored to the village. Last of all, Jones playfully lashes out with his whip to draw in the outwardly recalcitrant but inwardly yielding Willie, as Short Round appears on an elephant that squirts a stream of water at the happy pair. In abruptly shifting to Short Round's perspective, the film reminds us of its overt purpose, to take us back to those childhood years that Spielberg has elsewhere rhapsodically depicted as happy, carefree, and sexless.

What the film presents as its resolution is the reinstitution of the phallocentric Law of the Father, gaily packaged as kid stuff. Adventure and love, the two apparently independent plot lines, have come to structurally similar resolutions based on domination and submission. The light, adventuresome spirit of the beginning and end of the film, together with their carefree sexism and racism, are supposed to be legitimated by the central sequence in the Temple of Doom.

The film itself, however, points to a resolution of a very different nature that, while unrealized, is obliquely alluded to by a small but critical gap in the plot. To locate this absent presence, we must return briefly to the temple and to the scene in which the entranced Jones prepares to sacrifice Willie. As the moment of doom approaches, an anticipation arises, conditioned by the previous sacrifice, that he will be required to tear out her heart. We know that our hero can do no irreversible evil, and so we eagerly await the moment of his release, expecting it to come through the woman. Yet neither Jones nor the priest reaches for her heart, and she is lowered into the pit with her breast untouched. Why? Here at this juncture, where the plot misses a step, the film betrays its ideological project by unintentionally allowing us a glimpse of an alternative resolution.

Jones is saved in the film by phallic fire and boyish devotion. It is left to us to reconstruct the implications of the unselected path. Breaking the evil spell by touching the woman's breast would have meant overcoming the dominion of Kali by separating the erotic, life-bringing woman from the consuming, death-bringing one, separating desire from death, Eros from Thanatos. This in turn could have been the basis for a radically new masculinity, a masculinity no longer compelled to ally with little boys and to flee from women in adventures or to perceive sensuality as depraved. But as the masculinity that is constituted in the film is never transformed, it necessitates the continued phallocentric domination of everything female and the exclusion of sensuality. Western civilization's political victory over the Indian ruling class together with Jones's romantic conquest of Willie stand for the triumph of this undifferentiating form of masculinity over the fantasized threat of the female principle.

By including a latent alternate resolution, the film reveals that the values it seeks to legitimate are no longer securely grounded. Those values may once have been taken for granted but are no longer. In spite of itself, the film indicates the impossibility of returning to the past as if the present did not exist. Compelled as the film is to deny the present, its attempted return to the past requires the quasi-violent psychic repression of newer possibilities and sensibilities. What is repressed then reappears in projected form and seems all the more threatening. The inherent instability of such a resolution presages a future return of the repressed, which in turn would have to be denied and rejected all the more strongly. Whatever may be the film's self-understanding, the neo-American "heroic" ideals it clings to are not innocently nostalgic. Rooted as those values are in a sense of threat and vulnerability, they become dangerous in their anachronism. The "newly won confidence" of Reagan's America is threadbare. This way back is not the way out.

2

Redeeming Images:
The Wild Man Comes Home

F THE POWER of a received cultural myth has been tapped by several early 1980s films on the Vietnam War, these same films may inadvertently reveal the tensions latent in the process of ideology production.[1] The myth is the Myth of the Frontier, which shapes and is shaped by what Richard Slotkin (1973) has so compellingly analyzed as the principle of regenerative violence. The films that I have singled out for attention embody one of the more imaginative workings out of that principle. These films exchange the Vietnam War, as represented in earlier films, for a fantasy war. The fantasy may well have external referents (Nicaragua, for instance, or recent "hostage crises" involving Middle East countries), but it is immediately referred to earlier fictions about Vietnam. As this fantasy war unfolds cinematically, an enacted imaginary victory substitutes itself for a represented historical defeat.

Much of this chapter has to do with variations among the plot structures of three films, *Uncommon Valor* (1983), *Missing in Action* (1984), and *Rambo: First Blood, Part Two* (1985) (hereafter referred to as *Rambo*). These films share a common story line, which is easily summarized: Despite assurances from government authorities to the contrary, American soldiers listed as "missing in action" in Vietnam are still being held in Vietnamese POW camps. A hero or group of heroes believes in the existence of the captives and returns to Vietnam to rescue them. The authorities attempt to prevent the mission but to no avail. The hero finds the camp, kills many Vietnamese, releases the captives, and brings them home, where the people rejoice.

In all three films the metaphor for the state of the country in the aftermath of the war is captivity, a condition experienced literally by the passive agents of redemption, who are the MIAs. The symbolic captivity of the country is represented as the result of a collective refusal to confront and overcome an inglorious past, of which the MIAs are the lingering trace. So long as the MIAs languish in prison, their very existence denied, the country remains unredeemed, and the proper movement of history is suspended. In rescuing the captives, the hero effects a transformation of knowledge. An apparent fantasy (faith in the MIAs) turns out to be reality, within the terms of the films.

It is, of course, ironic that a represented relationship between reality and fantasy should figure so consistently in films that are packaged as escapist entertainment, upbeat substitutes for such unpleasant realities as lost wars or unrevenged terrorist attacks on Americans. With their flagrant disregard of history, the MIA films participate in a larger project underway in contemporary Hollywood filmmaking. The current state of the art, as Noël Carroll argues (1989), is characterized by an overwhelming tendency toward fantasy; nor is there at present any particularly vital "realistic" genre that might counteract the concerted cinematic "assault on the reality principle."

Such obviously enchanted cinematic worlds might be construed as refuges from a correspondingly disenchanted real world, a world that is, alas, "not like the movies." Indeed, Americans flocked to see *Rambo* at the same time as, according to the polls, a significant majority approved of Reagan's handling of the Beirut hostage crisis. The "reality principle" indicated that a rescue attempt would endanger human lives, and the "military option" was not widely favored. But if we turn to the administration's rhetoric during the crisis, the distance between "fantasy" and "reality" is reduced. Diplomacy had to be rhetorically constituted as an enactment of "standing tall." In effect, we were told that the resolution to the crisis was not diplomatic since "no deal was made."[2]

Fictional forms, of which mass entertainment cinema is one, contribute to the shaping of the symbolic values and plot structures to which worldly situations are assimilated as tokens of a type. If the United States does invade Nicaragua or the Philippines, such acts will almost inevitably be referred to mass fictions and may assume the cultural form of what Marshall Sahlins (1981) calls "historical metaphors of mythical realities." Richard Slotkin (1986: 16) has already shown how the Myth of the Frontier provided terms in which the Vietnam War was experienced by American participants who, at least initially, took the war as a sign of a "storied past." A related argument put forward by Bruce

Greenwald interprets the war as a response to socially generated "imaginative needs."[3]

Historical enactments of a given cultural myth, Sahlins reminds us, may sometimes result in the transformation of the myth and the culture it expresses. But in modern society there are mass cultural forms that interact with one another and intervene between the historical enactment of a cultural myth and its reproductive or transformative outcomes. The concept of genre provides a way of analyzing those interactions. The historical event of the U.S. defeat in Vietnam has been incorporated into a cinematic genre that deals with the figure of the Vietnam vet. This genre has already gone through a cycle, and my purpose here is to interpret certain shifts that have occurred in a relatively short period of time. As I understand the cycle, later films within the genre are at least in part intelligible as counterforces to forces released by earlier films. Hence the genre is as much a product of discontinuities as of continuities, and as it has unfolded over time, there has been a tendency to close off possibilities latent in its earlier state.[4]

The Renegade Vet

In one subgenre, represented by such 1978 films as *Coming Home* or *Deer Hunter,* a returning Vietnam vet is reassimilated into American society. Chronologically overlapping with these comparatively optimistic Return films was another subgenre in which the returned vet turns renegade and becomes a danger to society. Such inassimilable outcasts realize the structural potential of all frontier heroes. As men of the boundaries, these defenders of order partake of the nature of their alien adversaries and contain a version of that which they oppose. But unlike other frontier heroes, who are reabsorbed into society through marriage or else pass away with the Savage, the renegade vet is violently subdued, often in a sacrificial massacre. Figures of this latter type had become familiar from movies and TV dramas long before collective guilt over the treatment of real Vietnam vets was publicly acknowledged. Indeed, I suspect that fictional representations of renegade vets contributed to the belated recognition of "our forgotten heroes."

The film *First Blood,* retrospectively designated *Part One* (hereafter referred to as *First Blood*) is one variant of the hero-as-outcast subgenre. Based on a novel by David Morell and directed by Ted Kotcheff, *First Blood* tells the story of how blind prejudice and brutality unleash a force-beyond-control. That force is personified in John Rambo (Sylvester Stallone), former Green Beret, recipient of the Congressional Medal of Honor, "a goddam war hero," as Sheriff Will Teasle learns too late.

Teasle is a well-meaning but overdisciplinary small-town sheriff who can't tell a hippie from an Indian fighter. When he spots an unwashed, longhaired drifter, he promptly expels the undesirable Other from his town in the name of peace and order. Before driving away, Teasle paternally advises Rambo to get a haircut and a bath, but Rambo has other needs. All he wanted, as he reminds us later, was something to eat. Fulfillment of this desire is now freighted with rebellion against disciplinary authority, and Rambo promptly heads back into town. For this defiant act and for possession of a hunting knife, Teasle arrests him. In the sheriff's office Teasle instructs his deputies to "clean up" the prisoner. When a sadistic deputy attempts to beat him into submission, the brutality triggers traumatic war memories, and Rambo goes berserk.

He escapes with his knife and flees half-naked into the wooded mountains, where his first act is to fashion himself an Indian-style tunic. The film knows its myths, and as the posse sets out in pursuit, a young deputy remarks: "Isn't this where we went deer hunting last spring?" Teasle, who still believes in his version of the reality principle, looks out on the wilderness and mutters, "No problem." But before much time has passed, the brutal deputy has been killed, Sheriff Teasle's authority over his men is disintegrating, and Rambo has metamorphosed into a demonic spirit of the wilderness. In the words of the young deputy, "We're not hunting him, he's hunting us."

Teasle is drawn backward, against his will, into the anarchic world of the frontier, where personal loyalties and honor reign supreme. Despite appearances Teasle knows that his friend's death has turned the hunt into a personal vendetta, a "private war," as it is designated in the film. "I wanted to kill that boy," he confesses later, and the thirst for personal revenge "does not sit well with the badge." It was the same in Vietnam, he is told. Earlier, Teasle attempts to verbally reconstitute a hierarchical order of command. Upon learning that his deputies were "a little out of line" with the prisoner, he exclaims: "If some of my men were out of line, then the prisoner comes and complains to me, and I kick ass—*me,* the Law. That's the way it is. Not all this fucking around with the law." But he knows that he is in the grip of a regressive force, and his voice trails off. "Whatever possessed God or Heaven to make a man like Rambo?" he mutters.

From the doorway comes the crisp reply: "God didn't make Rambo. I did." "I" is Colonel Samuel Trautman, U.S. Army Special Forces, played by a polished, trim, genteel Richard Crenna, an icon of military virtues. Teasle and Trautman represent opposed social types, with Trautman as the embodiment of instrumental reason, authority, efficiency, and self-control. He belittles Teasle's provincial ignorance, and their statuses are visually marked in a scene where Trautman sips cognac while Teasle downs a shot of bourbon. Trautman's relationship to Rambo is overtly paternal. "I've come to get my boy," he informs Teasle. "I recruited him, I trained him, I commanded him in Vietnam. I'd say that makes him mine." His influence over his creation is twice enacted in the film in scenes where Rambo submits to Trautman's voice or presence. Trautman recognizes the emotional source of this dependency. "He trusts me," he says. "I'm the closest thing to family he has left."

Trautman's purpose is to get Teasle to call off the hunt (which by now has mobilized the state police and the National Guard). His logic is that if Rambo is allowed to escape, they can easily arrest him later in some other state without fuss or drama. Teasle refuses, despite Trautman's portrayal of Rambo as an invincible, man-made fighting machine. According to Trautman, Rambo is trained to kill indiscriminately, the "savage" mode of warfare, and to survive in the wilderness on food "that would make a billy goat puke." (There is a ludicrous cut here to Rambo carrying a raw haunch of meat into a cave.) But it is the machine-like efficiency that Trautman stresses in extolling the qualities of his high-tech Indian fighter. Rambo unites what is perceived as a force of nature with an extreme form of discipline that Trautman converts into submissiveness.

Both Rambo and Trautman implicitly equate the domestic conflict with the Vietnam War. Trautman warns Teasle: "Do you want a war you can't win?" And Rambo constitutes the entire country as a free-fire zone in asserting, "There are no friendly civilians." Domestic violence is modeled on the represented foreign violence, and the film makes a manifest attempt to identify the oppressive domestic forces with the Vietnamese war enemy. Still, it is Rambo who succeeds against all odds in the "private war." Escaping certain death, he returns to town to take his revenge. Soon the town is in flames, and the defeated Teasle lies prone on the ground with Rambo towering over him, gun in hand. Enter Trautman for the final dramatic scene.

Previously, when asked by Teasle, "Would you have kissed or killed your boy?" had they met, Trautman responded opaquely. When the two finally meet, the power of a kiss proves sufficient. "This mission is over, Rambo," commands Colonel Trautman; and then, paternally, "It's over, Johnny." Stallone braces himself for his longest speech in the film. "Nothing is over. You don't just turn it off. It wasn't my war. You asked me, and I did what I had to do to win, but somebody wouldn't let us win. And I come back to the world and see these maggots protesting at the airport, calling me baby-killer. Who are they to protest me? I was there, they weren't!" Trautman tries again to relegate the war to the past. Rambo negates the assertion: "For you, not for me. For me, civilian life is nothing without a code of honor. Over there I drove tanks, flew planes, I was in charge of million dollar equipment, and here I can't even hold a fucking job parking cars."

In articulating his abject dependency, Rambo breaks and enacts that dependency. He hurls away the gun, sinks to the floor, and tearfully relives the trauma of the hideous death of one of his battle companions in 'Nam. As he speaks, he grabs Trautman's hand and kisses it. Trautman watches in silence. His countenance, while not impassive, is enigmatic. Pity? Horror? Fear? Relief? The film ends with Trautman leading Rambo out through the shattered town, past Teasle on a stretcher, and into a waiting police car. Over the final credits a song is sung with the refrain:

> *It's a real war*
> *Right outside your front door.*

The song goes on to evoke the traditional image of the open road—the solitary space of freedom—but it is drawn back into the scenes of domestic violence.

Artistically *First Blood* is a badly flawed film, overdetermined, I suspect, by the casting of Stallone, who also shares credit for the screenplay. There is a tendency to reduce the plot to a vehicle for Stallone's narcissistic heroics, and the supernatural quality attributed to his skill undermines the dramatic effect of what is otherwise a realistic, downbeat retelling of the frontier myth. But viewed as a process of ideology production, *First Blood* is incoherent in interesting ways.

At the surface level, the level of the world that the text seeks to project, we are offered a familiar romantic critique of society. As instantiated in *First Blood,* the traditional plot structure of the heroic individual's rebellion against a corrupt system takes on neo-Fascist overtones. The film's conception of its superman hero as a force of nature perfected by a father-leader is grounds for suspicion, and Rambo's final monologue seems constructed to play upon working-class resentment. The primarily middle-class peace movement is designated by the emotionally charged metaphor of "maggots" and conflated with the sinister, nameless "someone" who allegedly interfered in the war and who, by implication, is also responsible for Rambo's postwar problems. The speech as a whole seems to operate as a "recognition scene," that is, a scene that acknowledges its intended audience and seeks to gratify what it takes to be their desires.[5] This is not to attribute a self-conscious Fascist ideology to either the filmmakers or their receptive audience. Disturbing continuities with Fascist traditions are there, but so far as intentionality goes, I assume no more than an appeal on the film's part to an audience defined in terms of class, age, and gender. Underprivileged, inner-city youth as well as "misunderstood" middle-class male adolescents would presumably be most receptive to this fantasy of the outcast's revenge.

The identification of the manifest enemy with overauthoritarian law enforcers would also resonate with the experiences of ghetto youth and works to mystify class frustrations. Inasmuch as the dramatic action is carried on by low-status rednecks motivated by personal psychology, any adequately social critique of class exploitation is short-circuited. Rambo is a working-class hero victimized by "deviant" authorities—the sadistic deputy and Teasle, who becomes the negative embodiment of the code of honor that Rambo follows. While the film invokes the conventional image of a corrupt system, it foregrounds a conflict between combatants of the same level, individuals motivated by the same values of face, personal loyalty, and revenge.

However, on the metaphorical axis that the film constructs, the violent individualism of Rambo and Teasle is implicitly resocialized. In self-consciously identifying the "private war" with the war in Vietnam, the film opens up a line of interpretation that it does not pursue. The Vietnam metaphor is by now a stock device in Hollywood films. It is used in *Year of the Dragon* (1985) and in the Dirty Harry films to legitimize police violence against the "criminal element," equated with the savage alien. *First Blood* wants to tell us that it is making the conventional identification of domestic corruption with savagery. But the plot structure places the hero and former Indian fighter in the structural position of the Vietnamese/Indians, fighting an enemy who, despite appearances, turns out to be inferior in both material and moral terms (not a bad "maggot's" description of the U.S. forces in Vietnam). In a plot structure of this type, the Vietnam metaphor has the potential to partially unmask the mythology of savagery and civilization that, by deflecting class tensions into imperialist wars, has historically preserved the fiction of capitalist development without class exploitation.[6] What Rambo leaves out of his resentful monologue is the very connection that he enacts, albeit in mystified form, between the objects of domestic and imperialist exploitation.

This unmasking potential is not realized in the manifest film. Rambo's manifest enemy is the regressive Teasle, whom he defeats. But Teasle is really the film's scapegoat in displacing attention from Rambo's conflict with Trautman, the film's true representative of social authority. Trautman, a character invented for the film, does not fit easily into the supposedly central heroic plot. Although he stands for the superiority of the military community over the civilian community, his function in the plot is to assist the civilian community in subduing the renegade. To achieve this end, Trautman must resolve the tension attributed to Rambo's nature in favor of authority, as opposed to "natural" violence. The result is a resolution that sits oddly with the larger tradition to which the film belongs. Within the terms of what appears to be the central plot, the film might well have ended with Rambo's defeat of Teasle, his manifest enemy. If the filmmakers already had a sequel in mind (as seems likely), Rambo could have escaped heroically into the wilderness, a mythical space that oral tradition currently populates with renegade vets who fuse the attributes of a Daniel Boone with those of a Charles Manson. Alternately, a coherent resolution would have been the sacrificial destruction of the hero (the option selected in the book), followed by some suitably moralizing Hollywood comment on the "tragedy."

First Blood's rejection of these traditional resolutions is one index of the ideological tensions generated in the renegade-vet subgenre. In this film, the stock theme of heroic individualism is undercut by making Trautman into the agent of Rambo's defeat. Trautman personifies the spirit of technical rationality and calculation. He is authorized to mobilize state power in its everyday, routinized, efficient forms, and he stands ready to use that power against his own "creation." His first appearance neatly identifies his cinematic origins. He is the scientist-father, the godlike human substitute for God, a contemporary Dr. Frankenstein come to reestablish control over the dangerous power that he has unleashed.[7] For Trautman to triumph is implicitly to subordinate Rambo's wild masculinity to a masculinity organized around rational control.

In the film Trautman triumphs through love or, more precisely, erotic dependence on authority. His mere voice reduces Rambo to the status of a needy child, and it is Trautman who ultimately checks the "private war," with its potentially subversive ideological significations. While Trautman's motivations are at best ambiguous throughout (assuming that we identify with Rambo), Crenna plays the character sympathetically. He exudes benign paternalism, and even as he conspires against Rambo, we are encouraged to feel that he is somehow doing the right thing. Opposed to the boorish and ineffectual Teasle, Trautman's very presence appeals to erotic longings for a good, all-knowing father, one who incarnates a just order and who will defend us against malevolent powers. Without belaboring the oedipal implications, I would note Trautman's own acknowledgment of the ambivalence of the father-son relationship. Had a kiss not sufficed, we may assume that the paternal protector would have killed the son and enacted his latent identity with the paternal persecutor.

The film does not take its own implications that far, no doubt in part to leave open the possibility of a sequel, but it takes them far enough to construct a distinctly unromantic and peculiarly unstable resolution that we are asked to accept as necessity. The only alternatives offered to Rambo by the film are to be the violent, antisocial individual or the obedient, submissive dependent. Trautman effects his transformation from the one extreme to the other, acting within the film's terms as the "reality principle." Although the split between Good Father and Bad Father in the film may be so ambiguous that some viewers experience Trautman as malevolent, his authority is placed beyond challenge. He does what must be done, which is to reconcile Rambo with "the world" of hostile civilians by forcing him to renounce the power of resistance. In short, "Trautman" is a force that partially inhibits the play of meanings within the film.

Innocence Regained

When President Reagan departed from his prepared 1985 Labor Day speech to remark that he would clean up the tax system "in the spirit of Rambo," I doubt that his intended referent was the hero of *First Blood*. While that film did well at the box office and on video, in the words of my one teenage informant, it may have had "too much of a plot." It was the sequel, *Rambo: First Blood, Part Two,* that became a media event. The second film was invoked by Reagan as a model for foreign policy; and in one particularly militaristic week in the wake of the Beirut hostage crisis, it was repeatedly alluded to in congressional debates on Nicaragua. In the interval between the 1982 release of *First Blood* and the release of *Rambo* in spring 1985, Hollywood did what Sheriff Teasle could not do. The dangerous renegade was "cleaned up" and reassumed his proper, unmarked role as the defender of the American way of life. At a deeper level, the theme of class struggle, so tenuously contained by the renegade-vet subgenre, was projected overseas.

The new Rambo joined the heroes of earlier MIA films, of which the first, to my knowledge, was *Uncommon Valor,* released in late 1983 and directed by Ted Kotcheff, who also directed *First Blood*. The song played over the final credits of *Uncommon Valor* indicates the shift in mood. In place of the domestic war outside our own doors, we are given a moral vision of redemption:

We're all brothers in the night
Reaching out for something right
At a certain time, a certain place
Man can redeem mankind's disgrace.

The means of redemption as it has just been represented in the film is a new and just war, the good old-fashioned, manly sort of war that leads, the song promises, to "peace at last."

While the idea of peace through war has an imperialist ring, the wars represented in the MIA films are not overtly imperialist. Their manifest purpose is not to fight communism abroad, but to rescue American captives and to restore the lost innocence of the nation. It is regeneration through violence but with a particular emphasis. The MIA films make the project of self-fashioning depend more on a neoromantic critique of authority at home than on the destruction of an alien other. While the action entails violence against a cultural alien, the significance of this violence does not derive primarily from the alien's character. In *Uncommon Valor* this structural tendency is most pronounced. The "Vietnamese" (who are actually Laotians, which comes to the same thing in the film's terms) are morally neutral. They are opponents to be overcome in battle, not villains to be eradicated. In *Missing in Action* the main Vietnamese character does have overtly negative (and distinctly un-Communist) attributes, but he is killed off early in the film, leaving the hero to face his bureaucratic adversaries, who include Vietnamese and Americans. *Rambo,* the most willing of the three films to gratify desires for alien-commie-bad-guys, provides suitably sensual, sadistic, and craven Vietnamese, as well as more efficiently villainous Russian-Nazis, but the same film also magnifies the conflict with domestic authority into a paranoiac fantasy that determines the plot.[8]

The heroes of the MIA films are also veterans, ill at ease in society. Rambo is initially encountered in prison. *Uncommon Valor* and *Missing in Action* begin with dreamlike prefaces set in Vietnam, which show us soldiers taken captive in battle and then cut abruptly to images of figurative captivity: Chuck Norris (*Missing in Action*) pacing up and down his seedy apartment, while a TV announcer drones on about negotiations with the Vietnamese; Gene Hackman (*Uncommon Valor*) sitting frozen and impassive before TV images of returning POWs, isolated from his handsome, well-bred, silent wife, oblivious to the tasteful decor of his middle-class surroundings, fixated upon photos of his soldier son. Norris throws the TV out the window and departs for Vietnam, ostensibly to assist a diplomatic negotiating team but really to set his own mind at rest by going back for the men he left behind.

Hackman, who plays retired army Colonel Jason Rhodes, sets off on a five-year odyssey through Southeast Asia in pursuit of information regarding his missing son.

These obsessive, restless heroes are anchored by their passive counterparts, the literal captives in whose existence they never cease to believe. The literary genre of captivity narratives provides models for this pairing of hunter and captive. In the literary tradition the captives are female, either in fact or in symbolic value, and they serve as agents for the resocialization of the hunter through marriage.[9] It could be argued that the MIAs are symbolically feminized by their captivity, but in my reading of the films the message is that they are infantilized. Given that Jason Rhodes is a father searching for his son, that Norris plays a paternalistic colonel fulfilling an obligation to his dependents, and that Rambo at least thinks he may be Christ the Lord, I suggest that we are invited to interpret the rescue theme as a fantasy of generation by means of the male principle.

At a psychosexual level the return of the captives is a redemptive rebirth. It is effected by males and infuses society with a vigor that has been lacking. But the MIA films are constructed to assign the major responsibility for the lack to domestic authorities rather than to the Vietnamese captors. If the latter could plausibly be identified with the antierotic negation of the maternal principle, that identification is not a developed theme, with the partial exception of *Rambo*.[10] The problem, however, is not simply to identify the psychosexual fantasies with which the sequence of captivity and release is charged but to examine how and with what effect particular psychosexual fantasies inhabit fictionally conveyed social ideologies.

All three MIA films understand themselves as offering a critique of a market society, but their critique is distinctly one-sided.[11] In the romantic understanding of society that the MIA films promote, the abstract is attacked in the name of the concrete. The object of criticism is a manifest abstract, not capitalism as a total social formation but capitalism as it is misrecognized by a mystified social consciousness.

This manifest or perceived abstract is identified in the MIA films with the cold, calculating reason of the marketplace, which has come to govern political life. The threat that menaces the country emanates from bureaucratic controllers who subordinate all transactions to the principle of profit and loss. Jason Rhodes states the case most eloquently when he compares the collective repression of war memories to moral bankruptcy. "You cost too much," he tells his men, "and you won't turn a profit. There's no gain in it." The films define and condemn negotiated peace as a commodity, an artificial, unnatural product of political transactions ruled by an economizing logic. The bureaucrats who represent America in these transactions are willing to lose face in international relations in order to secure domestic order and stability at home.

Such are the abstract forces that the films take to be capitalism. Against this manifest abstract stands a manifest concrete, constituted by personal loyalties and emotional commitment to "basic human values" such as blood and honor. The institutional locus of the concrete is the family and those social forms for which the family is the metaphor: fraternal devotion among battle companions, filial respect for a leader, patriotic love of country. These "natural" institutions are understood not as products of capitalist society but as anterior and antagonistic to what is perceived as capitalism. They are enclaves of concrete humanity, the counterforce that provides the means of renewal. Within their own mystified terms, the MIA films project nostalgic visions of innocence regained through a return to "earlier" modes of communal life. Rebar-barianization, in a word—the regressive route to perfection—appears as a way out of modern society's crisis.

Up to a point, the symbolism of opposition is identical in the three films. The antagonistic forces of abstract and concrete are instantiated in a relationship between words and deeds. What is done through words is abstract, negative, false, double. Speech is the instrument of political authorities who use or abuse their verbal skills to hide the real. Conversely, what is said through deeds is concrete, positive, true, single, a direct manifestation of the doer's inner being that penetrates the illusions wrought by duplicitous speech.[12] Norris and Stallone take antirationality to the extreme by practically renouncing the spoken word. They enact themselves in deeds, gestures, body movements, and the occasional facial expression—all iconic signs that bear a concrete resemblance to what they designate.

Missing in Action and *Uncommon Valor* code the basic opposition in the same way. These films perform the romantic reversal that associates the valorized concrete passion of deeds with masculinity and the devalorized abstract reason of words with femininity. From this follows a concise diagnosis of the negative social condition. The tyranny of abstract reason has feminized the nation. The traditional image of Woman the Peacemaker, the figure who soothes, pacifies, and conciliates, is projected onto authority to mark its negative character. Behind this representation stands a long tradition. In the literary mythology of the frontier the symbolic femininity of civilization is often contrasted with the masculinity of the wilderness, and the contrast is a convention of many western films. With respect to literary fictions, Leslie Fiedler (1962) has argued convincingly that adventurous flight from society entails a refusal of heterosexual love. But Fiedler goes too far in reducing adventure-romance to one psychosexual dimension and reading the tradition solely as male fantasies. The adventurous hero who flees a feminized, overcivilized society does so in the name of some social vision that both legitimizes and is legitimized by the hero's sexual conduct. The interplay is more apparent in *Uncommon Valor* than in *Missing in Action,* largely because the former film is a "platoon movie." In this type of story the heroic group overtly represents a form of communal life and eventually comes to terms with female society. Norris in *Missing in Action* is the conventional Lone Hero, whose omnipotence finds expression in a more radical, uncompromising exclusion of women from his world.[13]

Yet Norris's represented relationship to his men implicitly connotes a form of communal life. Norris is the noble patron whose relationship to his dependents has a feudal character. With his trim Robin Hood beard he evokes the swashbuckling heroes of earlier cinematic romances. He acts in the film as the righteous protector of the meek, who defies the inhibiting domestic authorities. In so doing he symbolically enacts his refusal of femininity. Even more than *Uncommon Valor,* this film emphasizes the negative female attributes of authority. The senator who tries in vain to restrain Norris's anger is marked as weak, timid, and ineffectual at his first appearance. In the next scene the hero's antagonism to what the senator represents is forcefully restated. When Norris arrives at Saigon, he asserts his hatred of feigning by refusing to participate in the status rituals of greeting. Rebuked by the senator for his lack of tact, his only reply is a contemptuous glance. We, of course, are meant to receive his coarse directness as refreshing candor—manly honesty that cuts through the cloying, effeminate double-talk.

Uncommon Valor seems more aware of its organizing oppositions and projects a distinction between two uses of language onto literal men and women. Masculine speech is empowering and has a therapeutic function. It undoes resistances, strips away defenses, uncovers and releases the male self's repressed emotions of love and rage. Jason Rhodes knows this. His own capacity to initiate action is conditioned by the silent understanding of his deferential wife. Others have not been so fortunate. In order to recruit his son's battle companions for the rescue mission, Jason must overcome the inhibiting force of female speech. The film makes the point in two symmetric scenes. Having easily recruited the team's bachelor member, Jason confronts in succession the melancholy sculptor, Wilkes, and the gentle pilot, Charts. Both men have wives who stand between them and Jason. Wilkes's wife is overprotective. Hers is the voice of defensive repression that begs Jason not to stir up the past. Unmoved, Jason insists on talking with Wilkes. When the reluctant Wilkes emerges, he and his bachelor friend reach out to each other, first in understated words, and then in the manly embrace that says it all. Charts's wife is underprotective and deploys speech as a weapon against her stay-at-home spouse. She makes no attempt to block Jason but asks how much Charts would be paid. At the predictable reply, "Nothing in dollars," she exits from the scene and the film.

Jason rescues these lost souls from two types of castrating women, who also exhibit the two negative qualities attributed to the authorities in the film. Thus the overprotective wife is criticized for attempting to suppress the past, while the underprotective gold digger would bring marketplace thinking into affairs of the heart. The scenes effectively establish the underlying theme of the endangered self. The reconstruction of a coherent masculine self-identity necessitates the suspension of heterosexuality and its replacement by sublimated homoerotic love among battle companions. In *Missing in Action* the refusal of heterosexual love is more casually enacted, as are most things in this thinly plotted film. Norris is befriended by a sympathetic woman senatorial aide, whom he treats with a sadism that is undermotivated in terms of the immediate situation. He allows her to imagine that his interest in her is sexual, whereas the supposedly real point of his entering her hotel room is to mislead the Vietnamese guards and buy himself time to gather information about his men. The enacted cruelty toward the woman reflects the film's denial of its own psychosexual fantasies, a denial that also finds expression in Norris's omnipotence. Femininity, whether embodied in women or sniveling diplomats, is represented on the film's surface as a minor nuisance, not as a serious threat.

Uncommon Valor goes on to develop the theme of restorative homoeroticism in moving scenes. At a training camp located in Texas the motley crew that Jason has assembled work and play their way back into life. The play is essential. The boot-camp scenes are a boys-town version of the battle lunacy depicted in *Apocalypse Now*. In *Uncommon Valor,* however, the background for boyish play is not the madness of war but the repressive, demasculinizing force of civilization that play counteracts. The boot-camp scenes also condense the film's psychosexual code with its manifest ideological concern. The camp is simultaneously a world without women and a refuge from the sociologically defined abstract. It is financed by a humane capitalist named MacGregor, whose interest is not profit but the recovery of his MIA son. In this reconstituted masculine space of the concrete, the flight from femininity and ordinary life appears as socially necessary. It is in the service of a just cause, which will redeem the country. "This time," Jason tells the men, "no one can doubt the rightness of what we're doing."

The plot structure of *Uncommon Valor* is not reducible to a simple opposition. By the device of recursivity the basic opposition between concrete and abstract is replicated in the structure of the rescue operation. Jason, a true entrepreneur, selects his men with an eye to both their brotherly feelings and their particular, socially acquired types of expertise. He puts together a sort of corporatized military community, racially mixed, heterogenous in terms of class, a bourgeois ideal of organic solidarity where each man is dependent on the special skills of all the others. It is established that the success of the mission depends on its rational design, as well as on passionate commitment to a cause. The point is first made when Jason recruits the film's only literal Wild Man, a convict named Sailor. A leftover from some earlier renegade-vet film, Sailor has no hope of reassimilation into society, and he begs Jason to enlist him. He identifies himself with the unadulterated, concrete force of nature, boasting: "I fuck nuclear waste." But Sailor's raw, untempered wildness is not to overwhelm the mission. "This is a precise military operation," Jason snaps, "not some bullshit biker's acid trip."

The latter part of this assertion could be read as a prophetic allusion to *Rambo,* while the first part is a wishful thought that does not go entirely unfulfilled. Motivated by love and honor, bound together by libidinal ties, the rescue team is also quintessentially professional. Within this rehumanized male world, the abstract is remasculinized in the form of the rational design of the mission. Nevertheless, the superior value of the concrete is consistently maintained, especially in the passage from plan to execution.[14] *Uncommon Valor* makes exceptionally good use of an element that figures in all three films: the attempt of the authorities to intervene in the heroic mission. In terms of plot the effect of the intervention is nil in Norris's case; it does not move the action but merely marks Norris with his manly attributes. But in *Uncommon Valor* the act has structural consequences. In Thailand the expensive modern arms provided by MacGregor are confiscated by a reluctant CIA agent, clearly sympathetic to their cause. A solution is quickly forthcoming. MacGregor has given each man a sum of money as his personal reward, a fact that everyone seems to have suppressed. Upon remembering that they do have money, they are doubly relieved. By pooling their resources, they are able to pursue the mission and to rid themselves of the embarrassment of mixing honor with profit. The act of pooling is also constitutive of community and reaffirms the solidarity of the men. Moreover, now that their funds are limited, they are obliged to rely on cheaper goods that carry a heavy symbolic load. The weapons they purchase are drawn from a pre-Vietnam military technology, or more precisely, from pre-Vietnam films about World War II. Jason's promise about the "rightness" of the cause is symbolically fulfilled through those old-fashioned weapons, which evoke traditional military virtues and a time when American wars were cinematically portrayed as just.

In the course of the mission itself, the men repeatedly enact their reliance on human skill and practical intelligence over technology and planning. Of particular significance for my reading is an accident that damages one of their radios. The damaged radio will transmit but not receive, which means that the party who is to attack the prison camp will not know for certain if the other party is coming with helicopters for the escape. Hence the attack party is obliged to regress to an "earlier" mode of mental functioning, hallucinatory wish fulfillment—Freud's concrete, primary process. The attack party must have faith in an ideal image of the desired event, and the plot device neatly recapitulates the larger theme of converting apparent fantasy into reality.[15]

Uncommon Valor incorporates the stock character type of the loyal native helper into its psychosexual code. The helpers are a truncated Laotian family, a father and his daughters. One of the women performs a somewhat unconventional role for an action film. That she is permitted to act with valor and courage is not unusual, but that her courage is never undercut is noteworthy. Moreover, she is not de-eroticized, as so often occurs with Hollywood characters of this type. Instead of the familiar boy manqué, we get a glimpse of a figure who is at once erotic, maternal, courageous, and efficient. She even speaks in the voice of positive rationality when she points out that the pilot Charts is too valuable to risk. The film encourages us to believe that Charts will exchange his bitch-wasp wife for this noble savage.

While the fantasy of gender equality remains confined to the film's other world, it is at least represented by allusion. The subplot is a minor "recognition scene" that acknowledges a liberal audience consciously committed to the restructuring of gender relations. But the dominant vision with which the film concludes is of a traditional patriarchal relationship. Jason is the only hero in an MIA film who completes the full circuit of journey and return. He has learned that his own son is dead, and we have seen him mourn, something else that no other MIA hero is allowed to do. Only *Uncommon Valor* takes seriously the issue of transition and manifestly links the movement of history to the succession of father and son.

Jason's own line will end, but he himself has previously identified his familial past with American military history, from Gettysburg to Korea to Vietnam. This past is wishfully displaced through the reconstitution of the MacGregor family triangle, signifying that a benevolent, rehumanized, peaceful capitalism will now preside. The film's final image is also one of peace. Against the background of collective rejoicing over the freed captives, Jason's wife moves toward him, and they silently embrace. For contrast, consider the final image in *Missing in Action:* Norris dragging an MIA into a Saigon conference room, where American and Vietnamese diplomats are about to sign a false peace. Norris's phallic force once more literally penetrates this effeminate verbiage. He smiles for the first time in the film, exuding untempered patriarchal satisfaction. Cameras flash around him, and we are left with a final image of the aggressive, phallic power of individual exploit over collective action and of concrete images over abstract speech.

Missing in Action is a silly film that would not merit attention were it not for the subsequent, more disturbing phenomenon of *Rambo*. It is in reference to *Uncommon Valor* that we must assess the latest development of the subgenre. *Uncommon Valor* understands and presents its resolution as the end of war through a regenerative conflict that closes the cycle of violence and reintegrates the hero into society. In its own mythical terms, it is a film about peace at last. Moreover, the film is notably free of racist hatred and does not appeal directly to nationalist sentiments. The restoration of the patriarchal family is the metaphor for the redemption of the country, but the film engages our emotions at the level of the family drama. It suggests that right action must be motivated by personal ties, not by an abstract commitment to a nation. Had I seen *Uncommon Valor* in some other context, I suspect that I would have found its romantic adventurism entertaining and mildly offensive. As it is, I wish only that the genre had stayed in this state.

Let us turn now to the best known MIA film hero, starting with the refrain to the final credit song:

> *Peace in my life, remember the call*
> *Cheerful my brothers, think of them all*
> *Home of the free, we'll never fall*
> *The strength of our nation belongs to us all.*

The film itself is more than adequate to this mindless conflation of sexism, narcissism, and patriotic chauvinism. The vision projected in *Rambo* is of a world of men, the loyal sons of the nation, led by an omnipotent hero.

The greater part of the film consists of flagrantly crude, cheaply made scenes of comic-book violence. The overall effect of the violence is one of accentuated disreality. In the long, poorly edited action segments, causes and results seem to be almost willfully disassociated, and the physical space in which the protagonists confront each other is radically disordered. There is, however, a pattern that organizes imaginary space in the film. Despite claims to the contrary, *Rambo* has a plot, a distinctive permutation of the basic MIA plot.

One permutation is in reference to *First Blood,* where Trautman mediated between the hero and the civilian government. In the "sequel" Trautman retains his mediating role, but the new premise is that the government has need of the hero's power. Hence Trautman, who previously brought about Rambo's submission, now secures his release from bondage. The film begins with Trautman arranging to get Rambo out of prison so he can participate in a special reconnaissance mission for MIAs in Vietnam. Trautman is once again "the only one that [Rambo] trusts," and this time the trust is not entirely misplaced. It is not only Rambo who has been "cleaned up" for this film but Trautman as well. His character, as it is revealed by the plot, has been softened and disambiguated, purged of the unresolved tensions inherent in the prototype. In the process, Trautman changes poles. Whereas Trautman's rationality marked the superiority of military authority over civilian authority in *First Blood,* in the "sequel" he becomes a personification of emotional loyalty to men and country.

Trautman's new adversary is far more dangerous than the backward Teasle. *Rambo* follows the other two MIA films in condemning a manifest abstract, once again embodied in economizing political authorities. The particular villain is named Murdock, and the office he holds is vaguely defined. His remark that "My committee cares" (that is, about the MIAs) suggests that he is a member of Congress, which is how Vincent Canby interpreted him, but that makes no sense given the powers attributed to him in the film, which suggests that he is a CIA agent in charge of the special operation. Of course, the film is under no obligation to make sense, and the vagueness of Murdock's office is really its point. He is a bizarre conflation of a pinko Congress with the bureaucratic ruthlessness and omniscience that some of us would associate with Central Intelligence. Surrounded by high-tech computers, which initially generated Rambo's name for the mission, Murdock is the perfect realization of that malevolent, shadowy, abstract force known as The System.

Despite surface similarities Murdock stands apart from the duplicitous authorities in the other films. The bad controllers in *Uncommon Valor* and *Missing in Action* are weaklings who resort to sneaky tactics coded as feminine. But in *Rambo* abstract reason is imagined in its unmarked, masculine form. Thanks to his computers, Murdock is all-knowing (except, of course, that he doesn't know Rambo); he is flanked by tough-looking dudes who, while they could easily be read as gay, are of a distinctly macho, heavy-leather variety. But above all, Murdock is masculine in the control he exerts over the mission for which Rambo is recruited. Murdock and his unseen associates have an excess of disciplinary power. They do not capitulate to external circumstances but rather actively manipulate circumstances to produce a desired effect. So far as we know, they never negotiate with Vietnamese. Instead, they devise a truly diabolical scheme to deceive the country.

The recon mission, you see, is a scam. Thanks to their computer technology, the authorities are able to monitor the relocation of POWs within Vietnam. The POW camp that they have selected for Rambo to reconnoiter and photograph is one that they believe to be empty. The hidden purpose of the mission is to generate photographic "proof" that there are no more American soldiers in Vietnam. Supposedly the authority of the photographs will be validated by the prestige of the magnificent war hero, whose previous incarnation as a renegade vet seems to have been made inoperative by Murdock.

Various scenes relate the conspiracy to the concrete-passion/abstract-reason scheme. The duplicitous Murdock characterizes the issue of the MIAs as "emotional" and assures Rambo that he "knows what the country feels." Shortly afterward, however, he lowers his mask a bit in Trautman's presence. He confides that he has little confidence in the success of the mission but notes pragmatically that "there are people who have to be satisfied." His cold, calculating tone gives this new Trautman pause, and he accuses Murdock of a lack of emotionality. Murdock shrugs off the charge. "It wasn't my war," he says. "My job is to clean up the mess." When the naked truth is revealed halfway through the film, Trautman's metamorphosis into the sentimental humanist is complete. He rails against the "goddam mercenaries" and "stinking bureaucrats" who value profit over human life. Vainly he asserts the countervalues of love, honor, and loyalty to "our men." "No, your men," says one of Murdock's thugs. "Don't be a hero."

Trautman cannot be a hero in this film, for his benevolent paternalism is rendered impotent by the superior power of Murdock's "machine." Murdock describes him as "just a tool" and places him under arrest. Murdock's commands have the force that Trautman's cultivated, honest, humane speech lacks. When Murdock speaks, the words are deeds and elicit immediate responses, whereas Trautman can only represent a wish that remains for his surrogate son to fulfill. "You've made one mistake," he tells Murdock: "Rambo." Like the wise old king in the fairy tales,

Trautman is reduced to dependency on the young hero. Their relationship as enacted in *First Blood* has been reversed.

The new Rambo tries to convince us that he's the same basically decent, unappreciated chap we met in the other film, but the way he goes about it is inadvertently revealing. In the earlier film the metaphor of the "war at home" remained ambiguous, with the potential to take in more than the film intended. *Rambo* drains the metaphorical reservoir of meaning. In what for him is a chatty mood, Rambo reflects philosophically on the "other war" going on at home. But he explicitly limits its victims to Vietnam vets and so undercuts the synecdochic representation of the exploited working class by the exploited vet. Moreover, the film as a whole reenacts the distinction between Vietnamese/Indians and Indian-fighter hero, thereby defusing the metaphorical correspondence implied in *First Blood*. Whatever those poor guys at home may be, they are certainly not Vietnamese.

Nor is Rambo himself a member of the community that he describes. He speaks about the war "against the soldiers" from a boat on a river in Vietnam, where he has once more assumed his Indian-fighter identity and where he will undergo trials beyond those of ordinary men. Prophetically, he foresees the persecution that awaits him. "I'm expendable," he says, and when the Vietnamese girl who has befriended him asks in Hollywood pidgin, "What mean expendable, Rambo?" his only response is a saintly smile. The film will play out the christological resonances of Rambo's "expendability" by seeing to it that all the evil in the world—whether emanating from Americans, Vietnamese, or Russians—is directed against the hero-redeemer. With godlike knowledge Rambo knows from the start that he is surrounded by enemies, set down in a corrupt world to which he himself does not belong. He is in the world but not of it, and this stressed apartness distinguishes the character from his earlier manifestation in *First Blood*. John Rambo was a man who suffered as men do—from hunger, from physical abuse, from traumatic memories, from loneliness, from the cruelty of an unfeeling world. The new Rambo transcends the human condition, from above in the film's terms, which would have us equate Rambo's sufferings with Christ's, from below in the generic terms that the film's presentation of its hero evokes.

Like Norris in *Missing in Action,* Rambo acts as the Lone Hero, but he also has other, less swashbuckling antecedents. Let us remember that he is the creation that threatens to escape its creator's control, the man-made monster endowed with superhuman powers. Teasle was close to the truth when he wondered what had "possessed God" to make Rambo, but it is the "sequel" that fully realizes the implications of the phraseology and gives us a conflation of the divine with the demonic. When *Rambo* replays the hunt sequence of *First Blood,* any attempt at realism is abandoned. In place of the crafty Indian fighter who entraps his pursuers, we see a self-avowed savior on a rampage of unlimited destruction. Apocalypse now, the film suggests, but the scenes are more reminiscent of horror films about the lunatic-in-the-woods.

In the first film Rambo incarnated a tension between savagery and civilization on the model of traditional frontier heroes. Even when forced to "regress" to his wilderness identity, he remained in contact with the civilizing force embodied in Trautman, poised between the two poles of the alien and authority. *Rambo* dissolves the tension. It is no longer a matter of resolving the opposition in favor of one or the other pole, for the new Rambo absorbs all the oppositions that the film generates.

This structure is neither that of *Missing in Action* nor of *Uncommon Valor.* The loner Norris embodies a pure, uncompromising masculinity that triumphs over feminized opponents and refuses relationship with literal women. *Uncommon Valor,* modeled on platoon movies, recursively replicates the basic opposition, with concrete, masculine passion as the unmarked term that stands for the whole. In that film the heroic forces can reestablish productive relationships with domestic society, as represented by MacGregor and by women. But in *Rambo* the fusion of opposites generates a third term that needs only itself. It is no wonder that Rambo's romantic alliance with the Vietnamese girl is almost immediately terminated. What need has our hero of the noble-savage woman when he already incorporates the attributes that she embodies? The point is anticipated in the disclosure of Rambo's ethnic origins. He is part Indian, part German—"a hell of a combination," as Murdock remarks. He fuses the stereotypical savage closeness to nature, egalitarianism, and quasi-mystical knowledge with those aspects of civilization assimilable to the concrete: efficiency, self-discipline, acquired mastery of military technology. This particular "combination" has a history. There is, for instance, Theodore Roosevelt's vision of an Anglo-Saxon cowboy who goes back to nature and is revitalized by the frontier experience.[16] But the more recent model, which the film seems unable to avoid evoking, is the Nazi vision of the union of blood and the machine.

As if disturbed by its own implications, the film hastily strips Rambo of his more highly coded attributes, the storm-trooper getup and ultraefficient equipment that Murdock has provided. Rambo, we are told, never really wanted all this gear, since, in one of the film's more ludicrous lines, he believes that "the mind is the best weapon." However absurd the line sounds in Stallone's delivery, it is consistent with the general scheme, for "mind" is conceived of as a concrete human attribute and opposed to the "artificial," overly abstract technology of intelligence. "Mind" is really the machine in human form, the perceived material aspect of industrial technology that is consistent with the glorification of the concrete.

The mission has barely begun when Rambo jettisons most of his heavy equipment. When we first see him in "Vietnam," it is in the true-blue American guise of the Indian fighter, half-naked, running silently through the Mexican "jungle," relying on his wits. He does, however, retain one piece of equipment that restates the point about his ancestry. Of all the "advanced weaponry" bestowed upon him, what he keeps is a sophisticated bow, first used with Indian-style arrows, but later loaded with exploding missiles that literally reduce the enemy to smithereens. This is no ordinary Indian fighter, despite the traditional elements of the symbolism. When Rambo finally unleashes his rage against the alien enemy, it is as the fusion of "blood-and-guts" savagery with machine-like efficiency.

But destruction of the alien, whether biologized Vietnamese race enemy or its hypercivilized Naziesque Russian accomplices, is not our hero's final objective. For all its inanity, the film never loses sight of its basic plot. Having stoically endured unspeakable savage and civilized forms of torture, the captive Rambo makes radio contact with the military base. His words and emphasis are: "Murdock, I'm coming to get *you!*" Rambo has good cause to be upset. The turning point of the film comes when he succeeds against all expectations in locating the MIAs. He rescues one of them and races to the agreed on "extraction point," with the Vietnamese in hot pursuit. The chopper arrives to meet him, carrying the loyal Trautman as well as Murdock's thugs, and word is sent back to the base that Rambo has been spotted with an MIA. At the base the technicians rejoice, thereby constituting themselves as The People. Murdock promptly orders them out of the room and aborts the mission, to Trautman's horror. Thus Rambo is stranded in the "other-world," like many a fairy tale hero. We next see him surrounded by Vietnamese tormentors, in a Christ-like pose that is clearly intended to identify Murdock with Judas.

Rambo is not a suspense film. Such gratification as may be provided in the action scenes does not have its source in a tension between the justness of the cause and the apparent improbability of its success.[17] Rambo's skill is so miraculous that we never doubt that he will succeed. The action scenes do not rely on a deferral of gratification. Instead, they *are* the first gratification of the desire for revenge aroused by the betrayal scene, which is intensely suspenseful. Its plot-generated tension is heightened by its capacity to arouse nightmare experiences of pursuit and primordial fears of abandonment.

The act of betrayal reveals the utter corruptness of the political power represented by Murdock, and it opens the final move of the plot: the hero's revenge. In this the film differs from both *Uncommon Valor* and *Missing in Action,* which end with rescue and return. The deeds of these films' heroes are sufficient in themselves to expose the weakness of the authorities, who passively defer to a morally superior force. But Rambo must actively defeat his domestic enemy in order to close the plot. The mode of closure reflects a relationship between hero and society unlike that constructed in the other films. *Uncommon Valor* and *Missing in Action* present two ways of reconciling heroism with ordinary social life. Reconciliation is metonymic in *Uncommon Valor* and metaphoric in *Missing in Action,* a distinction that derives from the films' specific generic antecedents. The heroes of a platoon film such as *Uncommon Valor* can be reintegrated into the society they redeem, whereas a Lone Hero like Norris will remain at the boundaries (the threshold of the conference room in the film). Nevertheless, Norris represents an ideal type who can be replicated in lesser tokens. Even if he himself rides away into the sunset, he has reinfused society with the phallic energy that it will henceforth contain in diluted or domesticated form.

But in *Rambo* no reconciliation is possible. The hero is neither contained by society nor is he a replicable type whose tokens could stand in some meaningful relationship to other social categories. At a psychosexual level, such resolutions are precluded by an underlying fantasy that is not the same as in the other films. In clinical terms there has been a passage from neurosis to psychosis that corresponds to the manifest contrast in the fictional resolutions.

A critical feature for my analysis is the permutation of the Teasle/ Trautman pair into Murdock/Trautman, which leaves Rambo caught between civilian and military authorities. The consistently oppositional structure of authority corresponds at a psychosexual level to a split between a persecutory oepidal father and a benevolent manifestation of the same prototype. There is, however, a significant difference in the way the two films realize the split. The Trautman of *Rambo* loses his association with instrumental reason and is rendered impotent. In place of the authoritarian resolution of the son's submission to the father, we are offered a double image of rebellion. Rambo defeats his persecutor and casts off his protector, thus enacting a fantasy of total freedom from dependence on others.

The film asks us to receive Rambo's omnipotence as a necessary response to the undependability of the outside world. From a clinical perspective, however, both grandiose self-images and the splitting of authority figures into good and bad appear as symptomatic formations, defenses against unconscious fears of dependence that originate in infantile rage at separation from the mother.

In this regard it is instructive to recall the trivial cause of the action in *First Blood*. Prior to Teasle's intervention all that Rambo wanted was "something to eat," a desire that went ungratified until he satisfied it by himself. In *Rambo* there is again a casual reference to the provision of food. Rambo refuses food offered to him by his female Vietnamese helper, even though, to our knowledge, he has not eaten since the mission began. Inconsequential as it is, the interaction momentarily brings the defensive function of Rambo's self-sufficiency to the surface of the plot. His apparent omnipotence becomes intelligible as a denial or repression of a feared condition of helplessness.

That fear returns in projected form in the film's realization of the theme of captivity. The Vietnamese treatment of the captives is represented as deplorable in the other films, but in *Rambo* it takes on a nightmarish quality that appeals directly to early fantasies of the Bad Mother. Whereas the other films include scenes of captives returning from work out in the fields, *Rambo* gives us to believe that the captives are perpetually confined inside a tiny cage, a condensed symbol of the womb as tomb. Yet if the gender identity of the captors is more strongly marked than in the other films, that of the deliverer is strangely indeterminate. The central characters in *Uncommon Valor* and *Missing in Action* are mature men, literal or figurative fathers, and paternal affection provides the model for the tenderness shown by rescuers to captives. Defined as the very paradigm of devotion, father-son love infuses homoeroticism with its sublime character. Even the weak, helpless captives quickly ally themselves with their saviors—as active combatants in *Missing in Action*, as consolers in *Uncommon Valor*, where Jason and the young MacGregor weep in each other's arms. But Rambo, who is identified as surrogate son to both Trautman and Murdock, exhibits a quasi-maternal concern for the captives, and the radical dependence of the captives on their rescuer is correspondingly emphasized. They can do nothing for him except adore him, while the only point at which the stoic hero momentarily hesitates is when the Vietnamese threaten harm to his charges.

The film openly invites us to code Rambo's compassion as spirituality and the boundless gratitude of the captives as veneration. A religious message is also implicit in a line that figured in the publicity for the film, "What you call hell, [Rambo] calls home."[18] Thus did Christ transform an evil world, but it should be noted that the task of homemaking is traditionally entrusted to women. Rambo the Deliverer is a composite figure, as much an idealized, internalized Good Mother as a penetrating, phallic force. The grateful captives exchange a negative dependence on their feminized captors for a positive dependence on their savior, who absorbs the maternal function.

Rambo loves the captives without reservation, as a narcissistic subject may unconsciously wish to be loved by the mother and, the film informs us, as he wishes to be loved by the country that once rejected him. "I want what they all want," he confides to Trautman in the final scene, "for our country to love us as much as we love it." The context for this admission is Rambo's triumphant return and defeat of Murdock. By implication "the country" is the stake in the oedipal struggle, the female object of desire, which now belongs by rights to the victor. But where *First Blood* opened with the frustrated desire for food, *Rambo* closes with the frustrated desire for love. Although Trautman promises Rambo a second Congressional Medal of Honor—the objectified token of the country's gratitude—the reward is not enough, not "as much" as Rambo claims to love. Norris could at least beam with satisfaction, but Stallone's Rambo remains sullen and refuses even that degree of relationship inherent in accepting respects and courtesies.

His last words are that he will live "day by day," outside of history, rootless in space. It is the traditional theme of the Indian fighter's disappearance into the wilderness (now the Third World) but condensed with both the religious savior's withdrawal from the world and the exile of the monster. The divine and the demonic remain fused to the end, and an image of flight from persecution is superimposed on the hero's voluntary rejection of society.

The film provides us with a checklist of the complex of factors that Freud associated with paranoia: fixation at the narcissistic stage (Rambo's manifest omnipotence and repressed fear of dependence), weakly sublimated homosexuality (his quasi-maternal relationship to the captives, which replaces the more manly, sublimated comraderie of the other films, not to mention the sexualized violence and violent sexuality conveyed in the image of Rambo pointing his knife at the prostrate Murdock), and delusions of persecution as the defense against the homosexual wish.[19]

In the Freudian model of symptom formation, the primary mechanisms are projection and distortion into the opposite. Motivated by a sense of threat, the subject withdraws his affection from the external world. The withdrawn libido then returns in projected form as "they hate me." *Rambo* systematically confounds the distinctions between internal and external, self and other, love and anger, omnipotence and helplessness. Subjective desires and fears return as an external danger to be overcome, and a repressed sense of powerlessness returns as a resolute will to power. So threatening does the world appear in the film that it legitimizes the rage from which the sense of threat originates.

Conclusion: Whose War Was It?

> *The experience of victimization,*
> *which justifies resistance, can also*
> *destroy the capacity for resistance*
> *by destroying the sense of personal*
> *responsibility.*

—**Christopher Lasch**

Lasch's immediate referent in the above passage from *The Minimal Self* is the film *Coming Home,* which he criticizes for its undiscriminating rejection of political causes. In the film's valorization of life at all costs, Lasch detects a blanket refusal of collective action, which he attributes to the wider culture. Viewed in the context of the liberal antiwar films of the 1970s, the emergence of the MIA genre adds a disturbing twist to Lasch's argument. For at the same time as these films indicate their predecessors' failure to contribute to a critical, historical consciousness of the war, they also demonstrate the power of mass fictions to empty political concepts of their oppositional content.

The MIA films began to appear in the aftermath of the Iranian hostage crisis, amid Reaganite assurances of the return of American confidence and pride. Their direct precursors, I have argued, were not the major liberal films about the horrors of war but less prestigious films and television shows involving the figure of the renegade vet. The Vietnam veterans represented in these films were permanent outsiders, inassimilable outcasts, who appeared in both divine and demonic manifestations as heroic crusaders (*Billy Jack,* 1971) or psychotic killers (*Rolling Thunder,* 1977). The divine and the demonic were fused in the Rambo character of *First Blood,* which I have treated as a paradigmatic member of the subgenre. But what needs emphasis is the persistent ambivalence in cinematic attitudes toward the alienation personified in the character type of the renegade.

The historical referents of the fictional renegades were the poor and underprivileged soldiers who fought in Vietnam and who were doubly victimized by the war. First, as many soldiers well understood, the responsibility for fighting the war was borne disproportionately by the working class. Second, Vietnam veterans returned to a country that largely denied them the traditional rewards of the warrior and to a government that failed to provide adequate forms of material support. As traces of a war that many Americans longed to forget (whether out of liberal guilt or damaged pride), Vietnam veterans were the object of a collective repression.

They returned in mass fictions, attached to the traditional mythic theme of the outsider, and in this form they became a potent symbol of discontent. Too potent, I have argued. Renegade-vet plots threatened, as did the war itself, to unmask the connections between imperialism abroad and class conflict at home. The tensions unleashed by fictional renegades were contained to varying degrees and by different devices. Renegades assimilated to the psycho type could be "legitimately" massacred by middle-class defenders of order, who were sometimes vets themselves. But in *First Blood* a subproletarian renegade moved to the center of the plot. This was no well-intentioned, countercultural crusader but a bundle of unsatisfied wants, whose tragedy is that he has no cause. "It wasn't my war," says Rambo to Trautman, "it was your war." If at *this* juncture in *this* film the son had rebelled against paternal authority, *First Blood* would have become manifestly subversive. Had Rambo turned on Trautman, as opposed to Teasle, and rejected "Trautman's war," the film would have openly solicited critical reflection on the class origins of imperialist and domestic struggles.

Instead, the rebellion is deferred. It took the MIA films to create a safe outlet for the social discontents embodied in renegade vets. What is most striking about these films is that they do not limit themselves to legitimizing violence against alien enemies. They also absorb and defuse the threat of domestic violence by incorporating the theme of resistance to authority into a basic plot. The MIA film heroes share a common distrust of abstract causes, an attitude that is also reflected in novels and memoirs written by Vietnam veterans.[20] Abstract commitments to nationalist ventures are distinguished in the films and in the literary works from the true community based on shared experiences and loyalty to companions. The MIA film heroes fight wars that are represented as "theirs"—deeply personal struggles, affairs of the heart. *Uncommon Valor* is particularly instructive in this respect, for its fantasy war is the one most closely modeled on cinematic versions of World War II, with one difference. The new platoon no longer fights its just war with and for the government but rather despite a government of weak appeasers, in defense of the private against the public.

There is a wider ideological process at work here, detectable in other mass entertainment films that dutifully criticize an overabstract, authoritarian system of control. To keep to the MIA films, their manifest message reverses a more traditional nationalist ideology. What we are told by these films is not that the nation's causes are the responsibility of individual citizens. Instead, we learn that personal causes are the true responsibility of a nation that has somehow strayed from its rightful course and awaits redemption. Lasch insists correctly on a connection between the sense of personal responsibility and the capacity for resistance, but the problem remains. The ideological conversion of public duty into desire provides a powerful instrument for eliciting consent to the dominant order.

Vietnam as historical referent recedes from popular consciousness. The films of the 1970s and the disillusionment they embodied are displaced by visions of a restored sense of purpose and mission. Inasmuch as fictional models of the past contribute to shaping images of the present and the future, the representation of Vietnam is the stake in a struggle. Whatever the shortcomings of the 1970s films, the war they represented did not lend itself to a militaristic nationalism. But from the just, private wars of the MIA films to military intervention in Grenada, Nicaragua, the Philippines, or Libya may not be so great a distance. It is all too easy to imagine a moment when such actions would appear, at least initially, as "personal responsibilities."[21]

Still, the outcome is not determined. *Rambo,* the most disturbing of the MIA films, may also prove the most difficult to control. With its paranoiac vision of a world in which all distinctions are confounded, it blurs the boundaries between internal and external enemies and can provide a model for limited acts of protest and resistance as well as for nationalist pride. On a television newscast last fall an escaped convict was assimilated to the Rambo character by a fellow prisoner; a more sophisticated appropriation is implicit in a story told to me of striking workers who designated security guards as "Rambo." An ethnography of the film's reception would doubtless uncover other appropriations, "secondary acts of production," as Michel de Certeau (1984) calls them. Meanwhile, a reaction is already visible in the mass media. Thus in a recent family sitcom, a middle-class suburban child is warned against acting like Rambo, who is made to stand for the negation of bourgeois values. Rambo's antiauthoritarian style does not provide a model for a progressive oppositional culture. Nevertheless, the rebellious tendencies he embodies are not easily contained, and it would appear that Reagan was only partly successful in appropriating the character. Fortunately for Reagan, there is always Rocky Balboa.

3

Secrets of Success
in Postmodern Society

*One could argue that . . . films bear
an intricate and woefully unanalyzed
relationship to their society.*

—I. C. Jarvie

ROM THE GILDED AGE ON, the
American fiction of the self-made man or success hero has been used to
reformulate an older republican dream of individual freedom in the
context of an increasingly organized, consumption-oriented, corporate
capitalist society.[1] My concern in this chapter is with one such refor-
mulation. From an analysis of four unabashedly minor Hollywood films,
I will abstract a certain ideological pattern that came into circulation
during the Reagan era.

The films were released between 1984 and 1987 at the height of that
era. They are: *All the Right Moves* (1984), starring Tom Cruise; *Ferris
Bueller's Day Off* (1986; subsequently referred to as *Ferris Bueller*),
starring Matthew Broderick; *Nothing in Common* (1986), starring Tom
Hanks; and *The Secret of My Success* (1987; subsequently referred to as
Secret), starring Michael J. Fox. These films are connected by similarities
in story, theme, and locale. All four are concerned with individual
mobility and success, as achieved in high school (*All the Right Moves,
Ferris Bueller*) or in the corporate workplace (*Nothing in Common,
Secret*). At a more abstract level all have plot structures based on an
opposition between youth and age, to which other oppositions are made
to correspond as the plots unfold. With the exception of *Nothing in*

67

Common, the films star teen idols and were intended for the biggest
ticket buyers of the 1980s, the 12- to 19-year-old movie audience. Hanks,
whose main appeal is to young adults, resembles Cruise, Broderick, and
Fox in an important respect. Along with a variety of young and youngish
stars, all four specialize in conveying a cool, breezy, highly verbal, yet
distinctly boyish style of rebellious independence.[2] In *All the Right
Moves,* however, Cruise is cast against this type. The film was a box
office flop. By contrast, both *Nothing in Common* and *Secret* did moderately well in their respective seasons, and *Ferris Bueller,* with its ultra-
ironist hero, was the smash hit of the summer of 1986.

In this chapter I try to contextualize the relative box office popularity
of cinematic images of success. My thesis, in brief, is that a fantasy
embedded in the commercially successful success stories appeals primarily to the young managers and professionals of today and tomorrow.
In short, I interpret the films as part of the making of the new middle
classes.

Before I develop this thesis, its theoretical foundations require definition. An anthropology of commercial film or other mass-mediated
forms of culture must be adjusted to the particular conditions of cultural
production in capitalist society. In a system where many forms of culture
are produced as commodities by the few for the many, the relationship
of cultural forms to collective experience is singularly complex. What,
if anything, connects the implicit meanings that mass cultural forms
may embody to the lived culture of receiving audiences? Assuming there
is a connection, what is its nature and how is it established? Do the
patterns of significance in mass cultural texts that analysis may uncover
originate in the imaginative needs of "audience subcultures" (Gans
1974), as a neo-Durkheimian reflectionist theory of mass culture would
have it? Or is the content of mass culture entirely determined by its elite
producers, the corporate owners and media professionals who control
what manipulationist theory knows as the "culture industry" (Horkheimer and Adorno 1972)?

In a lucid article on theories of capitalist culture, Richard Johnson
(1986–1987) argues that what requires study is a total process, a circuit
of production, circulation, and consumption of cultural forms. But
existing theories, he suggests, express only particular moments or stages
of the process. He asks: "What if they are all true, but only as far as
they go, true for those parts of the process that they have most clearly
in view? What if they are all false or incomplete, liable to mislead, in
that they are only partial, and therefore cannot grasp the process as a
whole? What if attempts to 'stretch' this competence (without modifying

the theory) lead to really gross and dangerous (ideological?) conclusions?" (45–46).

Reflectionist theory takes the viewpoint of the receiving audience, whose broadly shared values supposedly find expression in what these theorists tend to call "popular" culture. Among the limits of this viewpoint is its neglect of the culture industry and a resultant tendency to misrepresent the process of production as governed exclusively by market forces or, as the saying goes, as "giving the audience what it wants." But audience preferences are only one of many factors that influence production decisions. Producers also shape their work to conform to dominant sensibilities and values, including those of the producing community itself. Indeed, as Richard Slotkin (1984: 412) notes, among the most important audiences in film production is the "audience of fellow producers."

Moreover, the preferences of the mass audience can only influence production insofar as they are known, and the culture industry's favored instruments of knowledge (market-research techniques, ideas about public opinion circulating in the mass media) are notoriously unreliable (Gitlin 1983). Film audiences, in particular, went singularly underresearched for many years, perhaps, I. C. Jarvie (1970: 108) suggests, because a complacent film industry had grown accustomed to a seller's market.

Thus producers respond to an obscurely informed interpretation of audience needs, "a myth," as Slotkin (1984: 412) calls it, "about who the audience is and what it wants." As part of the raw material for cultural production, such a "myth of the audience" is eventually incorporated into cultural products and returned to consumers. What returns along this circuit is not a reflection but a highly selective version of collective sentiment, the culture industry's ideologically structured image of popular desires and fears. Active mass participation in the circuit begins at this point with the reception of cultural forms by social groups. To cite Slotkin (1984: 413) once more, "The mass audience does not make what it sees, but receives and reacts to what is produced by others."

Manipulationist views of mass culture as indoctrination never lose sight of the producers' activities. These views are limited, however, by what Johnson (1986–1987: 55) calls "productivism," a tendency to reduce the process of reception to that of production. The unwarranted assumption here is that whatever messages mass-media elites put into their texts are automatically realized in the consciousness of the receiving "masses." Reception, in this account, is no more than the passive, uncontextualized assimilation of ruling ideas by subordinate classes.

Ironically, in neglecting to account for how mass cultural forms are subjectively interpreted and situationally used, the older manipulation theory is unable to explain the power that it attributes to cultural forms (Ohmann 1981). For if audiences could not *re*cognize their ideals, beliefs, desires, or fears among the images circulated by the culture industry, why would they find those images compelling? The manufactured consent that neo-Gramscians call hegemony—ideological domination—is manufactured from the debris of common sense and recycled in a never-ending array of mass-mediated versions of the world (Hall 1982). For a given version to penetrate everyday thought and practice and so perform its hegemonic function, audiences must be able to relate it to their socially conditioned imaginative needs.

At this critical conjunction between the textualized goods of the culture industry and the private, everyday lives of their consumers, at least two modes of analysis would ideally converge. We need both systematic analyses of texts and cultural accounts of text-reception, studies of the structural properties of mass-cultural forms and ethnographies of their social uses. Such a Janus-faced study would explore the interactions between the commercial production of culture and cultural creation in everyday life.

Janice Radway's (1984) work on romances and their readers is an important contribution to this project. Radway begins with the social situation of actual readers and incorporates their insights into a highly original analysis of the narrative texts. But the passage may also be made in the other direction: from narrative texts to their receivers. An ethnographer who took this latter route could search for correspondence between patterns embodied in mass cultural narratives and the more loosely structured stories that people tell about their lives—their narrative constructions of personal and collective identity. In the process, of course, the ethnographer would probably come to revise the original textual analysis. Alternatively, I suspect that preunderstandings of mass-entertainment culture would help to elucidate the fictions through which people live their lives.[3]

Although the analysis that follows focuses on films as texts and not on actual processes of production and reception, it is informed by the model of the cultural circuit. Its framing questions are these: What brings particular story forms into circulation and makes them compelling to audiences at certain moments, and what implications might such stories have for lived culture? To answer these questions fully would require different forms of inquiry, supplementary studies of producing and receiving communities. But the assumption common to the present study and to those I have yet to undertake is that the answers lie outside of texts themselves, in the social and historical conditions of their production and use.

Vicissitudes of the Success Hero

The idea of the self-made man has done yeoman and postyeoman service in American culture. From Benjamin Franklin to presidential candidate Michael Dukakis's immigrant father, tokens of the type have been celebrated as incarnations of the American Dream—the dream of an open, mobile society where individuals rise through talent and achievement.[4] Conversely, the disappearance of the self-made man is a recurrent theme in twentieth-century literature, used to signify the negation of the dream.

Whatever his fate in social reality (where his presence has been greatly exaggerated), it is unlikely that the self-made man will disappear as an ideological figure. For success ideology has never been static, as its historians have demonstrated (Wyllie 1954; Cawelti 1965; Weiss 1969). It has existed in multiple versions, and these have changed over time, registering and responding to historically engendered cultural tensions. In all its versions success ideology has appealed primarily to the middle classes. Thus its history is embedded in the massive transformation of the American middle classes that dates back to the Gilded Age. Between 1870 and 1940 the development of corporate capitalism led to the displacement of the older, propertied, entrepreneurial middle classes by the new salaried middle classes of corporate employees. The latter classes have steadily expanded with the proliferation of the large organizations on which they depend.

The making of the new middle classes was a cultural as well as an institutional process. In its cultural dimension it involved a partial rejection of inherited ideas and values. What has unfolded over the last hundred years has been represented as a clash of cultures—a conflict, in Warren Susman's (1984: xx) expressive if slightly overcondensed phrase, between "an older culture, often loosely labelled Puritan-republican, producer-capitalist culture, and a newly emerging culture of abundance."

Although the crucial battles were not fought until the 1920s and 1930s, the conflict took shape in the Gilded Age. According to inherited middle-class morality, success depended on the disciplinary virtues of the Protestant Ethic—industry, thrift, sobriety, self-restraint—and was of less importance than the "character-building" effects of work itself. Success manuals and dime novelists such as Horatio Alger did their best to perpetuate this tradition under new conditions. But as American industry grew ever larger and more concentrated in the three decades after the Civil War, its very productivity weakened the Protestant Ethic.

Under this pressure, Alan Trachtenberg (1982: 81) observes, the image of success "accumulated its ambiguities." Successful businessmen who claimed status as traditional self-made men contributed to a secularized ethic of entrepreneurial success. For however attractive the image of the sober, industrious Businessman Hero might have been to new economic elites in pursuit of legitimacy, it failed to exhaust popular attitudes toward the business world. What more and more impressed the public was the aggressive competitiveness of the robber barons as well as the material wealth such men enjoyed. These attitudes are refracted in another traditional success hero popularized in humorous literature, a shrewd, enterprising, upwardly mobile rogue who succeeds by cunning and trickery and who is more concerned with material success than with self-improvement (Cawelti 1965: 63–73).

Industrious workers and materialistic men on the make have one thing in common: both types of success hero are radical individualists; they transform themselves and their social situation through personal initiative. In their spirit of independence and self-reliance, success heroes exhibit their kinship with the frontiersman, that archetypal individualist of American myth, whose self-transformation takes the form of mastering the savage in the name of civilization (Slotkin 1986: 86–87). While big business has often sought to exploit the affinity and represent the entrepreneur as the preserver of frontier individualism, critics of the new corporate society have used the same frontier imagery to attack it (Susman 1984: 32).

For incorporation in its early stages engendered what Alan Trachtenberg (1982: 84) calls a "cultural paradox," a tension between individualism and organization that persists into the present. The tension bears most heavily upon the new salaried, white-collar middle classes, whose common characteristic is their dependence on bureaucratic organizations.

With the proliferation of bureaucracies in business, government, and the professions, the organization of work underwent a radical transformation that C. Wright Mills (1953) named the "managerial demiurge." Mills isolated the centralization of knowledge and of control over labor processes as a fundamental feature of the white-collar world. The development of modern management entailed the appropriation of individual initiative and skills—what Harry Braverman (1974) called the separation of conception from execution. From this process, which reduces much of white-collar work to a form of manual labor, follows the increasingly hierarchical organization of the bureaucratic world. At the bottom are the de-skilled white-collar masses of office workers and service personnel. Above them are the hierarchically ranked managers and professionals who comprise a new professional-managerial class (PMC).[5] Between managed and managers a widening gap intervenes, maintained in part through the substitution of educational certification for practical experience as the means of mobility (Lash and Urry 1987: 73–74).

Within the ranks of the PMC, bureaucratization also affects criteria for advancement. In bureaucratic organizations such as large corporations, work is a necessary but not sufficient condition for promotion up the managerial hierarchy, a point that success manuals and middle-class magazines began to articulate around the turn of the century. Image or appearance became a central concern of the new success literature, displacing the older entrepreneurial values of self-reliance, effort, and achievement. With increasing frequency, young men were advised to develop self-confidence, willpower, magnetism, and charm—qualities designed to attract, please, and impress other people. These virtues are condensed in what became an obsession of the new middle classes, the widely circulated concept of "personality" as opposed to "character" (Susman 1984: 274–284).

Two tendencies of modern life intertwine in the preoccupation with personality. On the one hand, personality has been represented and cultivated as a strategy for success in the corporate workplace, a key feature of what sociologists call the "bureaucratic ethic." Since the 1950s sociologists have generally agreed that the entrepreneurial ethic was being eroded by corporate life. They have differed, however, with regard to the content of the new ethic and of the "structure of feeling" typical of the professional-managerial class. With the partial exception of Mills, sociologists in the 1950s singled out the bureaucratic emphasis on adjustment, harmony, and deference as an index of the "other-directedness" of the PMC. In this view, articulated by David Riesman (1950) and developed by William Whyte (1956), organizational life promotes cooperation and conformism at the expense of individualism and self-reliance. The new managerial type, his critics argued, was an overintegrated, compulsive team player, the faceless Organization Man whom the culture industry has alternately vilified and heroized.

In the 1970s, however, critics shifted the terms of the attack. Individualism, they argued, was not disappearing among the PMC but assuming a degraded form. Thus Daniel Bell (1976) held the consumerist values of late capitalism responsible for a new "hedonism," and Christopher Lasch (1979) detected a rising "narcissism," which he attributed to the interplay of consumerism with bureaucratic dependence.

Whereas Lasch offered a largely impressionistic account of the corporate workplace, sociologists of the professional-managerial class have
pursued a more empirically based mode of analysis (Bensman 1983;
Bensman and Vidich 1971; Jackall 1983). In the process they have
refined Mills's (1950: 118–146) model of the "bureaucratic entrepreneur." Like Mills, they interpret "other-directedness" as a self-consciously adopted mask, a strategic style assumed in the corporate struggle
for power. For in a world where achievement does not in itself confer
success, what is essential is the ability to mask and dissimulate, to project
the well-staged image at the well-timed moment. Self-control persists as
a virtue, but it takes the form of self-manipulation, as in Mannheim's
model of the "self-rationalized man" (Bensman and Vidich 1971: 49–
50; Jackall 1983: 124–125). Here we seem to have at least one factor in
the emergence of a "postmodern" self, a self who resides in the shifting
surfaces of a carefully staged personality.

Viewed from another angle, however, personality is not something
to control but to release. The notion of self implied here is not a set of
instrumental masks but rather an end or goal, an essence to develop,
cultivate, get in touch with, realize, and above all, fulfill. Like the
idealized performing self of the bureaucratic ethic, the version of success
as self-fulfillment has been primarily addressed to the new middle
classes. Embodied in New Thought and an array of therapies of release,
in the whole cult of leisure and relaxation that promises compensation
for the degradation of work, the self-fulfillment ideal is fundamental to
the consumption ethic of late capitalism.[6] Its roots are in nineteenth-
century self-culture and, more distantly, in Franklin's and Thomas
Jefferson's vision of natural elites who would create a just society by
realizing their personal talents. Since the turn of the century, however,
the idea of success as personal fulfillment has been privatized and
commodified. What Elizabeth Long (1985) calls the "corporate suburban" pattern of success gives narrative expression to the modern ideal.
Crystalizing in the 1950s, the pattern defined success as the product of
a partial retreat from the world of work into a familial world of leisure.
Its initiating work was the 1955 novel *The Man in the Gray Flannel Suit*
(subsequently made into a movie starring Gregory Peck), in which the
hero voluntarily limits his ambitions and trades career advancement for
the emotional fulfillment of a rich family life.

William Whyte interpreted the novel as a legitimation of the bureaucratic ethic. Such fictions, he claimed in *The Organization Man,* work
to reconcile the middle class to the limited opportunities for independence in corporate society. But as Long argues in her analysis of success
literature, there is also an oppositional content. In its nostalgic, mystified

way the image of the home as a refuge from a competitive, masculine workplace does provide a vantage point for critical reflection on capitalist society.

Long (1985: 181) goes on to argue that the quest for a univocal, monolithic middle-class consciousness is misdirected. In other words, as Todd Gitlin (1986: 159–160) also speculates, there may be no single structure of feeling out there in middle-class society. Instead, there would seem to be a number of interrelated currents, which the culture industry partially absorbs, packages, and returns to the public in various configurations. Let us turn now to certain images of success that were projected in the mid-1980s.

Career Training

All the Right Moves is an old-fashioned success story set in a Pennsylvania mill town. Its decent, honest, industrious boy hero, Steph (Tom Cruise), is the son of an equally decent, honest, industrious steelworker. Steph, the star of the high school football team, espouses a pragmatic version of the mobility ideology. He sees sport as it often appears to working-class students, as a means of admission to college. In Steph's carefully devised plan, his athletic abilities will bring him multiple football scholarships, from which he will select the one offered by the college with the best engineering program. His long-term goal is to convert manual ability into certification for a white-collar career.

The film contrasts Steph's rational, calculating drive toward self-improvement to the impulsive conduct of his best friend, Brian, who conforms to a Hollywood stereotype of the sensual but decent working-class youth. Brian winds up engaged to his pregnant girlfriend and obliged to forgo his scholarship for wage labor in the mill. In thus restricting his life chances, Brian performs the ideological function of the success hero's friend, which is to portray class difference as a product of differential individual abilities, characters, and choices. But Steph is not the unique author of his destiny. He is well on the way to becoming a self-made man, in his own modest terms, when a brief lapse of self-control threatens to rob him of all that he has worked to achieve. Steph's fortunes are reversed by the very event that would have foreshadowed his anticipated mobility and brought the plot of a more romantic success story to a climax, the Big Game against an upper-middle-class high school. Situated halfway through the film, this Big Game is lost, and the hero's decline is initiated.

In the locker room after the game, Steph, who played tolerably well himself, protests against the coach's unjust abuse of a teammate. For this impulsive display of solidarity, Steph is dropped from the team. He then gives in to a less noble impulse and joins an angry crowd in defacing the coach's house. The coach sees him and retaliates by black-balling him among college admissions officers.

His once-bright future abruptly blocked by the older man's hostility, Steph must enter the mill and resign himself to a life of manual labor. He is saved from this fate through the intervention of his girlfriend and the coach's wife. The women prevail upon the coach to put aside his anger; and when the coach's own hopes of mobility are fulfilled in the form of a position at Cal Poly Tech, he arranges to take Steph along. This happy news is conveyed to Steph in the yard of the mill, the symbolic boundary between blue-collar and white-collar worlds.

If Cruise's earnest Steph is reminiscent of earlier days, Matthew Broderick's Ferris Bueller may well be the first thoroughly postmodern hero of a teen comedy, the 1986 hit film *Ferris Bueller's Day Off.* The film was directed by John Hughes, the impresario of the teen-comedy genre, whose credits include *Sixteen Candles, The Breakfast Club,* and *Pretty in Pink.* But *Ferris Bueller* stands slightly apart from the rest of the Hughes oeuvre. Whereas teen comedies may be generically con-strained to subvert or in some way question whatever versions of adult values they present, in *Ferris Bueller* the antiauthoritarian impulse is carried to an extreme, leaving no space for any form of reconciliation between the generations. *Ferris Bueller* also contrasts with other Hughes films in its intentionally open, fragmented story line, repeatedly inter-rupted by Ferris's asides to the audience. With its self-conscious, ironic attitude toward the events it narrates, the film reflects a tendency of contemporary mass culture to appropriate "high" cultural forms.

Ferris is an appropriate inhabitant of this postmodern narrative universe. He is a creature composed entirely of surfaces, the product of the multiple masks he assumes. When the film ends, we know little more about him than we did at the beginning, or rather, we know him only through his artful stagings of self.

The film's setting is a prosperous, upper-middle-class Chicago suburb, at the other end of the class spectrum from *All the Right Moves.* It is similar, however, to the setting of Cruise's earlier film, *Risky Business,* in which the teenage hero goes briefly into business as a pimp in order to pay for damage he has done to his father's car. By contrast, Ferris Bueller's project is not work but play; destruction of a paternal car is not the motivation but the resolution of the plot; and the entrepreneurial virtues displayed in *Risky Business* are replaced by skills of another sort. In the person of Ferris Bueller, Tom Sawyer meets late capitalism, and "play" constitutes training for success in a bureaucratized, corporatized, high-tech society.

The plot, such as it is, turns around Ferris's desire to play hooky from school in the company of his best friend, Cameron, and his girlfriend, Sloane. In the first part of the film, Ferris overcomes a series of obstacles to his desire. First, he feigns illness to his oversolicitous but negligent parents; then he coerces the reluctant Cameron into joining him and persuades him to borrow his father's cherished Ferrari; finally, he and Cameron execute an intricate scheme to get Sloane out of school. This last maneuver involves them in a contest of wits with Rooney, the persecutory, none-too-bright high school dean.[7] Rooney's dogged pursuit of Ferris throughout the film contrasts with the permissive style of Ferris's careerist parents. But he is no more effective in controlling the truant, a computer whiz kid, who sets up a dense electronic screen of fake messages that anticipate and thwart Rooney's every move.

Rooney's avowed purpose is "to catch this kid and put a helluva dent in his future." Supposedly, what makes this particular exploit so risky is that it is Ferris's ninth sick day, and if caught, he will be held back for a year. In fact, however, that risk is eliminated early in the film, when Ferris breaks into the high school computer system and adjusts his absentee record, even as the outraged Rooney scans the monitor.[8] Such pleasure as the movie provides derives not from any suspenseful pursuit but rather from the escalating demonstrations of Ferris's omnipotence, which guarantees that all interfering adults will be made fools of, at best, and utterly humiliated, at worst.

The middle segment of the film chronicles the stolen day of leisure. In the film's most outrageously narcissistic fantasy, Ferris becomes the central attraction in a German-American parade. Standing on a float, surrounded by buxom blonds in peasant blouses, he delivers a rendition of "Twist and Shout," accompanied by a crowd of admiring blacks. Apparently, the blacks recognize the white boy's superior talent, a motif that is fast becoming a convention in the suburban-kids-in-the-city genre.[9]

The blacks are not alone in their admiration for Ferris. For reasons that the film never bothers to make clear, everyone adores him, with the partial exception of his resentful sister, Jean, and the ambivalent Cameron. Through Cameron, in particular, the film recognizes ambivalent feelings that its viewers may have toward Ferris. A middle-class Huck Finn, pressed into adventure by his bolder friend, Cameron's misgivings are compounded by doubts that viewers may well share regarding the authenticity of Ferris's friendship. Cameron's manifest singleness of purpose contrasts with Ferris's doubleness. Single-minded adults like

Rooney are fair game for Ferris's trickery, but his manipulation of the loyal Cameron is potentially more disturbing. Nor is the tension alleviated when Ferris presents himself to the audience as a therapist-surrogate, who compelled Cameron to take the Ferrari only in order to help him overcome his fear of his father. For Ferris assumes this role only to deny it by confiding that he also loves to drive the Ferrari.

In teen comedies the destiny of a paternal car is fixed from the moment that a son borrows it. What is interesting is the way in which auto destruction operates in *Ferris Bueller*. When Cameron accidentally sends the driverless car over a cliff, Ferris is (almost) visibly distraught and offers to take the blame. Cameron refuses, claiming that if he hadn't wanted to provoke a confrontation with his father, he would never have taken the car at all. Thus Ferris's "diagnosis" becomes Cameron's psychological truth. Through Ferris's agency Cameron is able to cast off his repressions and get in touch with the oedipal anger that he had been directing against himself. For Cameron, the day amounts to a session of assertiveness therapy, whereas Jean learns the inverse lesson, appropriate to her gender, and comes to understand her anger toward her brother as a defense against her own sexuality. I do not mean to dignify the film's psychologizing but rather to underscore the asymmetric organization of emotional development. Only the lesser characters have inner feelings, which are supposedly elucidated through their transferential relationships to Ferris. If Ferris operates at one level as a therapist surrogate, that role in turn symbolizes a condition of impenetrability, autonomy, and control—the celebrated "blankness" of pop postmodernism. To be the object and not the subject of transference; to know and never be known; to be needed and never to need; to manipulate the emotions of others without ever revealing an inner self: such is the condition of the success hero in this film.

Both *All the Right Moves* and *Ferris Bueller* derive from the boy-hero tradition, which links the achievement of success to an opposition between youth and age. Since success ideology began to shift in the late nineteenth century, that tradition has been distributed between two poles. At one pole, ambitious, industrious youths achieve success as a reward for toil, self-denial, and obedience to authority. Clustered at the other pole is an ever expanding assortment of more romantic, roguish heroes: boys who prefer play to work, who succeed through tricks or daring deeds like the adult men-on-the-make of humorous literature, and who routinely subvert established conventions and repressive authority. Over the course of the twentieth century, this latter type has come to predominate in success stories. Mark Twain, and not Horatio Alger, had sensed the direction of history.[10] From the perspective of

1980s success stories as well as that of the larger boy-hero tradition, *All the Right Moves* appears to have made all the wrong moves. First, the film's vision of success seems overly modest in the light of a tendency to replace the scaled-down dreams of 1970s success stories with more extravagant fantasies. It might have sufficed for Rocky Balboa to "go the distance" in the first *Rocky* film, and for Tony Manero simply to *get* to Manhattan in *Saturday Night Fever,* but the 1980s sequels to these films have transformed Rocky into a world-class champion and Tony into a Broadway superstar. By contrast, college admission, although it was a satisfactory resolution to the film *Breaking Away,* may now seem as mundane to middle-class audiences as it does to Ferris.

But a more serious problem has to do with the way that success is achieved in *All the Right Moves,* specifically with the hero's radical lack of autonomy. Steph's powerlessness contrasts most sharply with Ferris's omnipotence. It also distinguishes *All the Right Moves* from the moderately successful 1987 release *Hoosiers,* a second-chance story with affinities to the early *Rocky* cycle. *Hoosiers* also deals with high school sports and mobility. Its youthful characters are undisciplined farm boys who must learn the traditional values of strenuous effort, loyalty, and unquestioning obedience to the coach (played by Gene Hackman). But that move is completed in the first part of the film; the remainder concentrates on a string of victories over increasingly difficult opponents, culminating with the primarily black team of an Indianapolis high school. Thus submission to paternal authority empowers the boys, and the pleasure of the film derives from the vision of the underdog triumphant. As in the first *Rocky* films, moreover, albeit more subtly, an association of blacks with the superior social class plays upon white middle-class status anxieties and racist resentment.

All the Right Moves, in contrast, is a liberal film. Although it romanticizes the white ethnic working-class world it depicts, Steph's desire to escape into the middle class is positively represented, and the liberal view of education as a path to social mobility is not called into question. Had Steph's lack of autonomy been attributed to structural conditions, the message of the film would have gravitated to the left. Instead, both the cause and the solution of his predicament are an insufficiently bureaucratized educational system that is overly susceptible to personal influence. Not social conditions but the emotionally motivated acts of individuals—Steph's impulsive defiance of authority, the coach's vengeance and subsequent repentance—are what determine success and failure. But in projecting this liberal image of a society open to talent, the film diminishes its boy hero to a degree that audiences apparently found unacceptable. It is not the theme of patronage per se that is problematic (as we will see shortly), but the drastic restriction of Steph's ability to take control over his life. Even Alger's obedient heroes were rewarded for services freely rendered to powerful men, whereas Steph must passively await his benefactor's change of heart. In terms of the larger boy-hero tradition, the film reverses the antiauthoritarian drift in twentieth-century fictions. With its vision of limited opportunities and its almost willful refusal to gratify fantasies of individual empowerment, the film runs counter to a dominant ideological tendency in the Reagan era of optimism.

In contrast to the paternalistic resolution of *All the Right Moves*, *Ferris Bueller* projects a prolonged and exaggerated fantasy of freedom from supraindividual authority. In humiliating Rooney, "killing" the paternal Ferrari, and resisting the pangs of conscience and remorse, the teenage heroes rebel against all forms of repressive control, whether external or internalized. Disrespect for adult authority in the film entails a willful rejection of the Protestant ethic of self-improvement through work. For Steph that ethic is necessary but insufficient. In *Ferris Bueller* the work ethic is a thing of the past, rendered obsolete by the bureaucratized, denaturalized school environment and by the nearby city of pleasure and consumption that beckons to Ferris so seductively. Right conduct is defined in remissive terms as self-gratification, excess, indulgence, release, the playful overcoming of every obstacle to desire. At the same time the film implicitly assigns Ferris the considerable self-discipline and control required to operate his scams.[11] Ferris exemplifies the psychological type adapted to a world of commodified leisure and bureaucratized work. In Ferris the renunciative self of the old ethic is superseded by a self that is opaque, decentered, volatile, defined by a play of shifting surfaces as opposed to a fixed and stable inner core. His cool rebelliousness is not an expression of inner needs or a sign of some emotional struggle but a highly crafted and effective strategy for dominating others.

As a condensed expression of the double assault on the work ethic, *Ferris Bueller* provides both a narrative charter for the consumption ethic and a lesson in the qualities required for a successful bureaucratic career. The film operates as a form of what Richard Ohmann (1991) calls class instruction for elites, a narrative pedagogy that celebrates a seemingly rebellious but socially useful style. Ferris is a particularly uncompromising version of a new type of ironist hero, whose apparent individualism is in fact a qualification for success in the corporate world. His adult equivalent is Gordon Gekko, the ruthless, amoral corporate takeover artist in Oliver Stone's *Wall Street* (1987), with the difference that Hughes's film appeals to middle-class desire rather than middle-class morality and casts Ferris as its hero.

Well, sort of a hero. The film hedges its bet, appealing through Cameron to the cult of feeling that also characterizes middle-class culture. The inclusion adds a twist to the underlying libidinal structure of the narrative. Even as the film plays upon a fantasy of the rebelliously independent self, it also appeals to longings for a benevolent authority. Thus Ferris, who is a rebel to negligent parents and repressive school authorities, a pleasure ego breaking free of controls, is himself the omnipotent patriarch to Sloane, Cameron, and Jean. What is missing from this image of a restored surrogate family is any sense of tension with the corporate world of work. Is not the message that the corporate force embodied in Ferris will sustain us all?

Finding Fulfillment in Advertising

David Bosner, the hero of *Nothing in Common,* is well-versed in the manipulation of images. As played by Tom Hanks, David is the young, upwardly mobile creative director of a Chicago-based advertising agency. His job is to turn consumer goods into carriers of meaning, and his profession historically has promoted a consumption ethic for capitalist society. Since the 1920s, advertisers have stimulated demand by selling "satisfactions" rather than goods themselves (Marchand 1985). Consumer goods and services, in other words, are packaged as solutions to social dilemmas, vehicles of self-identity, means to self-fulfillment. In its daily practice advertising exemplifies the postmodern separation of substance from image.

Nothing in Common weaves advertising into a story of success and succession. David's father, Max, is a clothing salesman for a retail company. Played by Jackie Gleason, Max personifies an earlier stage in the corporate expansion of sales, when formerly independent agents were proletarianized by large corporations (Edwards 1979: 85–87). Like the door-to-door salesmen in *Tin Man* (1987), Max belongs to the past. His profession is being displaced by more modern marketing techniques, including advertising, and his individual career is winding down, while David's star is on the rise. In contrast to *The Color of Money* (1987), where Paul Newman as the Old Pro transmits his expertise to Tom Cruise, the Kid Successor, Max has nothing to pass on to David. The father operates in this film as a negative model for the son. As the plot unfolds, Max's constrictive machismo is contrasted to David's cultivation of a culturally feminine sensitivity-to-the-needs-of-others. Conversely, in the world of work, David recovers precisely what the proletarianized Max has lost, a symbolically masculinizing sense of independence.

When we meet him, David has come to a critical juncture in his career. Having just been promoted to an office with a window, he now aspires to a partnership. According to Charlie, his boss and benevolent patron, creativity alone will not advance him that far. To become a partner, Charlie advises him, he will have to "hustle clients." Thus begins a new stage in David's career as a professional seducer.

According to sociologist Joseph Bensman (1983), client-agency relationships in advertising resemble the relationship of king-and-courtier, although the agencies' self-representation of their compulsive deference as "client prostitution" might suggest "courtesan" as the appropriate image. In their pursuit of accounts, agency personnel must influence clients by attraction rather than coercion, seducing them with dazzling ideas and a pleasing, ingratiating manner. Under these conditions, insincerity becomes a culturally valued style.

David assumes the seducer's mask in his first encounter with a coveted client, an airline industrialist by the name of Woolrich. What keeps David amusing and attractive in these scenes is Hanks's ability to convey the essential doubleness of the character's conduct. With his breezy, ironic style, Hanks is able to make us admire David's skillful performance in pandering to a client. Yet even as the film solicits our admiration, it also insists on the feminizing implications of David's bureaucratic virtuosity by having him be picked up by Woolrich's executive daughter, Cheryl Ann.

Complicating David's work life is the collapse of his parents' marriage. After thirty years, his mother, Lorraine, has left the vulgar, uncommunicative Max and is trying to make a life of her own. Although Lorraine's abdication of the caretaker role is presented with some degree of sympathy, the film is structured by anxieties over the provision of maternal nurturance. Her attempt to create a life of her own is juxtaposed to the film's two opposed models of independent women. At one pole is the humorless, ambitious, masculinized Cheryl Ann. Her counterpart is David's high school girlfriend, Donna, a college drama teacher and director of experimental theatre, who represents the moderately independent, nonthreatening woman. The film makes clear that Donna's commitment to her work still leaves her abundant time to give David emotional support.

As a stubbornly noncommercial avant-garde artist (whose work is made to appear somewhat silly in our one glimpse of it), Donna also forms the third term in a ternary system of elite careers. Despite the film's self-presentation as a story about the conflicting claims of work and family, its main concern is with divisions within the public world of work. Donna represents the conventionally feminine world of cultural creativity, imagined as a precapitalist form of artistic production that stands opposed to the masculine world of corporate business. A second opposition internal to the business world distinguishes the newer, consumption-oriented, professional elites, represented by David and Charlie, from the older, production-oriented, industrial elites, represented by Woolrich and Cheryl Ann. A particularly elaborate scheme of oppositions defines this historically tense relationship and expresses the ambiguous character of advertising. The ambiguity is the product of the taxonomy, which situates the commercial artistry of advertising between the purely expressive, feminine art world and the purely utilitarian, masculine world of commerce. Like the mediating categories in ritual systems, advertising participates in opposed poles.

From one perspective, advertising is feminized, associated with the seductive labor it involves and also with more maternal images of nurturance and repose. This latter representation of the advertising profession as an indulgent, nurturing mother is conveyed through a series of scenes between David and Charlie, which take place in the agency's private health club and alternate with David's pursuit of the Woolrich account. The club is a circular, dome-covered, rooftop paradise, centered on an immense swimming pool, of which only a small portion is used for lap-swimming. The club's atmosphere of quiet and relaxation has therapeutic overtones and evokes a cult of emotional release. Thus yoga and tai chi are practiced in the club, whereas such ascetic forms of fitness culture as bodybuilding or grueling workouts are apparently excluded. The overall image is of an "abundance therapy" that channels and releases untapped psychic energy.

Juxtaposed to the oceanic health club is the rugged outdoors, where Woolrich summons the reluctant David for a combination duck shoot and business meeting. For Woolrich sport is a masculine, purposeful, productive activity, not a restful regression but a utilitarian extension of work life. David, who is appalled by this compulsive production, is heard protesting off camera that he doesn't *want* to lug dead ducks onto the plane. As he appears on screen, he is, of course, profusely thanking Woolrich for his share in the spoils of the hunt.

In opposition to the ethic of work and self-denial represented by Woolrich, advertising participates in the consumption ethic of self-indulgence and fulfillment that the profession has helped to promote. But the advertising profession has had an ambivalent attitude toward the consumption ethic and also toward the Consumer, that figure whom it invested with the culturally feminine traits of impulsiveness and

emotionality (Marchand 1985: 168). Advertisers themselves are producers, after all, of images and, ideally, consumer desires. Within the
process of production, identification with consumers is a manipulative
technique, a means to an end, and this encourages an ironic, sometimes
contemptuous sense of distance from consumers.

In the film this process is positively represented. Scenes of David and
his staff at work depict the creation of ads as a form of boyish play. It is
play with a practical purpose but nevertheless a basically pleasurable,
outrageous activity—something that, as David's director reminds him,
they would do "only as long as it was fun." On this axis of opposition,
advertising stands for a sphere of youthful freedom and creativity, poised
against a repressive industrial authority.

To be more precise, advertising and, by extension, the class of
professionals who produce it appear as a sphere where the principle of
paternal succession operates in a liberatory manner, in contrast to the
oppressive paternalism of the industrial elites. Cheryl Ann, the daughter
whose father "raised her to be a corporate executive . . . to be a man,"
is a mere extension of the Father's authority. Someday, as David tells her
at their parting, she will "make some corporation a hell of a CEO." But
this, of course, is precisely what Woolrich intends for her. Although the
masculinized woman will succeed in the corporate workplace, she is
denied the possibility of achieving autonomous selfhood by her old-
fashioned patriarchal father. David, the feminized advertising man,
finally rebels against Woolrich's authority in the name of familial ties.
When Woolrich insists that David make a presentation in New York on
the day that Max is scheduled to undergo surgery, David casts off the
pressures for deference, strips off his mask, and explodes at Woolrich,
man-to-man. Within the terms of the bureaucratic ethic, such a loss of
self-control is a fatal error, and indeed, Woolrich has David fired by
Cheryl Ann. But David's defiant choice of family over career is soon
rendered inconsequential, thanks to Charlie's intervention.

Charlie pacifies Woolrich, saves the account, and instructs David to
attend to his relationship with Max. After Max's operation, when David
announces that he is taking an indefinite leave in order to get to know
his father, Charlie conveys his warm support and promises to keep the
office with the window waiting for David's return. Charlie appears in
his final scene without any of the toupees that he had vainly experimented with earlier in the film. His bald, uncovered head expresses his
acceptance of age and signifies that the principle of succession will
operate properly within the agency.

Under these ideal conditions David quickly resolves the various issues
in his personal life. He makes a commitment to Donna and bids an

affectionate farewell to his mother. Lorraine has decided that she must go away to find herself, and she leaves her son with full responsibility for the care of his crippled, convalescent father. The final image is of David in his new role as maternal caretaker. He is wheeling Max out of the hospital and beaming with satisfaction, perhaps in anticipation of the quality time they will share.

Yet it is Charlie who makes it possible for David to find fulfillment in his private life, without costs to his career. The fantasy of overthrowing bureaucratic controls, reasserting masculine independence within a feminized workplace, and then combining career and family life is embedded in a fantasy of having an omnipotent professional protector who averts all harm. As the strong and caring patron who is both father and mother, Charlie's function undercuts the very tension between work and family on which the film is manifestly based.

Despite surface similarities to earlier stories of success as personal fulfillment, *Nothing in Common* transforms the message of the pattern it reproduces. The plot of *The Man in the Gray Flannel Suit* may have encouraged accommodation to restricted career opportunities. Nevertheless, the hero's choice of family over work also conveyed an oppositional theme—a critique, however partial and implicit, of the degradation of labor in the bureaucratized corporate workplace. In contrast, *Nothing in Common* projects a fantasy of unlimited possibilities, at least for the young, white, male professional class. The professional workplace of the film's imagination is open to talent, rewards independence, and encourages personal fulfillment. Its form is that of a family in which men are both father and mother.

Struggling Upward

If *Nothing in Common* reformulates the work versus family plot of the personal fulfillment tradition, *The Secret of My Success* identifies itself with the Horatio Alger boys' tales of individual mobility through work, ambition, character, and (the element that Alger never managed to eliminate) luck. Brantley Foster, the hero of *Secret,* played by Michael J. Fox, is a poor but enterprising Kansas farm boy who goes to New York to become a self-made man. By the end he has far outstripped the Alger heroes, who rise to moderate security and middle-class respectability. Brantley's rise knows no such limits and is effected by a combination of means that would have shocked Horatio Alger.

Secret opens with glimpses of the humble farm where Brantley was raised, intercut with shots of his arrival in New York. Brantley, who has already demonstrated his initiative by earning a college degree, recalls his farewell to his parents and looks forward to his new life in New York City as the opening credits roll.

The imagery of the prologue evokes the nineteenth-century self-improvement literature directed to aspiring small-town boys and farm boys. Brantley's rural origins (conveyed in a few shots of barns and barnyards) bespeak the traditional disciplinary virtues of industry, perseverance, honesty, abstinence, and thrift. His personal attributes are also implied in a special sense of obligation to his mother, the figure who typically molds character in the nineteenth-century inspirational literature (Wyllie 1954: 29–30). An iron that his mother insists on giving him ("You don't want to be wrinkled in New York") condenses the middle-class habits of neatness and order and may perhaps be read as an icon of the Protestant Ethic. Brantley accepts his mother's iron reluctantly, although he will have exceptional use for it later on. In the dream that he playfully shares with her, self-discipline may be a means but affluence is the end, measured in Jacuzzis, penthouses, and expensive women. Although his background links him to the old moralistic literature of work, the content of his dream evokes the consumption-oriented definition of success.

The dream is put on hold when Brantley arrives in New York and takes up residence in a slum apartment. The city is presented to us as a sharply divided world. Brantley's and the viewers' first impressions are of a colorful, volatile underclass, composed of ethnic and youth subcultures and featuring a variety of hookers with whom Brantley seems to feel a strange affinity. Yet a little later, when his own prospects have dimmed, the streets take on a menacing character. In what will be practically our last glimpse of the ghetto, it manifests itself to an unemployed Brantley as a place where violent crime is controlled by police surveillance, a separate world of transgression and repression. The poor function in the film as they do in the larger ideolology of consumption, as the negative self-image of the consumer (Bauman 1987: 186). Their situation is the threat that gives meaning to Brantley's struggle upward. Opposed to the motley world of the streets is the high-rising, streamlined business world with its ultramodern, glassy architecture and regimented flow of disciplined businessmen, whose ranks Brantley had hoped to join. But he soon discovers that he has come into an economy of scarcity. New York is no longer the mythical city of opportunity and free competition, where individuals rise and fall according to their merits. Once a testing ground for heroes, the city has become the site for a ruthless competition among giant corporations. To his horror Brantley discovers that the company that had offered him employment has fallen victim to a hostile takeover and his position has been cut in the ensuing shake-up.

Brantley has other unpleasant surprises in store for him. Personnel officers demand "practical experience" and display a negative attitude toward his educational qualifications more characteristic of the prebureaucratic work culture of the nineteenth century than of the corporate world that these officers represent. Brantley, however, is adaptable. On the model of Ferris Bueller, he promptly falsifies his resumé to stress the school of experience, only to be stymied by another obstacle. He has no ready answer to the last personnel officer's question: "Can you be a minority woman?"

Adversity, which first fanned his spirit of self-reliance, now dampens but cannot quench it. However, after a glimpse of the streets in their violent manifestation, he modifies his initial resolve to make it entirely on his own. His mother has given him the telephone number of his "Uncle Howard," a distant relative who turns out to be the forbidding Howard Prescott, CEO of the giant Pemrose Corporation, "a multinational conglomerate with twenty-seven different divisions, with products ranging from dog food to missile guidance systems." Despite his reluctance to trade on a kin tie, Brantley presents himself at Pemrose as the boss's nephew and so gains admission to see Prescott.

Apparently impressed by Brantley's self-confidence, Prescott gives the young man a job in the mailroom. Starting at the bottom is no stigma for an aspiring self-made man. The problem is the limited structure of opportunity. Passage from the lower to the upper strata of the corporate hierarchy is almost as difficult as from the streets into the business world. As Brantley is told by his co-worker, Melrose: "You can't even get paroled out of the mailroom!"

Melrose depicts Pemrose as a semifeudal society of status and privilege, governed by a strict hierarchical code. The white-collar masses of mailroom workers, clerks, and secretaries who make up the lower rank are not to "consort" with the upper rank of managerial elites, whom Melrose refers to as "suits." All this hierarchy, however, has produced chaos rather than order. In Melrose's prophetic words: "This place is a zoo. Nobody knows what anyone else is doing."

"Nobody" includes Rattigan, the dictatorial supervisor of the mailroom, who takes an instant dislike to Brantley and hounds him in a manner reminiscent of Rooney, the school dean in *Ferris Bueller*. The Irish names of these comic blocking characters are probably intended as references to police authority, and the ease with which the heroes evade their surveillance is a sign that such repressive control belongs to the past. And indeed, within the world of large organizations, personal domination is rendered obsolete by bureaucratic control systems.

The film's representation of Pemrose draws upon notions of bureaucracy as a multiple threat—to entrepreneurial values, to the possibility of finding personal satisfaction in work, and to the traditional ideal of a fully meritocratic social hierarchy. Melrose embodies the potential consequences of bureaucratic control at the lower echelons of the system, where narrowly defined tasks and limited mobility produce apathy (Blau and Meyer 1971: 61–71). Melrose's narrative function, however, is not to expose the negative impact of bureaucratization on worker motivation but to serve as a foil for Brantley's virtues. Cast from the same mold as a traditional Alger type, Melrose is the loyal friend who lacks the hero's courage and initiative but who stands by him and ultimately benefits from his success. Thus Melrose's limited ambition and his ironically deferential acceptance of the bureaucratic hierarchy underscore Brantley's identification with the self-made man of the old entrepreneurial ideology.

Brantley learns from Melrose that while the mailroom may be a prison, it is one in which the inmates do the surveillance. Mailroom workers, Melrose explains, have special access to the flow of information, and Brantley proceeds to take advantage of that position. Like Melrose, he can complete his rounds in a fraction of the time allotted, but the industrious Brantley puts his spare time to productive use. He pores over stacks of interoffice memos and research reports obtained from the corporate reference center. This intellectual activity, we are led to believe, reverses the effects of bureaucratization on work. Unwilling to be a cog in any machine, whether rusty or well-oiled, Brantley triumphs over the managerial demiurge. In a bureaucratized workplace, where knowledge is centralized and appropriated from above by management, Brantley reappropriates intellectual control over the work process. In a hierarchical social universe, however, the efficacy of knowledge depends on the status of the knower. Although Brantley has theoretically overcome the separation of conception from execution, he remains restricted in practice. His problem is how to enter the ranks of the decisionmaking managerial elite in a system that has broken the connection between merit and mobility. Brantley's New York experiences have taught him to be skeptical of the optimistic work-and-win ideology of the old middle classes. He turns instead to image-making.

Whereas the artful Ferris Bueller impersonated various figures of authority, Brantley goes one better. He simply invents an executive persona out of whole cloth or, more precisely, out of the signs of corporate status—an office, a nameplate, a secretary, and personalized stationery. In his capacity as mailroom worker Brantley requisitions these status symbols on behalf of one "Carleton Whitfield," which is the name of a cousin who, according to Brantley's father in the prologue, had returned to Kansas "with his head shaved and an earring stuck in his cheek." The real Carleton failed to make it up from the streets, but Brantley's creation is a rising executive, whose identity he assumes by the simple device of donning a suit. Clothes, as Melrose suspected, really do make the man.

Brantley's solution to his mobility problem is a fine parody of the bureaucratic ethic. For Brantley, however, manipulation of appearances is only a device to gain entry to the upper echelons of management. Once arrived, our hero boldly speaks his mind, albeit in Carleton's name. Whereas *Nothing in Common* contrasts David's old self to the new one, *Secret* contrasts Brantley's forthright, candid style to the submissive deference of Prescott's bureaucratic chieftains. With his creative intelligence and refusal to be controlled, Brantley bears a resemblance to Mills's bureaucratic entrepreneur. His displays of independence in the boardroom arouse anxiety laced with envy among Prescott's craven executive yes-men.

There is one yes-woman, as well, Christie Wills, an elite, Harvard-educated prodigy, who is also Prescott's mistress. Her presence in the pack serves as a warning of the feminizing effects of deference on men and, conversely, the masculinizing effects of ambition on women. Like Cheryl Ann, Christie is a mere extension of her powerful father-lover. She submits to Prescott both sexually and professionally, not, the film suggests, out of calculated self-interest, but under the influence of erotic attraction to authority. For women, submission in the workplace appears as a sublimated expression of the female Oedipus complex, a displaced version of what would be appropriate in the conjugal family.

Christie, however, will be liberated from her dependency by Brantley, who falls madly in love with her at first sight. She appears in his fantasy as the soft, feminine creature she really is, her compliant nature revealed in its proper, romantic form. Although Brantley does not know of her affair with Prescott, he observes her deference to the boss, and the first stage in his reeducation of Christie is to convince her of the superior rationality of his own economic policies.

We, of course, know that Brantley is Pemrose's future, but the content of that future is somewhat elusive. On the surface Brantley is the bearer of the entrepreneurial ethic, who will reinfuse an increasingly dysfunctional bureaucracy with the traditional middle-class virtues. In this code the boy hero from Kansas embodies the frontier spirit of independence. Under the influence of this spirit, as Brantley himself demonstrates, routinized and degraded bureaucratic work can be redeemed, made into an opportunity for self-creation and for the amelioration of society, as in the old entrepreneurial ideology. To this end the decadent bureaucratic authoritarianism that rewards deference over initiative must give way to the spirit of Jeffersonian and Jacksonian democracy condensed in Brantley's agrarian background. The promise is that a heroic individual from the producing class of small farmers will transform the static corporate hierarchy into a true meritocracy.

If, however, we follow the film's own cues and read gender into the scheme, the symbolic value of this transformation becomes ambiguous. Prescott's conflict with Brantley/Carleton develops around the question of how to respond to an imminent hostile takeover of Pemrose. Prescott's strategy for dealing with the threat is to institute drastic cutbacks in all departments, supposedly to amass capital for the company's defense. Christie and the others obediently set to work, earmarking departments and midwestern distribution centers for elimination, while Brantley/Carleton argues for a diametrically opposed approach. His strategy is not to contract but to expand—specifically, to expand distribution to the midwestern zone.

In case we have any doubts about the sexual significance of Prescott's defensive strategy, there are repeated references to the necessity to "cut hard and deep," and a freestanding phallic statue outside Prescott's office enforces the theme of castration. But if Prescott's timorous policy threatens to emasculate the company, it is less certain that Brantley's expansive solution is remasculinizing at a symbolic level. Let us note that the opposition is between a production-oriented economics of scarcity and a consumption-oriented economics of abundance. For Prescott, who sees the problem in terms of overproduction, the solution is to reduce distribution, whereas Brantley reads the problem as one of underconsumption and hence sees expanded distribution as the solution. Whatever vague reference is being made here, whether to supply-side economics or even to New Dealism, is less persuasive, I think, than the internal reference to intersignifying oppositions. The contrastive economic strategies refer us back to Prescott's style of fitness culture, on the one hand, and to Brantley's affair with Prescott's wife, on the other.

As in *Nothing in Common*, images of fitness culture have symbolic meaning, but the style of fitness favored by Prescott is at the other pole from the feminine cult of relaxation and release. The patriarch of Pemrose is a devotee of a masculine cult of strenuosity. The routines that he practices include jogging and running on a treadmill, both evocative of compulsive work and self-denial. He imposes these tastes on his subordinates, who are visibly infantilized by his strict discipline.

Prescott's recommendations for the company merely translate this ascetic code into economics. Brantley's rural roots notwithstanding, it is Prescott who stands for the old Puritan ethic. And in this film, too, the Puritan must die.

Brantley's real education does not take place at a desk. It is inaugurated in a swimming pool and a boudoir belonging to his "Aunt Vera," Prescott's beautiful, sensual, frustrated wife. Vera seduces a reluctant Brantley before she knows his identity. When he is revealed as her "nephew," the mildly incestuous aspect of the affair only increases her delight. Brantley's fear of Vera is treated playfully and is never projected onto her. "Just when I thought it was safe to go back in the water!" he cries, as she attacks him in the pool, to the leitmotif from *Jaws*. Later, still fixated on oral imagery, Brantley tells Melrose that being chased by a dog with "a mouth as big as my head" was the best thing that happened to him, while the worst thing was "getting laid." "Brantley," says Melrose for all of us, "I'm not sure you've got your priorities straight."

Brantley's priorities are what the film is all about. He thinks that he needs to take control of sexual relations, and to a point, the film solicits our agreement. We are expected to approve of his reeducation of Christie and at least to appreciate his virtuosity in conducting the noisy love-making of his next door neighbors to a phallocentric climax. But his increasingly frenzied attempts to exert control over Vera's sensuality indicate that the real problem is the release of his own. Before Brantley makes it to the top, he is purged of his residual Puritanism. His drive for perfection has to be detached from the compulsive resistance to pleasure, for which Vera repeatedly rebukes him. What comes naturally to Ferris and David must be taught to their country cousin. It falls to Vera to take the farm out of the boy by giving Brantley the truly practical education of a courtesan.

Brantley has more in common with Sister Carrie than with any upstanding Alger hero. His covert identification with the hookers in the prologue resurfaces in the affair with Vera. Repeated attempts to deny the identification only affirm it. Thus Brantley, trying to discourage Vera, pleads: "I'm not free any more!" "What!" cries Vera, "You mean you're going to charge me?" Or again, when Vera, about to introduce him to the rich and powerful, tells him to "do to them what you did to me," his automatic retort is, "I can't do that, Vera!"

But this remains to be seen. What Vera meant, she explains, is for him to use his "irresistible boyish charm" on her influential friends. To this he acquiesces. What goes overlooked is that Brantley had initially refused Vera's offer of patronage, with its connotation of a reward for sexual favors. These scruples apparently forgotten, Brantley embraces the role of the courtesan.

The testing of the courtesan takes place at a party at Prescott's estate. Included among the guests are three important bankers, members of the old upper class, to which Vera also belongs. Her father, we have learned, was the self-made founder of Pemrose, a true captain of industry who, while not exactly Met 400, would have conferred membership in elite society on his daughter.

Where *Nothing in Common* opposed a crass, philistine industrialist to cosmopolitan professional elites, the image of the class system projected in *Secret* has a nostalgic appeal. In the party segment, the status difference between the old and the new upper classes is visually underlined and slanted in favor of the older class fraction. Contrasted to Vera's self-confident, relaxed, and cultivated guests, Prescott and his executives appear compulsive, insecure, and common. This contrast is communicated through rock video techniques. Using music and images to tell the story, the scene shifts back and forth between two social groupings, an emergency business conference led by Prescott and a more leisurely company made up of Brantley, Vera, and the three financial magnates who retire to a gazebo. With Vera looking on, Brantley delivers a speech that we do not hear, but from the approving smiles of the audience, it is clear that they recognize the speaker as one of their own.

The visual structuring of this segment is important to the narrative, for it gives a new inflection to the content of Brantley's contribution to Pemrose. He is no longer the repressed midwestern farm boy but a "natural aristocrat," perfectly at ease among the business aristocrats of the eastern seaboard. It is as if he has taken on what Pierre Bourdieu (1984: 170, 172) would call a new "habitus," a structured and structuring system of dispositions, expressed through the very orientation of the body and also through the array of taste preferences that make up a "life-style." In a few hours he seems to have acquired the system of bodily movements, gestures, expressions, and consumption habits that distinguish the upper social class from the merely rich. We may well suspect that what bureaucracy needs from Brantley is something other than the rural middle-class virtues. Following the party the film moves rapidly to a conclusion. Brantley/Carleton is exposed and loses both his positions at Pemrose. In the process Brantley and Christie are estranged and then reconciled, each having learned of the other's affair. Despite a suggestion that the affairs cancel each other out, the effects of the reconciliation are not symmetric. In exchanging Prescott for Brantley, Christie does not transcend patriarchal love. She merely trades a crass, coercive master for one who is charming and considerate. For

Brantley, however, loving Christie means a double recovery of control. First, he has converted her from his rival to an admiring subordinate in the workplace. Second, through her he escapes the disruptive, uncontrollable attraction to the seductive mother.

The reconciliation of the lovers paves the way for a carnivalesque resolution to the success story. On the very day that Pemrose is about to be taken over by Davenport, a corporate raider who would destroy the company for profits, Brantley bursts into the conference room. Flanked by Christie, Melrose, and his ex-secretary, Jean, Brantley announces to the startled executives that the tables are turned. Pemrose is going to take over Davenport's company, with its strong distribution capacities, and thus realize Brantley's consumption-oriented plan. All this has been made possible by Vera, who has secured stock control of Pemrose and has persuaded her banker friends to finance the Davenport takeover for Brantley. Wearing a blouse that resembles a Matisse print, Vera glides regally into the boardroom, preceded by Brantley's new "financial advisors." With this array of patrician patrons behind him, Brantley wrests control of Pemrose away from Prescott.

It is a festive fantasy. As a vision of the redemption of the community, what is striking is the combination of egalitarian with hierarchical ideals. Brantley effects an alliance between the lowest and the highest social strata, the white-collar working class from the mailroom and the secretarial pool and the old upper class of the eastern seaboard. He acts as a cross between a populist leader from the plains and a young pretender to the throne. The film's epilogue suggests that the latter self-image prevails. Our last glimpse of Brantley finds him securely ensconced in a world of aristocratic consumption, which he shares with Christie, Melrose, and Vera. He has risen from the barnyard to the penthouse of his dreams, but his tastes have been upgraded along the way, perhaps by his elite women, and the Jacuzzi is replaced by a formal night at the opera.

The final scene alludes to the contrast between old and new upper classes and conveys a contrast between two ideas of the businessman. An opera-going Brantley evokes what Richard Hoffstadter (1962: 244–254) calls the American tradition of the cosmopolitan merchant, the civilized and civilizing businessman who was interested in and supportive of high culture. This mercantile ideal of gentlemanly leisure and cultivation as well as work was displaced in the nineteenth century by the ideal of the self-made man, a type viewed by the old elites much as *Secret* views its managerial villains, as vulgar and/or overascetic parvenus.

The opera scene in *Secret* is directly modeled on the Hollywood notion of "class" projected in countless movies and not on a historical social type. But what needs appreciation is that the film projects its negative image of the corporation from above, not from below. Despite the overt populist overtones, its critique of corporate bureaucracy is from the perspective of the highest social class. In short, it is the capitalists who will redeem capitalism.

At a psychosexual level, there is a similar blurring of perspectives. Brantley's usurpation of Prescott's position is an almost manifest oedipal rebellion against a jealous father who had hoarded all the available women, like some primal leader out of *Totem and Taboo.* Yet, like the fantasy of social rebellion with which it is condensed, the oedipal rebellion is embedded in a fantasy of authority. According to the family romance implicit in the film, the secret of Brantley's success is that he is really of noble birth, the child of Vera and the three bankers, and thus the true heir to Pemrose. Prescott, in this fantasy, is neither Brantley's relative (recall his real mother's vagueness about their connection) nor Vera's husband (an alliance that she in fact severs).

Thus *Secret* confronts us with the same ambivalence that we encountered in *Nothing in Common* and *Ferris Bueller* but not in *All the Right Moves.* Brantley, David, and Cameron are idols of consumption. They rebel against overdisciplinary, controlling males who still adhere to Puritan values of work, abstinence, and frugality (reduced in the case of Cameron's father to keeping an expensive car that he never drives). In each case the rebellion is presented as the central event in the narrative; less emphasis is placed on the condition of its possibility, that is, the enabling presence of an omnipotent, protective authority—Vera and the bankers, Charlie, and Ferris himself. Organization, it would appear, has become the guarantor of individual freedom.

Conclusion

Tension between individualism and organization is a persistent feature of twentieth-century American life. It was heightened, however, during the Reagan era. Following the lead of an undeniably popular president, political and economic elites joined in celebrating the entrepreneurial hero as the preserver of the old frontier spirit. With one eye on its potential audiences, the culture industry followed more cautiously. This latest burst of enthusiasm for the entrepreneur came at a time when entrepreneurialism was receding as a reality. For the culture industry's coveted young, middle-class audience, in particular, the bureaucratic corporation is the most likely destination, and it is the locus of anxieties that the industry has long known how to market. Among the most ubiquitous themes of mass culture since the 1950s is the subversion of our mobility, freedom, and humanity by an overorganized society. Our fictional defender against the bureaucratic threat is the Professional, an intergeneric figure who appears in action films as well as comedies and dramas. His constant attribute is his professional expertise and skill, which are his resources in the contest against the forces of Organization. That contest can be inflected in various ways. A convention of many films, for example, is to contrast the insidious doubleness of bureaucratic authority to heroic singleness of purpose. Speech, the quintessential instrument of duplicity, may then take on a negative value, in which case the hero will tend to avoid it and communicate through concrete deeds. Sylvester Stallone's Rambo character is an extreme form of this tendency and embodies a mystified critique of capitalism's abstract character.

In contrast, what is striking about the comic antibureaucrats analyzed in this chapter is that they possess the properties valued by the world they appear to oppose. Well educated, highly verbal, seductive, ironic, and adept at shape-changing, they revel in the gap between image and reality, exploiting it to their own advantage. Conversely, their opponents, who are notably deficient in the seductive virtues, only appear to represent established systems of control. Rooney, Woolrich, Rattigan, and Prescott personify the repressive ethic of compulsive self-denial that is now outmoded. In a postindustrial society, where the reproduction of capital depends more on consumption than on production, seduction replaces repression as a mode of social control. This point has been made persuasively, by Pierre Bourdieu (1984: 154) among others. What should not be overlooked here is the role played by the culture industries in shaping the consumption ethic on which they depend. Moreover, bureaucratic success requires skill at maintaining a seductive image, and one suspects that the producing community's own ideal self-image may have contributed to the latest version of the Professional hero. Who, after all, is more skilled at image manipulation than the Hollywood dream-makers? *Nothing in Common*'s idealized advertising world is an almost transparent substitute for the film industry, and there may be more than a little self-flattery in *Secret*'s fantasy of a bureaucratic community revitalized by a skillful young professional.

But if the fantasy referred solely to the producers' self-image, it would not appeal to audiences. These films, I have argued, address the hopes and anxieties of middle-class youth regarding the corporate work world that they have joined or are about to join. In the midst of the rhetorical Reaganite insistence on recovering the past and its frontier values, these films urge us to reconcile ourselves to the present—to live, in short, according to the standards of the corporate world of bureaucratic organizations. That world's potential dangers are selectively recognized in the films, and the emphasis is placed on the maintenance of gendered identities. Between the Scylla of dependence that threatens men and the Charybdis of ambition awaiting women, the films steer a course toward the comic resolution. Without any of the fanfare that attends the killing of the puritanical father, the permissive, corporate father is quietly reinstated, and young men and women take their places as his sons and daughters. Our moment of freedom, embodied in the hero's rebellion, leads us into a benign state of dependency.

4

Transforming Heroes: Hollywood and the Demonization of Women

AMONG THE MOST POWERFUL and dynamic of modernity's cultural narratives is the American myth or of the nineteenth century into a narrative charter for mobility ideology. metamyth of success. With roots in American Puritanism and in Franklin's secularized work ethic, the success myth developed over the course of the nineteenth century into a narrative charter for mobility ideology. Its hero, the self-made man, embodied the founding promise of America—the promise of a chance to try, restrained only by one's own capacity. Rising through talent, effort, and achievement, fictional self-made men brought an earlier dream of individual freedom into an increasingly organized society.

That dream has not come down unchanged. American success mythology has been notably open to its sociohistorical contexts, sensitive to shifts in the lived conditions that it claims to represent. In the first section of this chapter, I show how representations of the self-made man have articulated with different stages of and positions toward capitalist development. I then go on to analyze contemporary, mass-mediated reworkings of the narrative tradition.

During the 1980s Hollywood filmmakers turned with renewed energy to stories of individual mobility and success. The scaled-down dreams of 1970s melodramas such as *Rocky I* or *Saturday Night Fever* gave way to grander, generically comic fantasies of the unrestricted triumph of desire. Only men, however, enacted the more expansive dream. Unlimited ambition in women continued to be constructed as a threat, requiring either their subordination to the appropriate men or their expulsion from the imagined community. During the Reagan era, I argue, such representations of women were enlisted in specific ways in the fictional construction of identities. Briefly, a fantasized threat of female power, embodied in women and in feminized enemies, became instrumental to an ongoing ideological project of remasculinization. What is being remasculinized is not precisely "American culture," as Susan Jeffords (1989: 169) has suggested, but rather the gender identities of particular social classes.

In this chapter I connect the popularity of Hollywood films about dangerous women to what Michael Rogin (1987) calls the "political demonology" of the Reagan presidency. A continuing and, according to Rogin, central feature of American political life, demonization constructs political adversaries as monsters endowed with a mysterious power to subvert the body politic. In the countersubversive rhetoric of political elites, from the beginning of the cold war to the end of the 1980s, that threat takes a dual form. External danger from the Communist menace is paired more or less explicitly with the internal dangers of demonic women and the impending collapse of the family.

Hollywood filmmakers in the 1950s made the link explicit. In the essay "Kiss Me Deadly," Rogin (1987: 246–262) focuses on a cold war genre of anti-Communist films in which weak fathers and domineering mothers produce subversive sons whose sole redemption is the patriarchal national security state. But few of these films, Rogin goes on to note, were box-office successes. Explicitly anti-Communist films may have expressed the fantasies of their makers, but movie attendance figures suggest that science fiction films were more attuned to popular feelings. Transposed from the demonic mom to the strange reproductive powers of 1950s monsters, the theme of dangerous female influence appears to have tapped real social concerns. The monstrous reproduction of identical selves in science fiction films appealed, Rogin (1987: 262–267) argues, to widespread anxiety over the erosion of individual identity in mass society.

Rogin's analysis, to which I return in my conclusion, raises an important theoretical point. Mass culture, by which I intend the commercial products of the culture industries, may be viewed from the perspective of its elite producers or of its mass audiences. Over the history of the debate on mass culture, producer-centered studies have represented it as an instrument for ideological manipulation, whereas audience-centered studies find genuine expressions of collective beliefs and values. Taken in isolation, however, each of these viewpoints yields only a partial understanding of the object. What is obscured in both cases, albeit in different ways, is the cultural processes that mediate between and link elites and masses.

My critical practice is positioned between the older critique of mass culture as sheer manipulation and the pluralist model of authentic mass expression. Instead of separating manipulation from expression, the managed from the authentic, the ideological from the utopian, I attribute the appeal of mass-cultural products to the dialectical interaction of these polarities. From this perspective, mass culture does not directly express the socially conditioned wishes and anxieties of its audiences; rather, it selectively recognizes and actively transforms them. Mass culture, then, is that contested terrain where the contradictions of ongoing social experience are partially absorbed, reworked, and contained within dominant cultural forms. If the dominant culture is not all-powerful in shaping consciousness, neither is it without effect. In Stuart Hall's formulation, "The culture industries do have the power constantly to rework and reshape what they represent; and, by repetition and selection, to impose and implant such definitions of ourselves as fit more easily the descriptions of the dominant or preferred cultures" (1981: 232–233). That power of implantation works through the "utopian" appeals. That is, no mass-mediated "definition of ourselves" will be compelling to audiences unless they can re-cognize the longings and fears that it re-presents.

With this model in mind, I have been tracking 1980s films about mobility and success, paying attention to their intended audiences and to their relative commercial popularity as measured by box-office returns. In this chapter I identify and analyze certain narrative patterns that appealed to movie audiences in the late 1980s.

Workers and Shape-Changers: The Poles of Success Mythology

Let me begin with a common structure, a generative matrix of narrative possibilities. If the basic opposition in success mythology is between the open and the closed, the mobile and the static, then the negative forces of closure and stasis appear in antithetical forms. Aspiring self-made men are threatened from above by repressive authorities, rigid traditions, restrictive rules that limit individual initiative and freedom. From below, however, they are vulnerable to dangers of another sort and must guard against the distracting passions that dull the mind and blunt the will. Both threats are concentrated in the city, the ultimate testing ground, which is to the success hero what the wilderness is to the frontier hero.

Poised between law and desire, the success hero has two extreme choices: to mobilize law in the control of desire or to enlist desire in the overthrow of law. As is the practice of mythic mediators, most heroes arrive at intermediary solutions, compromises of some form that tend, nevertheless, toward one or the other of the two poles—law or desire, authority or freedom, respectful submission or defiant rebellion.

As the success myth began to crystallize in the Jacksonian period, it distributed its versions between these poles. At one pole clustered the lawful descendants of Poor Richard and his Puritan antecedents. Here were honest, plain-dealing workers, bearers of the disciplinary virtues of the Protestant Ethic, whose slow ascent from rags to moderate riches depended on industry and self-denial. Roguishly eyeing these sober figures from the opposite pole were an assortment of equally determined but less rugged individualists: guileful, smooth-talking men on the make who specialized in deflating pretense and subverting authority.

These distinct types of self-made men found their homes in different genres and appealed to different if overlapping audiences. The older, moralistic tradition was disseminated to the middle classes through Jacksonian rhetoric in praise of useful toil, sentimental novels, and self-improvement manuals addressed to aspiring young men. Antebellum comic theater and humorous literature nourished the more exuberant heroes. From such archetypal tricksters as the Yankee peddler and the sly backwoodsman are descended generations of hustlers, hucksters, con men, and promoters, right down to J. R. Ewing and Joe Isuzu.

What needs emphasis regarding the moralistic tradition is its ambivalence toward capitalist development and its increasingly residual character. Handed down from a preindustrial agrarian past, the tradition fostered values and attitudes of declining social utility during the age of industrialization, but it provided a vantage point for criticism of the society that was emerging. When Horatio Alger reproduced the work ethic as literature for children in the Gilded Age, he became the "nostalgic spokesman of a dying order" (Weiss 1969: 49). The critique to which Alger contributed is of a certain kind. It rests on a set of ideas about work that have the effect, as Marvin Meyers remarks of the Jacksonian version, of "distinguishing the classes not by their economic position as such, but primarily by their moral orientation" (1960: 31). Ante- and postbellum success traditions share a dichotomous moral economy that classifies occupational groups by their opposed modes and rates of accumulation. Wealth gradually accumulated through some manner of honest toil is regarded as a sign of virtue and marks off a composite laboring class of "industrious folk," which can include farmers, manual workers, merchants, and honest industrialists. Their opposite, the new "aristocracy" denounced in Jacksonian polemic, is a diffuse class of bankers, speculators, and financiers—all those who amass wealth rapidly, without toil, and who consume it conspicuously.

As the tradition entered the turbulent decades of the Gilded Age, anxiety over consumption intensified. The basic dilemma, as Max Weber recognized, was intrinsic to worldly asceticism, which produces the wealth that eventually undermines it. Caught up in this dilemma, middle-class success ideologists laced their praise of work and moderation with the old puritan-republican fears of the corrupting power of riches. Their obsession with the dangers of success is reflected in ambivalent attitudes toward the city. As the place of opportunity to which aspiring young men are summoned, the modern metropolis is also the place of temptation. Against the allure of urban fleshpots and easy wealth, hard work becomes a form of protection, thus weaving another strand into the ethic of salvation. Useful toil, the counterpart of shrewd speculation, appears simultaneously as virtuous in itself, as the legitimate means of social mobility, and as an instrument for control over the passions.

Within the dichotomous moral economy, concrete, productive labor is situated outside of and defined as antagonistic to what then appear as the more abstract, negative forces of capitalism. But the dichotomy of concrete and abstract forces is a notoriously slippery operator. Specifications of the scheme in U.S. history have united groups that could be divided (for instance, small farmers with big industrialists) and divided others that could be united (blue-collar workers from "paper-pushing" white-collar workers). From the Jacksonian "laboring classes" to the populist "producing classes" to the contemporary neopopulist concepts of the "working man" and "working woman" (Halle: 1984), we seem to be confronted with what Moishe Postone (1980) describes as expressions of capitalist discontent that leave capitalism intact.

At the other pole of success mythology, a certain quality of abstractness is celebrated rather than condemned. The archetypal comic success hero is a distinctive type of common man. Less fixated and compulsive than his industrious cousin, he is a trickster who succeeds through cunning, duplicity, and the artful manipulation of images. Speech is his instrument of control, and its "smoothness" typifies the style of individualism that he practices.

With his shrewd opportunism and his disrespect for tradition, the antebellum trickster expressed a sense of new possibilities in a period of rapid social change. Emancipated from collective moral controls, the comic hero of antebellum popular theater roved freely across the mythical spaces of opportunity known as New York and California, inviting audiences to marvel at his skill in the art of dissimulation. These transforming heroes prefigure the modern sense of the self as a construct for individuals to invent in performances. According to Donald Meyer, they taught their audience or, to be more precise, its male members, "that all identities were masks, and that freedom grew therefore in the ability to present as many of them as possible" (1987: 256).

I would add that by the time this lesson gained wide acceptance, its emancipatory potential had been largely absorbed and defused. If the concept of the performing self had origins in popular antebellum comedy, its future was tied to the growth of the professional-managerial class. During the twentieth century, an older delight in image-making would be incorporated into the bureaucratic and consumption ethics of late capitalist society.

Corporate Shape-Changers

If the creation of the consumer society eroded the ethic of self-denial, the bureaucratization of work dramatically altered the social conditions of mobility and success. Beginning in the mid-1800s and gathering force in this century, bureaucratization transformed the American middle classes from small producers into white-collar employees dependent on large organizations. Within these organizations the new work force was hierarchically divided. At the top there grew up an internally stratified, overwhelmingly male, class of salaried managers and professionals; at the bottom bureaucracy required an ever-increasing clerical labor force that came to be and remains dominated by women.

The cultural consequences of these massive changes in the organization of work have interested historians and sociologists for decades, and a considerable literature exists on the occupational cultures of modern bureaucratic corporations.[1] Central to my concern with success mythology is the position developed most fully by Robert Jackall (1988) in his important study of corporate managers. Jackall shows in fine detail how bureaucracy strikes at the very core of the old work ethic by breaking the connection between work and reward.

Under the semipatrimonial conditions of corporate bureaucracies, advancement after a certain point depends less on specific skills or achievements than on a multifaceted ability to please and impress those with power (Jackall 1988: 11–12; Kanter 1977: 73–74). Work alone does not confer success in the bureaucratic world; one's superiors must also appreciate the work one does, and this requires adroit self-presentation. For the aspiring corporate executive, the main task is to make oneself appear as one of the elect in the regard of others by projecting the well-staged impression at the well-timed moment.

In this distinctive version of the Protestant Ethic, mastery of the techniques of image management is essential (Jackall 1988: 192, 203). The persistence of egalitarian rhetoric within hierarchical organizations gives rise to a distinctive form of bureaucratic practice in which participants are required to mask the authority relations they enact. Thus one should defer to a superior without appearing deferential; the valued style for superiors is friendly and open, without loss of authority. External appearance and overall manner also contribute to making the right impression. Speech, dress, and bearing should convey a sense of poised ease—a quiet, relaxed self-confidence that distinguishes those at or bound for the top. In this managerial version of aristocratic style, disarming charm, cosmopolitan taste, and sophisticated wit enhance the crucial abilities to handle situations and people with agility and finesse (Jackall 1988: 46–59). Whether it is a matter of smoothly shifting blame onto a co-worker or of enacting frankness at precisely the right juncture in a dialogue, mastery of the dominant social style is an indispensable asset.

Where image displaces essence, one learns to manage appearances with unflagging vigilance. What matters is how closely one can transform oneself to meet the organizational ideal, and this requires relentless self-scrutiny and a capacity for self-rationalization (Jackall 1988: 59–62). Within the terms of the bureaucratic ethic—the largely implicit rules for survival and success in corporate bureaucracies—spontaneity of any sort is strictly proscribed, while an ability to mask subjective responses behind a public face is studiously cultivated and regularly rewarded.[2] At the bottom of corporate hierarchies, white-collar workers in nondiscretionary positions may experience their public faces as something imposed from above in the form of dress codes or prescribed behavioral styles. Toward the top, however, the masking ability is subjectively empowering. Jackall succinctly conveys the managerial perspective: "For them [corporate managers], the issue is not a reluctant donning of masks but rather a mastery of the social rules that prescribe which mask to wear on which occasion" (1988: 46).

Earlier studies missed the self-consciousness and intentionality with which business bureaucrats adopt the various masks they wear. When these trends first came under sociological scrutiny in the 1950s, they tended to be read as indexes of the decline of individualism.[3] Perhaps more fundamentally, the cultural equation of self-reliance and candor with masculinity brought the very manhood of the Organization Man into question. Deferential and self-effacing in the presence of superiors, obliged to rely on charm, seduction, and deceit, the dependent bureaucratic employee appeared to social critics to have assumed the feminine position.

Mass-cultural representations reinforced that impression. Corporate shape-changers first appeared in movies and television as spineless, emasculated victims of bureaucratic humiliation, used to identify masculinity with old-fashioned integrity and self-reliance. But the manly individualism of traditional paternal authorities had an increasingly nostalgic appeal. Such figures could not defuse the widely perceived crisis of middle-class masculinity in a bureaucratized society. Overdetermined by the seductive pressures of consumerism, by the therapeutic culture's assault on adult authority within the family, by the challenge to patriarchy embodied in the woman's movement, and by America's loss of political hegemony, the problem of masculine identity escalated during the 1960s and 1970s.

Hollywood experimented in the 1970s with sensitive, responsive men, who took on culturally feminine traits and learned to limit their ambitions. But since the return of pride in the 1980s, both the old paternal heroes and their sensitive sons have been superseded by another type. Boyish and determined, this new hero asserts his masculinity through practiced duplicity rather than manly candor or honest labor, and his ambition is unadulterated by any feminine traits that he may assume. Descended from the comic tradition of the transforming hero, proliferating variants of the type provide models of how to succeed as a man in an overorganized world.

Like his generic antecedents, the contemporary trickster combines skill at shape-changing with a playful disrespect for authority. In a common plot structure that I abstracted from a set of popular comedies about corporate success, a middle-class hero rises to the top through disguise, deceit, and seductive charm. Authority is represented in the plot as either oppressive or ineffectual, and the hero's apparent project is to cast off all restraints on desire, internal as well as external ones. As the plot unfolds, however, the corporate world that will assimilate his boyish individualism is constructed as a properly empowered authority, personified in a fun-loving, benevolent parental figure. Rebellion, in short, becomes a form of accommodation to corporate society.

Embodied in blockbusters such as *Ferris Bueller's Day Off* (1986) and *Big* (1988) and in other well-received comedies including *The Secret of My Success* (1987), this pattern governed the success stories produced at the height of the Reagan era. Political elites might celebrate the entrepreneur as frontier hero, but Hollywood tailored its products for young audiences embarked on corporate careers. With their seductive charm, verbal dexterity, and mastery over their public faces, comic tricksters provide a narrative lesson in the dominant social style. But what makes the lesson at once compelling and ambiguous is the antiauthoritarian fantasy with which it is condensed. The hyperrebellious, defiant style of the heroes also appeals to popular ambivalence toward bureaucracy and, specifically, to social anxiety over gender identity in white-collar workplaces.

Any commercially successful cultural commodity constructs multiple, if not unlimited, positions from which it can be meaningfully viewed, and reception is likely to vary along lines of class as well as gender. For professional-middle-class audiences, already positioned to experience image-manipulation as empowering, the films construct bureaucratic seduction as a positively valued style for men while simultaneously discouraging its cultivation by women, whose career ambitions are ritually tamed in the basic plot. I suspect that lower-middle-class male audiences, however, may ignore the "pedagogical" message and seek gratification in the antiauthoritarian fantasy of masculine defiance. What this suggests is that cultural commodities produced for maximum profit take on a differential and differentiating ideological function. In this case, they educate some segments of their audience in the requirements for corporate success while systematically miseducating others.[4]

An explicit and less successful type of pedagogy was attempted in Oliver Stone's *Wall Street* (1987), a film that made its seductive, masculine shape-changer into a villain. An intended return to the countertradition of moderate success through honest labor, *Wall Street* presents itself as an attack on the abstract from the standpoint of the concrete. Yet such appeal as the film has emanates from the supposedly negative dimension of capitalism personified in Michael Douglas's Gordon Gekko, the dazzling, dynamic corporate takeover artist who knows how to turn illusion into reality.

Douglas's performance (which won the film's only major Oscar) overpowers the plot. It is as if a transformer from the other pole of success mythology had somehow wandered into a cautionary tale and then proceeded to wreck it, as easily as Gekko wrecks the companies he buys. Gekko's potency is marked by the very multiplicity of the forces arrayed against him. Under his magnetic influence, Bud Fox, an ambitious broker played by Charlie Sheen, succumbs to the temptation of easy, unlimited wealth. But at every step in Bud's descent, a stern, symptomatically mixed crew calls him back to the moral ideal of productive labor. There is Bud's father (played by Martin Sheen), a hardworking, relentlessly honest airline machinist who hopes that jail will teach his son to value creativity over the easy buck. He has a counterpart at Bud's firm, a pious stockbroker played by Hal Holbrook in a reprise of his Abe Lincoln role. The broker lectures Bud interminably on such fundamentals as the (fetishized) danger of money (it "makes you do things you don't want to do"), the importance of "character" (it keeps man from the "abyss"), and the true role of the stock market (to create jobs by enriching industry). Finally, there is Gekko's opponent within his own sphere, a responsible speculator who buys companies to develop rather than to destroy them.

One effect of these redundant dichotomies is to void even the one-sided critique of capitalism of any critical social content. The film celebrates a composite class of industrious producers who share a moral orientation toward work, which in principle is available to all occupations, including speculators such as Gekko. Still another effect of the redundancy is to reduce poor Bud Fox to an utterly abject position, hemmed in by moralizing paternal authorities. If the comic transforming heroes evoke a pleasure-ego breaking free of controls, in *Wall Street* the superego returns with a vengeance to preach a distrust of conspicuous consumption more consistent with the Carter 1970s than the Reagan 1980s.

Considering the combined clout of its stars and its hot, Oscar-winning director, *Wall Street* was a disappointment at the box office. Even in the wake of the stock market crash, audiences seem to have been largely indifferent to the film's patriarchal call for moral restraint. Subsequent productions, however, have more successfully reintroduced the theme of moral discipline into success stories. The formula turns out to be simple: Identify the dangerous, uncontrolled forces loose in society with the independent, upper-middle-class, professional-managerial woman.

A Job for Working Men and Women

Peter Biskind and Barbara Ehrenreich (1987) connect Hollywood's rediscovery of the working-class world as a subject for major films in the 1970s to a crisis of masculinity in the professional middle class. In the context of intensifying corporate domination and unsettled gender roles, Biskind and Ehrenreich argue, the patriarchal, male-bonded, ethnic blue-collar community was constructed as a locus of defiant masculinity, which could then be evaluated in two ways. Attacked and repudiated in liberal films such as *Saturday Night Fever,* spectacular working-class masculinity was romanticized in the conservative *Rocky* films and used as a standpoint for condemnation of an overpermissive society. In both cases, however, by associating working-class masculinity with ethnic neighborhoods, the films marked it as something vestigial and destined to pass away.

When working-class heroes reappeared in the 1980s, they had lost that vestigial quality. No longer confined to ethnic neighborhoods, the new working-class characters operate in the heart of middle-class society, from Beverly Hills to New York City, where the specific virtues they incarnate are urgently required.

Two films in particular, both released late in 1988, found receptive audiences for their stories of working-class success. *Working Girl,* a comedy directed by Mike Nichols, stars Melanie Griffith, Sigourney Weaver, and Harrison Ford. The film opened to generally favorable reviews and, amid sporadic grumblings over its sexism, was even nominated for several major Oscars. The film also did well at the box office. It stayed among the top ten films for more than two months and grossed over $62 million in eighteen weeks in release. Whereas *Working Girl* was directed primarily at adult women, *Cocktail,* starring Tom Cruise, was a late summer release for the teenage audience, primarily boys. Panned by the critics, Australian director Roger Donaldson's moral tale about the struggles of a young bartender became the ninth top-grossing film released in 1988, with a total domestic gross of $77 million. At first glance, these two films seem poles apart. *Working Girl* is a self-consciously liberal comedy that identifies upward mobility with personal emancipation. It politely but firmly rebukes working-class males for patriarchal oppression, while celebrating the liberated, cosmopolitan life-style that its heroine assimilates. In *Cocktail,* by contrast, urban society is depicted as decadent and is attacked in frankly sexist, neoconservative terms, while the patriarchal working-class family appears as the source of moral restraint.

Yet *Working Girl* is in some respects the closer of the two films to the conservative, moralistic tradition. Horatio Alger himself would approve of Tess McGill, the spunky, hardworking, congenitally honest secretary played by Melanie Griffith. Tess shares many qualities with Alger's boy heroes, such as compliance, obedience, submissiveness to bourgeois norms, and willingness to serve powerful men.

What Alger would make of Cruise's Brian Flannagan is another matter. On the surface, *Cocktail* tells the story of Brian's rescue from a dissolute life-style and his domestication through marriage. Alger could only applaud the film's resolution, yet he might justifiably protest that the lad demonstrates none of the disciplinary virtues in the story that the film relates. Brian's languid struggle upward involves seductive charm, predatory sexuality, and a series of increasingly defiant rebellions against male authorities. Thus the quality of submissiveness attaches to a comic transformer, while the industrious moral hero takes on the rebellious style.

The Secretary and the Boss from Hell

Working Girl's Tess McGill has a twofold problem. On the one hand, she must free herself from a warm and close-knit but restrictive working-class community, with its norm of feminine deference to masculine desires. On the other hand, she reenacts the immigrant journey (as the establishing shots of New York harbor remind us), setting out each day on the Staten Island ferry to toil as a secretary in a Wall Street investment firm. Intelligent and industrious (she has a night-school degree in marketing and takes speech classes to upgrade her image), she is stuck at the bottom of a white-collar bureaucracy as indifferent to mere merit as it is to hard-won, second-rate credentials.

Tess must also deal with sexual objectification at home and in the workplace. This is a film that tries, with its head if not with its heart, to treat the working-class characters with a measure of sympathy. Mick Dugan (Alec Baldwin), Tess's tattooed, blue-collar boyfriend, is not a bad fellow. We may assume that he genuinely cares for Tess in his way, which is simply as limited as his taste in lingerie. Nevertheless, when the film cuts from a bedroom scene between Mick and Tess to a limo where Tess must fend off a sleazy manager, it connects Mick's kinky working-class sensuality to more brutal forms of sexual exploitation. Tess demonstrates in the limo scene that she is not *that* kind of "working girl," a point that the film visually undercuts. With their elaborately teased hair, heavy eye makeup, and short, tight skirts, the secretaries are made to look like hookers, as Pauline Kael (1989: 81) observed. Tess, however, takes prompt revenge on the low-level sleazoid pimp of a boss who had tried to set her up. The scene in which she teletypes her assessment of his manhood for all the office to read is wonderfully gratifying and endears her to audiences. It also tells us quite a lot about Tess's future in a bureaucracy. Consider how a shape-changer might have handled a similar situation. Ferris Bueller, for example, or Brantley Foster of *The Secret of My Success* would easily have manipulated the computer technology in such a way as to humiliate their superiors without exposing themselves to retribution. Compared to these more advanced types, Tess is clearly a beginner in the art of defiance.

Class and gender conspire to keep her honest, even when she dabbles in disguise. *Working Girl* employs a variant of the device used in *Secret,* a parody of the bureaucratic ethic wherein reliance on hard work and achievement is exchanged for image manipulation. In *Secret,* Brantley simply dons a suit, gains access to an unused office, and invents an executive persona, complete with secretary, personalized stationery, and nameplate on the door. Tess keeps her own name but borrows the office, wardrobe, and style of her new boss, Katherine Parker (Sigourney Weaver), an ambitious, patrician executive. Tess resorts to trickery only in retaliation for Katherine's attempt to steal her business idea. Upon discovering her boss's treachery, Tess resolves to steal Katherine's symbols of executive status and make the deal herself while a skiing accident keeps Katherine away from New York.

Tess has considerably more difficulty carrying off her ruse than did Brantley. The Kansas farm boy effortlessly assimilated the dominant style of relaxed ease, but for Tess the masquerade is an ongoing struggle against dispositions rooted in her female, working-class habitus. Repeatedly in the film, she temporarily loses her confidence and poise, as when she almost faints upon hearing that the cocktail dress she is about to don costs $6,000. ("It's not even leather!" exclaims Cyn, her best friend and reluctant ally.) While there is a certain realism to Tess's uncertainty, this is, after all, comedy, where fluid shape-changing expresses a spirit of freedom. That spirit, as Donald Meyer (1987: 559) reminds us, has long excluded women, and Tess is the exception that proves the rule. Embarked on a new career as what Cyn calls "a total imposter," Tess is recurrently restabilized, fixed in identities other than those she seeks to assume.

Consider the outcome of her ill-fated choice of the cocktail dress for a business party where she hopes to make professional contacts. Tess, who has listened to Katherine quoting Coco Chanel, extols the dress to the doubtful Cyn: "It's elegant, simple, and yet . . . makes a statement. Says to people, *confident*. A risk-taker. Not afraid to be noticed." But Tess has learned only the langue of elite fashion, not the parole, for the dress is wrong for the occasion. It indeed attracts the notice of Jack Trainer (Harrison Ford), the investment banker whom she wants to meet, but not in the way she had intended. Where Tess had anticipated a professional encounter between colleagues, she is instead converted into the object of the masculine gaze. Says the admiring Jack to Tess: "You're the first woman I've met at one of these goddam parties who dresses like a woman and not like a woman thinks a man would dress if he were a woman."

With the sure instincts of the gamesman, Jack automatically conceals his identity from Tess, the better, as he admits later, to direct their interaction away from "acquisitions and mergers" and toward "lust and tequila." To this strategy, which quite confounds her own, Tess can offer only passive resistance. Having taken some of Katherine's valium to calm her nerves, she gets smashed on the tequila, confides to Jack that she has "a head for business and a bod for sin," and then passes out in a cab, obliging him to carry her up the stairs to his minimalist brownstone apartment and put her gently to bed.

The distance Tess will traverse is thus clearly circumscribed. Still an object to voyeuristic men, she has found in Jack a more nurturant and refined voyeur, one able to sublimate his passion in aesthetic contemplation of her sleeping form. Moreover, in contrast to Mick's inexpressive, old-fashioned masculinity, Jack combines rational business skills with a quasi-maternal capacity for affection and concern.

Tess's awkward attempts at self-transformation contrast with the polished performance of the true shape-changer, who is, of course, none other than Katherine herself. Before the skiing accident, Katherine instructs the eager Tess through word and deed. Adopting the apparently participatory style of the enlightened executive, Katherine deftly manipulates Tess into the position of a loyal dependent. Katherine is equally as adept at manipulating male rivals as female subordinates. With Tess looking on, she easily deflects the sexual advances of another executive, while suggesting that she may bestow her favors on him later in return for admission to a deal he is arranging. Quips Katherine to the admiring Tess: "Never burn bridges. Today's junior prick, tomorrow's senior partner."

Such farsighted and manipulative smoothness is precisely what Tess lacks, but Tess is not alone. Katherine is a relatively unusual type. In other workplace comedies, such as *Nothing in Common, Secret,* and *Big,* the negatively qualified career women are extensions of powerful father-lovers. They occupy the role that Rosabeth Kanter (1977: 234–235) calls the "seductress," the executive woman who allies herself with a high-status male "protector." In the movies such women are usually liberated by the heroes, which is to say, they shift their allegiances to more charming masters and are feminized in the process. Katherine, however, is a more predatory seductress. She is under no one's protection and is not the extension of any male ego. A free agent, she dispassionately includes sex among the resources at her disposal for controlling others, including Jack, with whom she has contracted a mixed business-pleasure alliance.

The device used to get Katherine out of the way interacts oddly with the character initially established. From the moment that Katherine prepares for her skiing trip, the film directs attention away from her managerial skills and onto her privileged, upper-class background. When she speaks German on the phone to an innkeeper, it is as if the film expects us to resent her cosmopolitanism, and the resentful, disapproving tone intensifies after the accident. Peculiarly unpleasant scenes portray Katherine in a hospital room, surrounded by lascivious doctors and festive patients, apparently reveling in her forced recruitment into the leisure class.

Onto the character of the scheming career woman these scenes superimpose another familiar type, the spoiled rich girl or society lady, whose frivolity deserves contempt. Detached from the corporate workplace, where impeccable self-control is one of her prime assets, Katherine abruptly metamorphoses into a self-indulgent, decadent pleasure-seeker, languishing in the hospital while Tess and Jack busily promote an important deal. Katherine's identity as an independent working woman is undercut in small ways as well. We learn, for example, that she is living in her parents' opulent, vacant townhouse, and when Tess snoops through Katherine's correspondence, she turns up a reference to Wellesley rather than to a Harvard M.B.A. Katherine's regression into hedonism is only temporary, but it introduces into the story the old moralistic critique of decadent leisure. Additional images of upper-class excess are provided later on when Tess and Jack crash the lavish and oddly tasteless wedding of the daughter of a wealthy industrialist. Both Janet Maslin (in a generally favorable review in 1988) and Pauline Kael (in a hostile one in 1989) criticize this scene for making the society people look unnecessarily foolish. What they do not go on to observe is that Tess and Jack proceed almost immediately from the wedding to a business meeting with the industrialist, Oren Trask (Philip Bosco). Here, in Trask's offices, everything is dignified, stately, and refined. However nouveau the wedding may have appeared, walnut-paneled walls, gilt molding, oil paintings, and marble stairs bespeak old wealth and an atmosphere of quiet, sober productivity.

Upper-class society, in other words, is once more split, this time into degraded, leisured women and honest, industrious men. Unlike the first wave of 1980s success comedies, *Working Girl* rejects the fun-loving rich of the screwball tradition who legitimize a spirit of release. Instead, it condemns idle play and reserves its approval for the hardworking plutocrat with a heart of gold, a type reminiscent of Frank Capra's comic fantasies (Sklar 1975: 207).

Tess's alliance with Trask is anticipated in the film's title, with its allusion to the ideology of productive labor. The business deal that Tess masterminds obliges Trask to limit his ambitions by buying into radio rather than television and has an old-fashioned, ascetic character. Profit is to be subordinated to the values of stability and security, a theme echoed in representations of the southern owner of the radio station they want to buy as a traditionalist who will sell to Trask over other competitors because he cares as much for character as for profit. But *Working Girl* handles its economic morality more circumspectly than did *Wall Street*. Whereas the latter film personifies the moral dichotomy of destructive and productive capitalism in contrastive styles of masculinity, in *Working Girl* the dichotomy is displaced onto oppositions between unrestrained and restrained women.

Whatever its manifest purpose, Tess's alliance with Trask is contracted *against* women of the dominant class. Tess is the film's condensed, wishful substitute for Trask's empty-headed daughter and for the overambitious executive woman. Less frivolous and extravagant than the one, more docile and compliant than the other, the dutiful girl from the working class will diffuse an imagined threat of female power.

Katherine, who concentrates and personifies that threat, is everything that Tess is not. In the corporate workplace she gives the staged appearance of ease that distinguishes the rising star. With a facility rooted in a privileged background and extensive social training, she always knows what to do, as she demonstrates when she uncovers Tess's scheme and swiftly turns the tables. By contrast, Tess remains an indifferent shapechanger to the end. Exposed and unjustly accused by Katherine, temporarily abandoned by Jack, she almost slinks out of Trask's conference room, an icon of defeat. Self-effacing, deferential, conscientious, and remorseful, Tess is limited by dispositions rooted in class, gender, and social trajectory. Although somewhat diluted as the plot unfolds, these dispositions are never shed, and they position her in relation to the elite characters, with their staged self-confidence and public appearance of relaxed ease. Like Alger's heroes, Tess achieves moderate success through the intervention of a paternal protector. Whatever promise may be held out for the future, it is hard to imagine her rising to the top. The qualities attributed to her in the film qualify her for relatively low-level, low-discretionary managerial positions, the very positions that, as Rosabeth Kanter (1977: 55) found, women in corporate bureaucracies are more likely to occupy.

Katherine, who has the qualifications for a top-echelon position, is blocked and expelled, the manifest cause being her duplicitous professional conduct. But the film inadvertently exposes itself when it converts the corporate gameswoman into a decadent and aggressive hedonist. After the accident Katherine's predatory sexuality ceases to be one resource among many and appears instead as her life project. With her leg perpetually rigid in its cast, she snatches at flirtatious doctors and comes close to raping a terrified Jack. Oddly, the film's only explicit reference to motherhood comes at this juncture, when Katherine alludes by way of a proposal to her biological clock. But when she makes a grab for Jack's pants, gleefully asking if Big Jack can "come out to play," her transformation into the pre-oedipal phallic mother is complete.

"The secretary and the boss from hell" was one of the publicity slogans for *Working Girl,* and albeit in a comic register, the film participates in the demonization of the independent woman more graphically effected in *Fatal Attraction.* Generated out of reawakened infantile fears of being under female power, the fantasy of the demonic woman splits female sexuality into what then appear as lawful and unlawful forms, represented in *Working Girl* by Tess and Katherine, respectively. Not the least of the film's achievements is to have transposed the joyously sensual and erotic Melanie Griffith into a "good," passively sexual, oedipal daughter, while turning Weaver into a version of the monstrous female sexuality that she herself defeated as the Rambette of *Aliens.*

Katherine's defeat in *Working Girl* comes in fairy-tale form through the motif of the false bride. Tested for knowledge she does not possess, she is exposed and expelled like the witches in the tales. Witches decisively lose their shape-changing abilities at such junctures and stand revealed as what they really are, fixed in their dreadful, devouring rage. Katherine was originally to have played out her affinity with the witch. In the film script she is last seen "losing it" in the elevator, "with a mighty wail, a gnashing of teeth, cursing the fates and pounding the walls."

In the narrative logic from which that vision proceeds, Katherine personifies the danger of the early Mother, against which the Law of the Father, personified in Trask, appears as the necessary and legitimate resolution. In fairy tales, exposed witches are usually put in spiked barrels, which are rolled down mountain slopes or dragged through the streets by white horses. *Working Girl* settles for a more symbolic phallic punishment. It is inspired by Tess, who in the heat of anger makes reference to Katherine's "bony ass." Trask subsequently appropriates the insult, and his authority lends it potency. He uses it as a metonymic transformer that deprives Katherine of her dangerous, seductive sexuality prior to her expulsion and forces her to regress further to the purely destructive monster we were to have glimpsed. However the decision was made to cut this scene, its absence opens up a small space for resisting the narrative logic. Without that image to provide closure, the expulsion scene may be received as excessively cruel. Professional women, in particular, could conceivably identify with the abused but outwardly graceful and defiant Katherine and proceed to separate her from the projected threat.

The film's final image depends on the sense of a threat contained. It is a shot of Tess, seen through the window of her new executive office, while on the soundtrack Carly Simon and a women's choir burst into exultant song. As the camera draws back, the office is revealed as a tiny box in the middle of a skyscraper containing row upon row of identical boxes. Debate over whether or not any irony is intended here seems to me to miss the point. At one level the rows of offices suggest that corporate society, like the frontier of old, provides unlimited opportunities for industrious citizens.[5] At the same time, the image appeals, I suggest, to anxieties over unlimited ambition in women. In the image of the woman successfully contained within a corporate bureaucracy, the film offers its ideal solution to the imagined threat of female power.

The Defiant One

Yet another version of the success myth is whipped up in *Cocktail,* a frothy blend of misogyny, homophobia, right-populist resentment, and antifeminism. Dispensing with the pseudoliberationist appeal of *Working Girl, Cocktail* claims to be about the loss and recovery of moral restraint. That, however, is not the main thrust of the story it actually tells.

The film opens on a rural highway, somewhere in the West, where a car filled with boisterous young men is in pursuit of a bus. Brian Flannagan, the film's sometimes less-than-noble young savage, has just been discharged from the army. Freed from disciplinary controls, he longs "to be wild again," the soundtrack informs us. He is heading for New York City to make his fortune, in the tradition of self-made men. We soon learn that Brian is a local boy, born and raised in a run-down, ethnic blue-collar neighborhood in Queens. His uncle, Pat Devine, owns a neighborhood tavern, to which Brian returns for a brief visit and some quick character establishment. It is the standard meeting between youthful vigor and senescent authority. Pat incarnates the surly, ascetic virtues that would have enabled his own ascent to the lower-middle class. A miser whose strategy for accumulation is never to buy a drink, he illustrates Pierre Bourdieu's definition of the petit bourgeois as "a proletarian who makes himself small to become bourgeois" (1984: 338). Although we are given to understand that Pat is a decent and honorable man, he has had to limit ties of neighborly solidarity in the interest of mobility. Thus his tavern bears little resemblance to the convivial place of male fellowship portrayed in beer commercials. Its function in the narrative is to characterize the world that Brian wants to leave as a place antagonistic to pleasure and in need of revitalization. Staring across the river toward the city, Brian appears as a typical romantic success hero—ambitious, impatient of restraints, charged with unlimited desire.

The city, however, proves inhospitable. Although he is well-supplied with easy self-confidence and charm, Brian is barred from the corporate world for lack of educational qualifications. The film portrays his exclusion through a montage of meetings with unresponsive personnel officers, many of them black or female, who one by one advise him to go back to school. An earlier script appealed more directly to neopopulist resentment. It placed him briefly in the copy center of a firm called Swedlin, Vogel and Mintz, in which he soon decides he has no future, having neither an M.B.A. nor a Jewish name.

In both versions Brian temporarily withdraws from the corporate world, intending to acquire educational capital. Thus he wanders into another type of story. Set not in overbureaucratized offices but in shiny palaces of consumption, this story presents the city in its other guise as the corrupt and corrupting place of temptation.

Brian is initiated into the ways of this other city by Doug Coughlin, head bartender in an Upper-East-Side night spot where Brian takes a part-time job. Coughlin is typed from the outset as the ambitious but cynical and dissolute Irishman, a type well represented by Australian actor Brian Brown in the film's shopping-mall mentality.

Coughlin's character is a blend of class resentment, misogyny, and machismo. His distinctive style of self-indulgence, implied in the red-eyes he is making at his first appearance, has class as well as gender qualities. A hard drinker, with the emphasis on the hard, Coughlin drinks Remy from a shot glass and compels Brian to follow suit, thus conscripting the yuppie status drink into the working-class rite of male fellowship. Drink, Coughlin explains, is part of Brian's training. According to him, he who can maximize his capacity is positioned to prey upon weaker hedonists, the rich and loose women who flow into the bar at night.

A poor man's Gordon Gekko, Coughlin espouses the hustler's version of success without labor. New York is the center of action for both characters, but in Coughlin's scheme of things the "investors" are women and the capital to be deployed is predatory sexuality, whether his own or Brian's. Endeavoring to entice Brian with his vision of success, Coughlin speaks like a pimp recruiting a hot new talent: "You see, the name of this game is Woman. The little darlings come in panting, their little hearts pit-a-patting for the handsome, all-knowing bartender. In their wake, a parade of slobbering geeks, one hand on their crotches, one hand on their wallets. Just get the women, you'll get the bucks. You got 'em. Buttons were popping. Skirts were rising. When you can see the color of their panties, you know you got talent."

Officially, the film disapproves of Coughlin's easy way to wealth, and it will punish him severely, in due course. Nevertheless, it also shows us middle-class pleasure seeking through his eyes. The world that turned Brian away returns to him and to us transmuted by Coughlin's resentment, revealed in all its effete decadence. In this nocturnal world of the film's imagination, hostile men snarl at the bartenders and watch jealously over their female companions, whose eyes are riveted on the real men behind the bar. Women predominate among the clientele. Their lurching steps and uncontrolled bodies, repeatedly captured by the camera, accentuate the poised precision of the bartenders, who stand erect and self-contained against the flow. The film has surely concocted one of Hollywood's more creative images of spectacular working-class masculinity. In what must pass as the film's high moments, Cruise and Brown display their prowess, whipping the crowds into frenzy with performances that evoke a male striptease. They toss their glasses and blender containers into the air in perfect unison, twist and shake to the blaring music, and pivot from the customers back to face each other, proudly twirling their bottles.

The plot, however, requires our hero to struggle against the ethic of pleasure in which he participates. Positioned between an overly ascetic work ethic, represented by Uncle Pat, and the dream of easy riches that Coughlin holds out, Brian searches for a middle path. To find it proves difficult. Brian's plan for success is repeatedly revised as the film unfolds, its content becoming ever more elusive in the process.

Initially he submits to rules imposed from above. He enrolls in a business program, intending to bring himself to the point where Tess already is when her movie begins. But Brian's good intentions are obstructed by an arrogant and domineering professor. When this petty tyrant belittles the students, Brian rebels and brings his brief college career to an end. His defiant nature drives him away from the ascetic pole of industrious work and back toward the pole of rapid success, where Coughlin is waiting.

Brian, however, does not capitulate at once. Abandoning his aspiration to a corporate career, he comes up with an entrepreneurial scheme in which he and Coughlin will start their own business. This, of course, takes money, and here the film devises a truly ingenious, not to mention photogenic, version of the work ethic. Brian's brainstorm is that the two of them should go down to Jamaica, where they can live cheaply, earn vast sums as bartenders, and within a few seasons accumulate the capital they need.

For Coughlin, this is still too slow and industrious. Moreover, for reasons that remain opaque, he disapproves of Brian's new girlfriend, a well-to-do journalist. To prove to Brian that she is nothing but "an assembly line hump," he seduces her himself, and their friendship collapses. According to an outraged Brian, Coughlin has violated the sacred code of male loyalty, which in this film is reduced to one proscription—not to sleep with your buddy's woman. "Where I come from," says Brian, "you don't do things like that to your friends."

It is hard to avoid the conclusion that Coughlin has violated an even weightier taboo. His hostility toward the woman is undermotivated unless it is read as jealous rage. This, I submit, the film invites us to do, both through its plot line, in which Coughlin twice disrupts Brian's relationships with women, and through its visual imagery. Women interested in Brian are repeatedly seen from Coughlin's point of view, fixed in his cold, suspicious gaze. If this interpretation is accepted, Brian's angry departure for Jamaica should be read as a homophobic flight.

A dissolve signifies miles and years passing. Part two opens on a Jamaican beach, where Brian works in a posh outdoor bar, to the accompaniment of a lilting Caribbean soundtrack. Coughlin appears as a man of leisure. He has risen to become the husband of a wealthy woman, whom the film hastily types as a promiscuous bitch. As the class-conscious Brian tells us, she "was looking for a way to get even with (her parents), so she married a bartender."

Despite himself, Brian is impressed. His own progress has been slow. He keeps a "how-to-succeed" manual behind the bar, but in this idyllic atmosphere his entrepreneurial dreams have gone on hold. The funds he had hoped to accumulate are dissipated in the pursuit of nocturnal pleasures, and Brian is increasingly afraid that he may be stuck in his bartender station.

Complicating the picture is his romance with Jordan Mooney (Elizabeth Shue), the poor, struggling artist who is really a Park Avenue princess in disguise. Their budding relationship provides the occasion for a montage of exotic island locales that contribute greatly to the film's glossy look. Plotwise, the romance serves to remind us of Brian's still untamed nature, which recoils at Jordan's domestic chatter.

As before, Coughlin is on hand to tempt Brian away from responsibility. Coughlin taunts Brian with being a congenital worker and bets him that he can't hustle an elegant woman who is sitting at the bar. Brian wins the bet, loses the good girl, and wins the affections of the other woman. She turns out to be the owner of a successful import business in which Brian hopes to make his fortune. Freed at last from his commitment to autonomous achievement, he returns to New York as a kept man.

Narration in what David Bordwell et al. (1985) call the classical Hollywood film encourages specific spectatorial activities. By what Bordwell refers to as the "primacy effect," first impressions of a character provide the basis for expectations across the film. They invite us to code departures as temporary deviations and to anticipate that vagrants will return in the resolution to the path from which they have strayed (Bordwell et al. 1985: 37–38). As a film in the classical style, *Cocktail* never leaves Brian's recovery in doubt. What needs specifying is the nature of the self to which he returns.

The achievement of a narrative resolution in the film has little to do with the manifest opposition between workers and hustlers. Although the surface plot requires Brian to learn the value of work and moderation, no such lesson is provided. As the plot approaches resolution, the film's economics grow increasingly vague. In Jamaica, Brian broods over his inability to save money. Back in New York, when he finally proposes to the pregnant Jordan, he tells her that with the money he has saved plus a loan from Uncle Pat, he now has enough to start his own business. Perhaps so, but his alleged achievement of self-discipline has gone on entirely off camera. What is revived and celebrated in the concluding sequence is Brian's quality of rebellious defiance. After a predictably brief stint as a managerial woman's lapdog, he recovers the wildness, purity, and natural vigor attributed to him in the prologue, and he revolts against male representatives of the dominant classes. These include a sneering artist, who doubles for the tyrannical professor, and Brian's most formidable adversary, Mr. Mooney, Jordan's father.

Mooney is a composite of the class enemy and the persecutory oedipal father. He lives in elite surroundings—a Park Avenue penthouse complete with hardwood floors, piano, antique settees, and original artwork. His casual clothes hint at country leisure, which would be the film's idea of upper-class taste. He treats Brian with aristocratic contempt for the fortune hunter, expressed in the cutting tone of a harsh father belittling a pretentious boy. With his imperious attitude, Mooney represents hierarchical class distinctions that appear to be collapsing. He is portrayed as an evil king who locks the princess away in a tower guarded by ogreish doormen, whom he must repeatedly rebuke for negligence. In this world where authority is at once repressive and ineffectual, the very precautions that Mooney takes signify his inability to control his bohemian daughter.

What separates Brian from Coughlin is not their respective attitudes toward work but their responses to authoritarian men of the dominant social classes. Brian's rebellious defiance of Mooney underlines what, in the film's terms, is wrong with Coughlin's strategy. Coughlin seeks to bypass the dominant males and obtain access to wealth and power through females. This, however, perpetuates and intensifies what the film defines as a social crisis, a crisis of patriarchal control among the upper classes.

In Jamaica, Coughlin tells Brian that, thanks to his wife, he no longer needs to "steal the key" to mobility and success. Back in New York, he discovers that he was wrong. Without that key, Coughlin is swiftly unmanned. Unable to control either his wife's money or her sexuality, bankrupt and cuckolded, the fortune hunter dies by his own hand. He pays the price generically exacted of the fallen woman, whose narrative role he has usurped.

Coughlin's death sends Brian storming back to Mooney's apartment to steal the key as well as the woman. He almost literally wrests Jordan out of her father's arms, thus decisively separating himself from Coughlin, and carries her away to Uncle Pat's tavern, where they celebrate their wedding. In a final scene that takes place in Brian's new establishment, a respectably festive crowd witnesses Jordan embrace her reproductive function (she has conceived twins), while a proud, domesticated Brian assumes the role of paternal provider. If he hints that he will be a disciplinarian to his daughters, we may be sure that he will also be a generous patriarch. With his last words, "Drinks are on the house," he firmly projects Uncle Pat's asceticism into the past.

What is striking is how two such different films as *Working Girl* and *Cocktail* arrive at closely related patriarchal resolutions. Both films project a vision of moral breakdown, overcome from above in *Working Girl* and from below in *Cocktail*. In both cases, moreover, an imagined threat of uncontrolled women drives and legitimizes the authoritarian movement of the plots, while the contents of the respective patriarchal visions recognize their intended audiences in interesting ways.[6] *Cocktail,* geared to the Middle American tastes of lower-middle-class audiences, tries to defend the traditional values of hard work and self-restraint. At the same time, however, its neoconservative version of patriarchy selectively absorbs features of the consumer culture. As the fully enabled paternal figure, Brian fuses the repressive authority that Mooney no longer commands with the spirit of pleasure that Uncle Pat never had and that Coughlin had in excess. The most explicitly authoritarian of the commercially successful tales about success, *Cocktail* also amplifies its hero's rebellious qualities and dilutes its disciplinary message with elements of the ethic of pleasure. However hardworking, sober, and chaste our redeemed hero may be, he is, after all, part of the service industry, in the business of marketing fun.

In *Working Girl,* aimed at more cosmopolitan, professional-middle-class tastes, the patriarchal vision receives a significant twist. In the process of exchanging Katherine for Tess, Jack progressively reveals a feminine side to his nature. As the man who claims to know better than women do just how a man would dress if he were a woman, Jack cross-dresses metaphorically throughout the film. On one occasion, he follows Tess into a women's restroom and nonchalantly uses the facilities with no trace of the embarrassment that she had exhibited when forced into the symmetrically transgressive position. Unlike Tess, who has no flair for transgression, Jack easily appropriates culturally female spaces and roles in a manner reminiscent of Dustin Hoffman literally cross-dressing his way to success in *Tootsie.* Jack's "gentlemanly" treatment of Tess at their first meeting bespeaks a capacity for maternal nurturance that surfaces as the film unfolds. We last see him tenderly handing a child's lunch pail to Tess to sustain her on her first day at her new job.

Janice Radway (1984: 147) has suggested that tender, nurturing male characters in popular romances are exercises in the transformation of masculinity to conform with female standards. While this explanation works well for literature marketed almost exclusively for women, the appropriation of women's roles by men is now a widely distributed theme, familiar from Vietnam films to television sitcoms about male single-parenting (Jeffords 1989: 168–169). Viewed as part of a broad, patriarchal resurgence, the refined, upscale, nurturant masculinity imagined in *Working Girl* also evokes the ultimate refuge from female power, a world where men can divide gender identities among themselves and need no longer depend on women even for their physical selves.

Conclusion

The independent woman as a demonological symbol is not an invention of 1980s Hollywood movies but a recurrent theme in American history, a specter that periodically returns to haunt cultural production. Michael Rogin (1987) has traced anxiety over fantasized female power through a variety of historical settings, including Indian removal, cold war anticommunism, and the Reagan presidency.

Focusing on the discourse of the countersubversive political leader, Rogin shows how the leader's political appeal is rooted in a diffuse sense of vulnerability and threat. Fear, in short, is what makes the message compelling, and fear of a certain general type—fear about sexual desire and bodily integrity; about change, flux, transition; about lost identities, uncertain boundaries, shifting and unstable social roles. Such socially generated fears and anxieties may reawaken the psychosexual fantasy of the devouring, engulfing, pre-oedipal mother. Thus it is that the represented triumph over hidden enemies and restoration of social order on the part of the political leader tends to appear at the psychosexual level as the defeat of the dangerous early mother by the protective oedipal father.

Over the course of the Reagan era, cultural elites brought a specter of female power to the surface of mass-cultural productions. The demonic woman appears most dramatically in adventure and horror films such as *Indiana Jones and the Temple of Doom* (1984), *Aliens* (1986), and *Fatal Attraction* (1987). She is also, I suggest, the absent presence in the 1987 blockbuster comedy *Three Men and a Baby,* a film that invites us to imagine a world without mothers. In this chapter I have focused on her insertion into stories of mobility and success. My specific problem has been to elucidate how a critique of "permissiveness," most forcefully articulated by the New Right, was absorbed into mass-cultural forms that, judging by their commercial success, had considerable popular appeal.[7]

In the second half of the 1980s, Hollywood filmmakers returned to the moralistic version of the success myth, which had seemed to have been superseded. Where the first wave of comic success stories revolved around the overthrow of disciplinary controls, *Wall Street, Working Girl,* and *Cocktail* appeal in their various ways to fears of moral breakdown, and they assert the need for moral restraint. But conservative rhetoric and the tradition from which it derives were reworked in the pursuit of contemporary mass audiences. Instead of celebrating the values of work, self-denial, and repressive authority, the films that struck a responsive chord concentrate on attacking the negative forces of excess projected onto women. Once women are constructed as the source of social problems, their expulsion offers an imaginary solution. Demonic women also create the narrative situation in which men can legitimately appropriate such feminine qualities as seductiveness and nurturance, in a sense offering themselves as substitutes for what is (wishfully) repudiated. It may be that the most enduring legacy of these films and of the Reagan era is to have brought together under the sign of the masculine peculiar combinations of patriarchal control with the ethic of self-indulgence.

Women's vulnerability to demonization is not directly attributable to pre-oedipal fantasies, as these can attach themselves to other disadvantaged groups. In our own period the perception of woman as demonic other is mediated by interrelated social conditions, including the wom-

en's movement, changes in family structure, and the increased participation of women in the work force. To analyze these and other factors
is beyond the scope of this chapter. But the disturbing implication of
the analysis presented here is that antifeminism has become a privileged
discourse of popular discontent.

5

Who Will Do the Caring?
Domestic Men and
Independent Women
in the Movies

SINCE THE 1950s a struggle over the family has gone on at multiple levels, waged by scholars, politicians, media elites, and ordinary women and men. At stake in this struggle are the dominant cultural constructions of gender, what it means to be a man or a woman, what qualities, activities, or spheres, if any, are to be classified as distinctively masculine or feminine.

The cultural form this struggle takes is shaped by the traditional ideology of domesticity and the gendered social universe that it produced. Also known as the ideology of the separate spheres, this belief system arose with early capitalism and provided the framework for the emergence of the middle classes in Victorian England (Davidoff and Hall 1987; Armstrong 1987) and America (Cott 1977; Smith-Rosenberg 1985). Legitimation of the new bourgeois way of life involved a redefinition of women as domestic beings, with an innate capacity for nurturance that required proper cultivation. The virtuous woman improved herself through work; but whereas her industrious mate labored in the marketplace, she was uniquely qualified for work in the home, which came to be seen as woman's proper place or "sphere." Thus under the influence of the gender system, the split between home and workplace that capitalism imposed took on the appearance of a natural division, adjusted to fundamental differences between the sexes. Woman's role in this scheme was to stabilize society from within by exerting a moral influence on household members. Her industrious service within her own sphere complemented her husband's productive labor and also distinguished her from the women of other social classes. Opposed to aristocratic vanity and to working-class lust, the ideal of female domesticity was part of the production of the middle classes.

More than a century later this ideal has lost its hegemonic status and is hotly contested from within the new middle classes. Although the traditional family retains zealous defenders, full-time domesticity is an option that few contemporary women can afford, and many of those who could afford it have rejected it on ideological grounds. Briefly interrupted in the 1950s and then accelerating once more, the long-term trend over the course of the twentieth century has been toward women's movement out of the home and into the workplace (Gerson 1985).

Some women have always worked in America, but in the past the majority were from the working class, and their productivity was determined by the household's needs. Women's work, moreover, was typically part-time or confined to particular stages of the life cycle and remained subordinate to women's domestic role (Tilly and Scott 1978). What has emerged since the abortive postwar revival of domesticity is a new work pattern in which growing numbers of women of all ages, single and married, with and without children, pursue or aspire to full-time careers. The potential consequences of this pattern for family life in general and child care in particular are enormous and they are only beginning to unfold. But in a society that has traditionally defined nurturance as a female responsibility, careers for women inevitably raise the question of who will do the caring.

For those opposed to the new trends, the growing fear is that no one will. Since men are indifferent nurturers in the traditional ideology, the specter of women leaving the home in ever-rising numbers arouses fears of abandonment that fuel antifeminist politics. Moreover, anxiety over nurturance also haunts proponents of careers for women and indexes the persistence of traditional beliefs about motherhood.[1] But there is another, more optimistic response to the perceived dilemma, one that presupposes a human capacity to change. In this emergent vision, women and men will cooperate as equals and learn to do the caring together.

Shared parenting remains an experiment that in most cases stops somewhere short of equality and is largely confined to a small circle within the professional middle class.[2] In the absence of public provisioning of child care, it is a course available only to those with flexible work schedules and/or the financial means to hire domestic help. As it is currently practiced, shared parenting is predicated on the availability of cheap, primarily female labor and represents a privatized, middle-class solution to the problem of expanding women's choices without reducing the care provided to dependents. Nor will shared parenting in itself bring an end to gender domination, as feminist advocates of the strategy concede. Asymmetry in parental roles, Lynne Segal (1990: 46–49) observes, is as much or more the product of extrafamilial forms of gender inequality as it is their cause, which means that reorganizing the family is at best a limited strategy for undermining male dominance.[3] Jessica Benjamin (1988: 123) also recognizes that traditional parenting is not the sole foundation of gender domination, but where Segal stresses the multiplicity of institutional practices that make up a gender regime, Benjamin calls attention to their common underlying structure. In her theory shared parenting can mute but not dissolve a deep-seated dualism that works at psychic and cultural levels to construct male and female as polar opposites. According to this argument, the critique of the traditional family is part of a wider attack on the polarity principle that feminizes nurturance and dependency while masculinizing authority and freedom.

For Benjamin and Segal alike, men's more active involvement in child raising is an important part of the ideological struggle against gender polarity and the practical struggle for equality between women and men. Those struggles, however, go on at many levels and in sites other than the family. To focus on Benjamin's point, the psychic efficacy of changes in parenting practices depends in part on the dominant cultural representations of gender, and these are not reducible to the actual forms of family life. Briefly lapsing into an uncharacteristic pessimism, Benjamin darkly observes: "At times it even seems that regardless of what real parents do, the cultural dualisms sustain the splitting of gender and recreate parental images as polar opposites" (1988: 217–218).

But the reproduction of cultural dualisms is also a social process, and the contested character of contemporary family practices is inscribed in culture produced in commodity form. Mass-cultural representations, the products of the culture industries, neither directly reflect nor totally control the ways that people represent and experience their daily lives. Rather, we need to see the culture industries as active participants in ongoing social struggles over representation, and my project in this chapter is to look at how the mainstream Hollywood cinema participated in the family and gender politics of the 1980s.

As in the preceding chapters, I approach mass-cultural forms as selective reworkings of popular desires and fears, but I want to begin with a relatively close examination of specific social concerns that the culture industries have attempted to rework. In other words, before moving to the texts themselves, I will investigate their social contexts of reception in some detail, distinguishing the diverse audiences for mass-produced fantasies about family life. Gender and family issues, I will argue, posed a special challenge for a movie industry motivated primarily by commercial profit. In an era characterized by mounting antifeminism and widespread nostalgia for traditional family forms, on the one hand, and by a continuing struggle for gender equality and ongoing experimentation in family practices, on the other, attracting the widest possible audience was no simple matter. With considerable ingenuity, in my view, the openly conflicting and ambivalent expectations of the mass audience were incorporated into movies about family life. One implicit strategy for commercial success was to appeal to widespread anxiety over women abandoning their traditional place in the home while offering a nontraditional form of fatherhood as the ideal solution.

Women and the American Dream

Women and men take positions on the traditional family in the process of navigating the conditions that have called it into question. Foremost among these are the following: the greatly expanded but still limited and unevenly distributed opportunities for women in the paid labor force (Tilly and Scott 1978; Gerson 1985); rising standards of consumption that pushed middle-class women back into the labor force in the mid-1950s and contribute to the ongoing proliferation of two-career families (Ehrenreich and English 1979; Hood 1983; Hertz 1986); the heightened instability of marriage, indexed by high divorce rates, a rise in the number of children born out of wedlock, and an overall increase in single-parent families since 1960 (Levitan and Belous 1981; Ehrenreich 1983; Weitzman 1985); the erosion of social supports for the traditional domestic ideal by suburbanization, corporate employment patterns, and the increasing privatization of family life (Wolfe 1989); and the availability of new reproductive technologies that potentially allow women a greater degree of choice over motherhood, both within marriage and outside of it (Luker 1984).

Such interrelated changes in women's work and family roles have helped bring into being a new social type whom Kathleen Gerson (1985) calls the "nondomestic woman." This latest version of the New Woman may be married or single, with or without children. She is defined by her refusal to be contented with an exclusively domestic function and by her pursuit of the culturally masculine goals of independence and career achievement. As an emergent ideal, she has sources in the feminist movement and in the middle-class ideology of success through individual initiative, which liberal feminism helped to extend to women.

One result of that extension is that contemporary women may not need an ideological commitment to feminist politics to launch them on a nontraditional path. Both Gerson and Rosanna Hertz have shown how the pushes of economic need and domestic isolation or instability combine with the pulls of expanding workplace opportunities to draw middle- and upper-middle-class women into corporate and professional careers, which Hertz describes as "an intersection of feminism and the American dream" (1986: 197).[4] In many cases, women who play out the dream of mobility and success become advocates of change in domestic organization, especially when they choose to combine career commitment with parenthood. Although not all analysts concur, these and other studies suggest that economically successful women in dual-career marriages are particularly disposed to demand a more equal sharing of household tasks and, most importantly, to insist that men become more involved in child care.[5] Domestic inequality persists, even in families committed to the new arrangements, and there are major economic as well as cultural and psychological obstacles to the equal sharing of housework and child care between men and women. Nevertheless, while the actual division of domestic labor in society remains asymmetric, closer cooperation between women and men in the home is emerging as an ideal for the professional middle class.

Meanwhile, nostalgia for traditional family life has grown stronger among women who have experienced blocked or downward mobility. As Gerson discovered in her research, when the limited opportunity structure of female-dominated occupations restricts income and mobility and erodes career aspirations, women are more likely to orient or reorient themselves toward domesticity. Trapped in low-level white-collar jobs, Gerson (1985: 99) argues, many women experience dependency on a male breadwinner as liberation from boring work. Such women become staunch defenders of traditional domesticity, seeking in marriage and motherhood satisfactions that work has failed to provide. Given their past experiences in the workplace and their poor job prospects, these women have an interest in preserving a family system that offers them economic support and a meaningful role within the domestic sphere.[6]

Domesticity, however, has been devalued in the larger society, while nontraditional paths for women, although not without their difficulties, have acquired a certain prestige.[7] To select the traditional feminine path is to reject the new alternatives, and under these conditions, Gerson observes, domestic women "find themselves embattled, forced to justify a position once considered sacrosanct" (1985: 212). Conversely, non-domestic women have to defend their choices against the residual but still powerful ideology of full-time motherhood, whether by discounting the negative aspects of childlessness or by redefining what good mothering entails. The contradiction between work and motherhood generates a situation of "structural ambiguity" (Gerson 1985: 123) in which each group of women feels threatened by the other and is under pressure to repudiate the other's way of life as unnatural.

What varies, among other things, is the concept of nature deployed. Domestic women attack their counterparts in the essentialist terms of the ideology of separate spheres, invoking what Nancy Cott (1977: 195) calls its central distinction between feminine self-denial and masculine self-assertion. From this standpoint, both childless career women and full-time working mothers have denied their true nature by putting "masculine" self-interest before selfless devotion to dependents. As the dark pictures painted by Gerson's (1985: 188–189) informants suggest, such "unnatural" creatures are vulnerable to demonization. By contrast, nondomestic women are among the most recent heirs to the rationalist Enlightenment ideal of a common, self-realizing human nature. In this viewpoint, popularized by Betty Friedan (1963), the housebound woman's nature remains undeveloped, stunted, and stifled by her "unnatural" confinement to the domestic sphere. Gerson's nondomestic informants regularly reproduced this stereotype, perhaps, she suggests, projecting their own fears of domestic entrapment onto the figure of the bored and boring full-time mother.

At a deeper level, according to the model I will set out later on, such fears reflect the split between mother and father that is imposed in oedipal socialization. I agree with Gerson that women's choices are not determined by early childhood but are conditioned by the particular socioeconomic conditions in which they are made. I would add, however, that from a psychoanalytic perspective, her nontraditional informants who construct the mother as the enemy of freedom appear to be haunted nonetheless by early fantasies of the role that they have rejected.[8]

Whereas Gerson and Hertz interviewed women who reached adulthood in the 1970s, a recent study by Ruth Sidel (1990) deals with young women who were in their teens and early twenties during the Reagan era and whose choices lay ahead of them. Sidel (1990: 10, 52) encountered ambitious, career-oriented women in all social classes, but she also notes that many of these "New American Dreamers," as she calls them, were upper middle class.[9] Optimistic, adventurous, individualistic, these young women aspire to elite, "masculine" careers and affluent life styles, which they intend to achieve through hard work and determination. But what strikes Sidel most is their obsession with one particular strand of the American Dream, the importance of self-reliance. "Above all," she writes, "they believe that they must be prepared to go it alone" (1990: 29).

It is this acute sense of aloneness that intensifies the felt pressure to succeed and gives their version of the Dream a peculiarly anxious, distinctively 1980s quality. Wearing their extravagant ambitions like a mask over a deeper fear of dependency, Sidel's New American Dreamers seem to have received the dual message of the Reagan era, which promised abundance to the privileged and showed contempt for those in need. Ironically, while Reaganism aligned itself with conservative "family values," some young women appear to have taken its praise of rugged individualism as an invitation to renounce the father and rely only on themselves.[10]

The Family in Conservative Politics

The family is not only a concern in the daily lives of ordinary people. It is also central to the organizational strategy of the conservative political movement that emerged in the mid-1970s and went on to achieve a relatively broad populist appeal. Right-wing populism had its basis in resentment against the liberal reforms of the early 1970s, resentment which became concentrated among the lower middle- and blue-collar working classes. From these class positions such gains as were secured by women and minorities could all too easily appear to be at the expense of others and to pose a threat to social order. To capitalize on popular discontent, the New Right, as the movement is known, emphasized certain parts of its program over others. In place of the economic and national security issues foregrounded in an older style of American conservatism, "social issues" such as abortion, the Equal Rights Amendment (ERA), pornography, busing, and school prayer became critical instruments in the New Right's attempt to build a broad conservative coalition (Ehrenreich 1987: 162–163; Himmelstein 1983: 24–30). By emphasizing these issues, the New Right sought to tap nostalgia for the traditional family and resentment of independent women. These efforts did not go unrewarded. In great part, Rosalind Petchesky (1981: 203) argues, the ideological legitimation of the New Right derives from its aggressively antifeminist "pro-family" campaign.

If the family needs defending, it must be under attack, and the New Right identified the enemy as the "liberal" or "intellectual" elite. According to theories first propounded by neoconservative intellectuals in the 1970s, liberalism is the instrument of privileged and power-hungry professionals who compose what has become known on the right as the New Class. In fact, as Barbara Ehrenreich (1989: 152) points out, this is not a class but "a set of suspect occupations," an arbitrarily selected portion of the professional middle class designed to include assorted liberal "intellectuals" and to exclude the generally more conservative corporate employees. Nevertheless, New Right leaders hold this putative social group to blame for a massive moral breakdown in the wider society.

According to this view, the effective cause of the incipient crisis is "permissiveness." This corrosive condition of moral laxity is being rapidly injected into American society through assorted "liberal" policies and ideas, including abortion, affirmative action, antipoverty programs, prison furloughs, loose sexual standards, the secular curriculum in public schools, and the relativist attack on "basic values" in the universities. Eclectic as this notion of permissiveness may seem, it rests on a single metaphor drawn from family life.

New Class liberals, in this metaphor, are bad parents; they are spoiling properly subordinate social groups with their projects (notably women, young people, minorities, criminals, and the poor), just as they spoil their actual children and as they themselves were spoiled by their own permissive upbringings. What began as neoliberal backlash against student radicalism, Barbara Ehrenreich (1989: 168–173) argues, was turned into an attack on liberalism itself simply by reinflecting the family analogy. Where backlash theorists castigated student activists as spoiled children, the New Right also condemns the "parents" who do the spoiling through overindulgence and neglect. In this view, the moral laxness that threatens society as a whole is concentrated in the liberal family, where weak fathers fail to exercise authority and selfish mothers no longer find fulfillment in caring for others.

If the liberal family is the problem, then returning to the traditional family is the solution. Loyalty to families of the traditional type is the mark of Middle Americans, the New Right's version of the populist "producing classes." These sober and upright folk are the natural adversaries of the dissolute New Class, preservers of the traditional values of hard work and self-denial that are the moral counterforce to permissiveness. Their families appear as bastions of order, stability, and discipline in an increasingly decadent society.

What supposedly distinguishes conservative families from their liberal counterparts is a strong and strictly differentiated parental presence. Within the Middle American households of New Right imagination, nurturing women devote themselves to physical and emotional caretaking, while responsible male breadwinners personify autonomy and self-control. Whereas men participate in both the private and the public spheres, women's identity is ideally defined by their family role. Within their own domain, women may exercise considerable authority in ideal and practice, but ultimate authority over the family as a whole is exercised in theory by the paternal provider. In the idealized traditional family, as in the larger society, the Law belongs categorically to the Father.

Defenders of the traditional family ideal contrast its ever-present mothers and watchful fathers to the negligent parents of permissive households—the ambitious working mothers, determined to "have it all," and the irresponsible, absent fathers, caught up in their own affairs. Although both parents are held guilty of neglect, their sins are asymmetrically evaluated. According to the underlying logic of the ideology of the spheres, a man who puts self-interest before familial duty gives in to his masculine nature whereas a woman denies her femininity when she commits a similar offense, and her "unnatural" conduct warrants the strongest sanctions.

To put the distinction another way, motherhood is essential to women in a way that fatherhood is not to men. Maternal nurturance is defined as a natural female capacity, rooted in an innate disposition to self-denial and developed to different degrees by particular women. From this viewpoint, a woman may go against nature and pursue an independent life, but she achieves true fulfillment only in accepting the sacrifices of motherhood and devoting herself to others.[11]

In this contemporary version of the Victorian denial of women's subjectivity, desire and agency belong to men. As in the nineteenth-century model, men are represented as naturally aggressive and predatory, driven by strong sexual impulses that they laboriously subdue in assuming the role of family provider. A woman's nature is reflected in motherhood, but a man's is ideally transformed through paternal responsibility. In binding men to dependent women and children, family ties convert aggressive male sexuality into a productive economic competitiveness that benefits society as a whole. Thus the breadwinner role that came to validate middle-class masculinity in the nineteenth century is what separates the beasts from the bourgeoisie.[12]

According to another convention handed down from the Victorian era, women play a major role in the crucial process of "civilizing" men. Part of their traditional role as wives and mothers is to exert a regulatory, moral influence on their more active and impulsive charges. What they cannot do in this ideology is provide their husbands or sons with the constitutive qualities of masculinity: independence, assertiveness, ambition, and rationality. If women participate in making men, the ideology also implies that men must make themselves by consciously accepting responsibility and modeling it for other males.

What I am driving at is the importance of narrative in constructing gender identities and the problem of hasty equations of women with culture and men with nature.[13] In the rationalist narrative resolved by marriage, nature is not what men represent but what they conquer, inside themselves and outside in the world. Although this was the dominant gender-defining narrative in the nineteenth century, the same matrix of oppositions generated a romantic narrative that presents nature in a different light as the refuge to which men return in search of their true masculine selves. Predicated on male escape from female domesticity, romantic masculinity is the symmetric inverse of the masculinity validated by the provider role. Leslie Fiedler (1962) has analyzed literary versions of the romantic dream, and a similar fantasy underlies the ubiquitous barroom jokes about the ball and chain. In all such representations, the antagonism implicit in the gender opposition predominates over complementarity. From the masculine perspective, women appear to exercise a power that robs men of their essential selves, and real men are those who refuse to submit.

During the last few decades, Jesse Bernard (1984) has observed, resentment of the provider role began to be more openly expressed among middle-class men, some of whom went on to repudiate their traditional responsibilities.[14] Barbara Ehrenreich (1983) links what she calls the "male flight from commitment" to an upscale version of romantic masculinity constructed by the consumer culture. Thus at the same time that women were demonstrating their own abilities to provide, the consumer culture began to address new and seductive appeals to men, encouraging them to consume in less responsible, more self-fulfilling ways.

To conservatives, any such neoromantic male flight from commitment signifies a dangerous regression, and certain commentators on the right, men as well as women, have constructed a singularly gloomy vision of male psychology. Fixing on the image of male desire in its unbound state, conservative male-bashers like Phyllis Schlafly (1978) and George Gilder (1975) discern within even the most reliable of providers a predatory beast who could break out at any moment. All it takes is sufficient temptation, and this, say the critics, is provided by sexually and economically independent women. These seductive usurpers of the breadwinner role offer what every man secretly desires: pleasure without responsibility.

Reasoning in the logic of the traditional gender system, New Right critics of permissiveness arrive at the antifeminist conclusion that what threatens social order is not men's lust but women's independence. A similar displacement of anxiety occurs among the primarily female members of the mainstream, grass-roots antiabortion movement, the so-called "right-to-life" coalition, which, as Faye Ginsburg (1989: 46–48) emphasizes, maintains a tense, uneasy relationship with the New Right (see also Petchesky 1981: 218–219). Antiabortion activists in local communities such as Fargo, North Dakota, understand their activity as an oppositional practice, a defense of "female" values against what they see as the threatening "male" forces of the market (Ginsburg 1989: 10–11, 215–216). However, what Ginsburg (1989: 17) calls their "embedded cultural critique" remains enclosed within the ideology of the spheres, merely reversing its terms to idealize the "female" values of nurturance while denigrating the pursuit of self-interest as "male."[15] As a consequence, the antiabortion activists' discontent over the devaluation of nurturance in society fails to engage the antiwelfare policies advocated by their New Right allies and is displaced, as Ginsburg observes, from men onto masculinized women. For the moral reform movement the most highly condensed and emotionally charged symbol of the negatively valued masculine sphere is the inverted female who puts sexual pleasure over reproduction and autonomous achievement over sacrificial motherhood, the ambitious career woman who selfishly aborts her "unborn child."[16]

In New Right discourse, emphasis on paternal discipline gives the "pro-family" campaign a sharper patriarchal thrust. Whereas the fetus in "right-to-life" iconography is a helpless dependent in need of maternal nurturance, in the New Right's inflection it requires paternal protection against bad mothers, notably poor minority women whom the Reagan government effectively deprived of access to abortion services. Conservative generosity toward innocent "unborn children" has its counterpart in the disciplinary attitude assumed toward the poor, whose negatively "childlike" traits are invoked to legitimize the attack on the welfare system (Ehrenreich 1987: 176–177).[17] What is more, drawing together the implications of the New Right's "purity crusade," Rosalind Petchesky (1981: 230–231) concludes that protecting the fetus is less fundamental than the concern to " 'protect' young women from sex," in other words, to reestablish male control over wives and children.[18] Thus, the circle closes. From one side of the gender polarity, it takes nurturant women to keep men from reverting to their natural, predatory selves, while from the other side, it takes strong paternal disciplinarians to keep unnaturally independent women from repudiating their proper role. The individualism preserved in the traditional family is reserved for males alone. The conservative defense of the family as matrix for the self-reliant, autonomous individual rests on what Jessica Benjamin calls the "hidden gender clause," namely, that women "create the framework for the autonomous individuality of men" (1988: 201). She continues: "Thus, while men can have a career and 'more,' subsidized by the care and labor of the wife-mother, women should realize that this offer is not open to them. Their role is to *produce* autonomous individuals (boys) who can balance their public and private lives, not to *be* such individuals."

According to Benjamin, the inequality that underlies complementary gender roles has its source in the process of oedipal socialization.

Oedipal Socialization and Gender Polarity

Benjamin's case against the traditional family derives from feminist object relations psychoanalysis and rests on a closely argued critique of the oedipal model of psychic development. Building on work by Nancy Chodorow, Dorothy Dinnerstein, and Carol Gilligan, among others, Benjamin isolates the institution of women's mothering as a key factor in gender development.

According to object relations theory, the early stages of infancy and childhood are critical to psychological development, which is understood in terms of the unfolding relationships between self and other. Under the existing gender relations that assign nurturance to women, the mother is the initial figure of identification for children of both sexes. But from the earliest period, Chodorow (1978: 91–110) argues, her relationships to boys and to girls tend to differ in systematic ways. Independence is more likely to be encouraged in boys, facilitating their identification with the more remote but active and exciting father who represents the outside world. By contrast, the greater difficulty mothers tend to have in separating from their daughters compounds the problem girls encounter in identifying with the early father. During the oedipal period, these tendencies contribute to the production of gender difference as the masculine and feminine complexes unfold to asymmetric resolutions. In what the oedipal model constructs as the ideal, girls sustain the maternal identification, whereas boys repudiate it and make a decisive shift to identification with the father.

For the dominant psychoanalytic theories of gender identity (including nonfeminist versions of object relations), successful development proceeds by this model and entails following the oedipal injunction to identify only with the same-sex parent. By contrast, from the critical perspective characteristic of feminist psychoanalytic approaches, the project is to unmask the hidden assumptions that make the oedipal routes to identity appear necessary. According to Benjamin, what is hidden is nothing other than gender polarity, the principle that constructs gender difference as a polar opposition between the engulfing mother of dependency and the liberating father of separation.

Benjamin's central contention is that the classic psychoanalytic viewpoint is distorted by gender polarity and can only see individuation as separation. In her alternative vision of psychic development, the ideal for children of both sexes would be a balance or creative tension between unity and separation, connection and autonomy, dependence and independence, mutual recognition and self-assertion, nurturance and freedom. Under the influence of the polarity principle, however, these contradictory impulses appear as antagonistic opposites, and oedipal socialization assigns gender to the split. The nurturing mother becomes the representative of dependency, while autonomy is represented by the father as freedom from her regime. The consequence of this split, Benjamin argues, is failure to recognize the mother as an independent subject. Reduced to an object, she is no longer authorized to validate individual strivings for independence, and this polarity of male subject and female object lays the basis for gender domination. Powerfully inscribed in the traditional asymmetric organization of parenting, gender polarity also permeates the culture as a whole and works pervasively to equate subjectivity with masculinity while denying it to women.

Women's constructed lack of subjectivity gives rise to what Benjamin calls the "oedipal riddle," the repudiation of femininity by which masculinity is constituted in the oedipal model. Against the necessity for repudiation in the classic viewpoint, feminists emphasize its defensive character, which Benjamin takes as symptomatic of psychic splitting. It is the construction of gender difference as polarity that retrospectively defines maternal nurturance and the feelings associated with it as what is not masculine. In the male Oedipus complex, early experiences of dependency, emotional attunement, and connection with the mother come to appear as dangerous regressions, threats to independence that must be overcome in order to achieve autonomous masculine selfhood. Under these psychic conditions, renunciation of femininity is insufficient. That would mean balancing acceptance of gender difference with recognition of likeness or, in other words, retaining the early maternal identification while also identifying with other males. In repudiation, difference triumphs over likeness, and the maternal identification is repressed. Thus masculinity is negatively constructed by rejecting the feminine as "the other."

Like Chodorow (1978: 181–182), Benjamin connects the oedipal repression of "feminine" qualities within the masculine self to the devaluation of women and femininity in society. With the maternal identification blocked, the source of nurturance is projected outside the self where it appears in symmetrically distorted forms as an idealized and desirable object to be dominated and kept available or as a demonic force to be either eluded or destroyed. Corresponding to the rationalist and romantic masculinities that I distinguished earlier, these representations reflect a common structural dilemma. As a consequence of gender polarity, to assert masculinity is to deny dependency on the feminine world of nurturance. Psychoanalysis becomes complicit with that denial when it takes the oedipal male as the model of the individual and defines individuation in "one-sided" terms. It avoids confronting the oedipal riddle, Benjamin (1988: 165–166) argues, "by defining differentiation not as a tension or balance, not in terms of mutual recognition, but solely as the achievement of separation: as long as the boy gets away from the mother, he has successfully become an individual."

If to become a subject is to separate from the mother, a child's ally in that great endeavor is the oedipal father. In the oedipal model the father is the progressive counterforce to maternal power, the embodiment of development and growth who intervenes to save the (male) child from "limitless narcissism" or merging with the mother.[19] Benjamin's objection to this scheme is twofold. First, she notes a tendency in psychoanalytic accounts to confuse symbolic representations with actual practice, since real mothers play an active role in encouraging children to develop. Second, and more fundamentally, while fantasies of paternal rescue from maternal danger are indeed pervasive, permeating both psychic and cultural representations, they should be viewed symptomatically as products of the polarity principle, not as reflections of how developmental processes either actually or ideally unfold.

It is the denial of female subjectivity that makes early dependence on the mother appear as loss of self and creates the apparent necessity for paternal intervention in the mother-child relationship. In oedipal socialization the counterpart to devaluation of the mother is idealization of the father as the principle of individuation, "the only possible liberator and way into the world" (Benjamin 1988: 140). According to Benjamin, this privileging of the father's role in development occurs in almost every version of the oedipal model. Whether emphasis is on the self's internalization of paternal authority, as in the Freudian theory of the superego, or on its progress toward independence and reality, as in the contemporary psychoanalytic theory of oedipal separation, the common assumption is that only the father can take us higher.

From a sociological perspective, the desirable styles of paternal intervention seem to vary along class lines. Among the old middle class and the blue-collar working class, parents tend to emphasize the importance of discipline, and the strong, authoritarian father persists as a cultural ideal (Kohn 1977; Baritz 1982: 216–218). This is the father whose waning is deplored by the New Right as the root cause of moral breakdown. In his absence, according to his defenders, there is no one to model the disciplinary virtues, so that desires go unmastered and individualism is undermined.

On closer examination, however, it is not individualism that is endangered but rather the particular version of manhood that the authoritarian father represents. Since the 1950s, changes in the organization of work and of family life have helped consolidate a new masculine ideal among the professional middle class. At work, the traditional self-reliant masculinity has been eroded by bureaucratization, which requires and rewards skill in pleasing others (see Chapters 3 and 4). At home, theories of child raising that became dominant in the 1950s reflect the larger culture of self-fulfillment and emphasize understanding and responsiveness to children's needs over the disciplining of their desires. No longer an authoritarian figure, the new father is expected to support his children and guide them toward their adult identities.

More recently the image of the supportive father has been reworked into the nurturant and caring father of the 1980s, the man who takes over qualities and duties traditionally assigned to women. Significantly the importance of fatherhood has been culturally reasserted as men's actual hold over women and children has declined and as antifeminism has pervaded political culture. The conjuncture, as Lynne Segal (1990: 57–59) observes, is not unproblematic for women. The new emphasis on fatherhood can be deployed against them in legal contexts to take away custody from single mothers or to assert the rights of men as fathers to control women's bodies. The culture industries have pursued a less authoritarian but similarly problematic strategy by representing the nurturing father as the protector of the child against bad mothers. Consistent with Benjamin's critique of the oedipal model, the deeper assumptions of gender polarity survive and remain embedded in the new paternal ideal.

Hollywood and the Return of the Father

The authoritarian backlash of the 1980s has left its mark on mainstream politics and culture, but it has not restored the image of the strong, disciplinary father to hegemonic status. As president, Ronald Reagan used the image cautiously, in selective contexts, and not without a trace of "postmodern" irony. Standing tall against the Communists (or other appropriately "savage" enemies), sternly slashing the welfare budget in order to educate the poor in self-reliance, Reagan cloaked himself in the hard, rugged, patriarchal masculinity celebrated by the New Right. But Reagan also wore the kinder, gentler face of the "'overconsumptionist' demiurge" (Pfeil 1985: 290). Those of the professional middle class who were assimilated to the new conservative bloc responded to the promise of abundance that the Reagan administration enacted in its ritual practices.

Hollywood negotiated the rightward turn circumspectly, paying particular attention to its implications for gender identities. Mass-mediated versions of masculinity and femininity incorporated a range of cultural trends and recomposed them into patterns that were aimed at particular audiences. Beneath the diversity, however, a broadly identifiable process was underway. During what Mark Crispin Miller (1990: 219) calls the "epoch of revision" in Hollywood, movies rehabilitated patriarchal authority along nontraditional lines.

Looking back over the most popular films of the 1980s, we find no revival of the rugged, authoritative masculinity still conjured up by such names as John Wayne or Gary Cooper.[20] No doubt in deference to the youth market, most action heroes in the first half of the decade were positioned as sons. There were rebellious sons, like John Rambo, Axel Foley, and other renegades, as well as more dutiful, submissive ones, like Luke Skywalker, Indiana Jones, and the Karate Kid, but they shared a disposition to acknowledge an authority of a certain type. Acceptable authority in the most successful 1980s movies wore a kindly, noncoercive, paternalistic face. It was vested in figures who were either identified as outsiders lacking structural power (Yoda, Mr. Miyagi in *The Karate Kid;* Colonel Trautman in *Rambo*) or who masked their coercive force behind a playful, impish, fun-loving manner.[21]

Comedy, with its generic movement toward festivity, is particularly suited to characters of this latter kind. During the 1980s, television sitcoms as well as movie comedies perfected the figure of the permissive, playful patriarch. A spirit of release, he incarnates the inflated promises of fulfillment of the high 1980s. He presides over the expulsion of assorted butt-figures who represent what the narratives construct as outmoded systems of disciplinary control. In opposition to repressive, tyrannical "bad dads," his main qualifications are his relaxed, indulgent manner and his childlike sense of fun. As the gracious corporate leaders in *The Secret of My Success,* the playful CEO of *Big,* the charismatic teacher of *Dead Poet's Society,* the affluent, easygoing dads of 1980s family sitcoms, the permissive patriarch holds out infinite possibilities for the future.

I have discussed this pattern in Chapters 3 and 4 (see also Miller 1986), but one point needs repetition, and that is the differential access of sons and daughters to the fantasy of unrestricted desire. In workplace comedies, ambitious women who cannot be domesticated by the romantic hero must be expelled from the festivities. This task falls to the permissive father and requires a residue of the old patriarchal power. Thus in *Working Girl* (1988), just before the CEO turns his kindly face on the docile heroine, he metes out harsh justice to her more assertive, upper-middle-class rival, and this is not an isolated case. The problem of female ambition also surfaces in movies that feature a subtype of the playful patriarch whom I call the domestic man.

Father Knows Best

Nancy Armstrong (1987) has connected the rise of the domestic woman to the making of the middle class. The counterpart of this figure, the domestic man, arose during the mid-twentieth-century crisis of masculinity among the new, or professional, middle class. The underlying conditions of this crisis are well known and have already been noted: the bureaucratization of work, which appeared as an attack on traditional, self-reliant masculinity, and the expansion of the consumer culture, which led to the pseudoempowerment of the managerial mother and made indulgence into a virtue for men and women alike.[22]

In *For Her Own Good*, a study focused on women, Barbara Ehrenreich and Deirdre English (1979: 235–265) also discuss the predicament of middle-class men at midcentury. Their sense of masculinity endangered at work, men were encouraged to renew it at home in newly distanced, suburban castles stocked with power tools and outdoor barbecues. At home, however, men would confront another problem, the American woman, who had long been mistress of the private sphere and who ruled ever more imperiously in popular imagination over the consumption-oriented household.

As told in *For Her Own Good*, the story of domestic man unfolds amid intensifying gender anxieties at work and rising levels of misogyny at home. In the late 1940s and 1950s, the (overwhelmingly male) "experts" who elaborated "scientific child raising" withdrew their earlier confidence in maternal instinct and became obsessed with the potential consequences of bad mothering. An extreme form of this anxiety had been popularized by Philip Wylie in his 1942 best-seller, *Generation of Vipers*. According to Wylie, the real threat to American manhood emanated not from the workplace but from the home, where domineering wives and overpossessive mothers drained the male of moral fiber. "Momism," as it became known, was a conservative fantasy, but anxiety over the domestic power of women took many forms and haunted the postwar cult of domesticity. Domesticated masculinity was presented as the liberal solution to an incipient crisis in the "father absent" middle-class family. During the 1950s parental advice columns and other mass-mediated forms of therapeutic culture called on Dad to reassert his masculine presence at home in the interest of the child.

What was envisioned was not a fundamental reorganization of parenting but a modest expansion of the paternal role. Thus men were to retain their breadwinner role while supplementing it with new, potentially rewarding domestic responsibilities. These, however, were strictly circumscribed. Division, not sharing, was the guiding principle in the distribution of household labor, with the result that men's increased participation did not undo the ideology of separate spheres. On the contrary, as Lynne Segal observes of the new domestic partnership, "the separate worlds of women and men are reconstituted inside the home itself" (1990: 6). Both in representation and in practice, studies suggest, 1950s husbands took little responsibility for day-to-day housework or child care, which continued to be defined as the constitutive work of women. Around the house, men were assigned irregular or special, readily masculinized tasks, such as skilled repair work, heavy jobs, or outdoor labor in the new patios and yards. As fathers, their participation was equally selective. Overwhelmingly, men opted for play and entertainment over routine physical child care, thus preserving and reinforcing the image of the father as the more exciting parent.[23]

According to the experts, Dad had two main functions to perform. In the more liberal and potentially liberatory trend, the experts connected good sex with good parenting. Using a logic not without sexist overtones, they reasoned that a sexually fulfilled wife would not overwhelm her son with excessive maternal devotion as the overpossessive mother was feared to do. Given this premise, a man's course was clear. In Ehrenreich and English's account: "It follows that it was the husband's duty *as a father* to keep his wife sexually satisfied" (1979: 243).

Dad's second and properly instrumental function was to inculcate children with their appropriate "gender" or "sex" roles. The new terms derived from social psychology and implied a diluted version of oedipal socialization. In the view of the experts, Dad could dispense with the authority that precipitates castration anxiety, repression, and individuation in the orthodox Freudian model, nor was he required to incarnate the disciplinary virtues of the conservative family ideal. He had only to project a properly masculine image, to provide a "role model" whom sons would want to imitate, and to be an attractive personality whom daughters would strive to please.[24]

Although the ideal father contributed to the socialization of both sexes in this Parsonian model, it was the boy's masculine identification that appeared as a special problem. A girl identified with a mother who was, or was expected to be, continuously available to her family, but a boy had to deny his earliest attachment, while simultaneously developing his identification with a relatively remote male breadwinner. But the experts had a simple solution to the problem of father absence. A father, they argued, compensated for the limited time that he could spend at home with his expert, rational handling of highly charged developmental issues. To encourage masculine role learning in his son, he simply needed to display his own masculinity in highly concentrated, condensed forms— for example, through the mechanism of the all-male ritual of sport. During the 1950s, Ehrenreich and English (1979: 247) observe, Little League games and father-son excursions to the ballpark became privileged sites for the enactment and transmission of masculine identity. These developments weakened the cultural polarity between female nurturance and male autonomy, but they did not dissolve it. Traditional patriarchal control was displaced onto the new ideal of the responsive professional father, skillfully guiding his children into their appropriate roles and in the process enjoying a sense of mastery that was at risk in the white-collar workplace. Domestic manhood, however, proved to be a highly unstable solution to the masculinity crisis. It required a definition of masculinity that was contested from the outset, needed periodic amplifications, and proved notoriously difficult to contain.

Hollywood played a major role in redefining masculinity, as Peter Biskind (1983) demonstrates in his skillful ideological decoding of 1950s cinema. Biskind distinguishes mainstream or "centrist" films of the period from "extremist" films on both the left and right, and he isolates an internal conflict between liberal (or "pluralist") and conservative versions of the dominant centrist consensus. Among the struggles this grid elicits is one between competing, cinematically conveyed ideals of manhood (1983: 250–333).

In the 1950s, Biskind observes, older stars like John Wayne, Gary Cooper, Gregory Peck, Humphrey Bogart, and James Stewart took their tough-guy roles from previous decades and replayed them as neurotics, psychotics, or at the least, troubled, worn-out men. Usually heightened by a contrast to a younger and different type of man, the message was clear. Rugged, hard-driving, "inner-directed" masculinity had become a thing of the past. It was embodied in an array of negative forms: the obsessive revenge character, the compulsively acquisitive businessman, the overauthoritarian leader, and of course, the tyrannical bad dad who stifles his children's individuality. In the liberal viewpoint that constructs these characters, an oppositional scheme marks their obsolescence. Taciturn and closed rather than affable and open, rigid rather than flexible, competitive rather than cooperative, tense rather than relaxed, cold rather than warm toward women, hard and insensitive rather than soft and responsive, oriented toward career rather than family, the characters offered negative models of what it meant to be a man in the corporate-suburban world.

The contrastive, positively valued qualities were embodied in a new masculine type. A more sensitive and caring man with a heightened capacity for tenderness, he was variously interpreted by a new generation of actors that included Montgomery Clift, Rock Hudson, Anthony Perkins, and James Dean. These new men were attuned to others and to their own emotional needs, or at least they were capable of achieving such attunement, with help from the right sort of woman. Heroes in liberal 1950s movies needed spunky, assertive wives, who were not afraid to remind them of their moral duties, as Elizabeth Taylor does for Rock Hudson in *Giant* or Jennifer Jones for Gregory Peck in *The Man in the Gray Flannel Suit,* both released in 1956.

According to Biskind (1983: 271), liberal movies feminize men and masculinize women, but I would prefer an alternative formulation. It is, I think, consistent with Biskind's wider analysis to view the androgynous drift as a possibility that the dominant cinema both reflected and struggled to contain by various means, only to have it surface elsewhere in the grid.[25] From this perspective, although the liberal construction of gender identities was chiasmic, the crossover was asymmetric and strengthened the masculine position at the expense of the feminine.

Such "masculinization" of women as took place in movies was strictly circumscribed. Independent career women retained the negative, threatening character they had assumed in 1940s film noir, and both liberal and conservative movies punished them for their transgressions. Indeed, Biskind (1983: 264–265) notes, any female resistance to domesticity was pathological in liberal movies and required the intervention of male therapeutic authorities.

An alternative solution was for women to ally themselves with therapeutic culture and become agents of social control. In liberal movies women who stayed or returned home were rewarded with power over the domestic sphere and incarnated the therapeutic values of the dominant culture. Their narrative role was to civilize men and instruct them in moral duty. Men being what they were in these plots (initially deficient in the pluralist virtues), the civilizing role took strenuous effort and called for a strong-willed, assertive heroine, whom Biskind (1983: 271) characterizes as masculinized and empowered.

Biskind (1983: 273–274) also notes that women's domestic power in many liberal movies was explicitly derived from male authority figures, and where he emphasizes the delegation of power, I would stress its historical expropriation. Since the construction of the domestic as a separate sphere in the nineteenth century, moral influence had appeared as a natural vocation of woman (Cott 1977: 63–100; Epstein 1981: 80–85). It was the twentieth century that made moral development into a science and entrusted it to male experts, whose authority rested on the denial of women's autonomous sources of knowledge (Ehrenreich and English 1979: 1–98). What women had once seemed to do by instinct, men had mastered through the use of reason; and with the triumph of the therapeutic in the high 1950s, women became increasingly dependent on male expertise. Embodied in countless books and magazines, the experts monitored a woman's every movement, weakening her sense of autonomy in her own sphere.

Although woman's place was still at home, home was no longer uniquely woman's place. At the level of representations, a one-way erosion of the ideology of separate spheres continued to bar women from the male sphere, while instructing them to make room for men within their own. Liberal movies about the family confirmed the new advice of the experts. They called on men to become more involved in parenting and celebrated domesticity as the route to reconstructed manhood.

The most dramatic appearance of the new domestic man was in what has been called the "corporate-suburban" version of the American Dream (Long 1985). Based on the convention of the home as refuge from the world, the pattern redefines success as a partial retreat from the workplace into the domestic sphere. The hero—a new, less-compulsive type of self-made man—asserts his individuality by limiting his drive for worldly achievement and discovering fulfillment in family life. *The Man in the Gray Flannel Suit*, a 1956 movie based on a best-seller by Sloan Wilson, enlisted no less a personage than Gregory Peck to enact the choice of family over career. Peck plays Tom Rath, a troubled World War II veteran who turns down a promotion and settles for a midlevel position that allows him to devote more time to his wife and kids. By making Rath transcend in the narrative the type of man that Peck himself used to play, the movie uses the star's image to persuade us that it takes a real man to live the domestic life.

This claim to manhood was not universally acknowledged, as Biskind (1983: 296–333) shows in detail.[26] Even within the centrist cinema, the softened, relaxed domestic man had competition. Conservative movies endorsed a hard, strong, authoritative figure who preserved the older disciplinary virtues. Actively residual rather than traditional, the patriarchal hero of 1950s movies was defined against the dominant liberal ideal. He became the adversary of permissiveness, which in conservative plots endangers society, the family, and in particular, men.[27]

Within the family, conservative movies reasserted traditional gender roles. They subordinated women and children to patriarchal authority and repudiated the domesticated man as effeminate. To the right of the center, extremist movies intensified these trends, celebrating hard, masculine antidomestic loners who dominated women with ease and showed scant interest in family life of any kind.

On the left, women were also subordinated but to a different type of man. Soft rather than hard, he was an exaggerated version of the liberal ideal, imbued with definite if limited oppositional meanings. Left-wing 1950s movies amplified the feminized qualities of the domestic man and assigned them to lower-class outsiders—assorted drifters and drop-outs—coded as natural men. These free spirits rejected mainstream sexual morality. Their liberatory energies were typically concentrated on uptight middle-class women who had repressed precisely what the men possessed—their sensual and nurturant feminine selves. Hence, the new twist in these plots, which Biskind (1983: 328–329) neatly identifies, is not that men must teach women to be women, for this they do in movies of all persuasions, but that men themselves already *are* what women need to become. To put this a little differently, the polarity between nurturance and autonomy is modified to the point that nurturant femininity becomes a sign of masculine autonomy.

During the 1960s and 1970s the mainstream cinema itself shifted both to the right and to the left, and the image of the domestic man, Biskind (1983: 336–348) concludes, shifted accordingly. Conservative backlash converted him into a psychotic, most memorably in Alfred Hitchcock's *Psycho,* released in 1960. But in the late 1960s and 1970s left-mainstream movies presented sensitive, feminized men as heroic countercultural opponents of the dominant order.[28]

Superdads of the 1980s

When the domestic man reemerged as a hero in 1980s movies, he was no longer an outsider but an insider, usually a successful professional with an upscale career. Moreover, measured against his 1950s antecedents, he had penetrated considerably deeper into the female sphere. What drives him to new extremes is the fictional threat of the independent woman, a type who reverses the corporate-suburban success pattern by choosing career over family, workplace achievement over the self-sacrificing nurturance of dependents. Such ambitious, rejecting mothers create the gap that men are asked to fill in 1980s movies.

Since *Kramer vs. Kramer* initiated it in 1979, a cycle of movies has celebrated the nurturing, caring father. As this cycle unfolded, it came under the influence of the fantasy of unrestricted desire, with the result that the sacrifices involved in male parenting were steadily reduced. In *Kramer vs. Kramer*, Dustin Hoffman permanently curtails his career ambitions, in effect becoming a working mother who is economically outdone by his ex-wife. By contrast, Michael Keaton merely puts his career on hold in *Mr. Mom* (1983) while his wife attempts, unsuccessfully, to advance her own, and he takes over as primary breadwinner in the resolution. Then came the 1987 blockbuster comedy *Three Men and a Baby*, the movie that showed us what fun mothering can be when it's done by the right men. In *Baby Boom*, also released in 1987, Diane Keaton has to sacrifice her executive position in order to care properly for her foundling, but in *Three Men* the baby of the title fits as easily into the upscale professional lives of the playboy heroes as she does into their penthouse playground overlooking Central Park. Men, in this film, no longer choose between family and career. All that they need renounce is their hedonistic singles lifestyle, which in the moralistic atmosphere of the late 1980s they willingly trade for the joys of parental responsibility. While marking the moral superiority of its altruistic and self-disciplining heroes, the film also resolves the economic contest with women in men's favor by making the baby's mother a poor, struggling actress rather than a masculinized businesswoman. This construction of the rejecting mother as potential dependent permits a festive reconciliation in which she is paternally welcomed into the ménage as an adjunct mom.[29]

What is repressed in this fantasy returns in distorted form in the menacing power attributed to more aggressively independent women. In such movies as *Fatal Attraction* (1987), *Working Girl* (1988), and *Cocktail* (1988), women with "masculine" sexual drives and career ambitions are eliminated or replaced by female rivals whose assertiveness, like that of the repentant mother in *Three Men and a Baby*, takes more containable, less-threatening forms. Embodied in rejecting mothers, psychotic seductresses, and overambitious career women, "excessive" female desire appears as a problem in Hollywood movies of the

1980s, a danger to the family and to society. By contrast, male desire was openly celebrated in the first half of the decade, and when Hollywood moviemakers subsequently took up the conservative attack on permissiveness, they continued to give differential treatment to men and women. Whereas uncontrolled feminine desire requires some form of masculine intervention in Hollywood's moral tales, overindulgent men reform themselves and learn to exercise self-restraint. Men may change, however, in opposite directions, becoming harder or softer according to the version of manhood constructed in the plot. Domestic men repudiate the repressive authority that the more traditional heroes of *Fatal Attraction, Cocktail,* and *Wall Street* reabsorb and devote themselves instead to releasing their untapped nurturing capacities.

Although not without basis in social reality, the image of the new fatherhood in the movies provides an instructive instance of how the culture industries selectively recognize social concerns. There is evidence that male participation in child care has indeed increased and that many men are finding as much or more personal satisfaction in family life as in career.[30] But what is represented in the movies as a noble masculine response to the abandonment of domestic responsibility by working women is in practice more often achieved through the efforts of working women to divide domestic responsibility on more equal lines. Although shared parenting does not go entirely unrepresented in the mass media, it has been subordinated to what Lynne Joyrich (1991: 181) calls the "purely fathered family" as a vision for family reform.

Drawing on Tania Modleski's analysis of *Three Men and a Baby,* Joyrich interprets the appropriation of women's nurturing role by men in mass-cultural fictions as a response to men's anxieties over their paternal position and the decline of patriarchy. I do not disagree with this interpretation of the general tendency, which in my terms is to annex female nurturance to the pole of male autonomy, thus reconfiguring gender polarity rather than dissolving it. Nevertheless, I believe that greater attention needs to be paid to particular versions of the nurturant father, on the one hand, and to the diverse audiences who receive them, on the other.

Three movies about family life released between August and October of 1989 all became commercial successes. Two of them, *Parenthood* and *Uncle Buck,* stayed among the top ten for more than a month, and their cumulative domestic grosses reached over $90 million and $60 million, respectively. The third, *Look Who's Talking,* was the sleeper hit of 1989, a blockbuster that grossed almost $140 million in its long domestic run.[31] All three movies deal with male domesticity and female independence, and judging by their popularity, they found receptive audiences for their contrasting treatments of these themes. In the interpretations that follow, I approach the domestic man and the independent woman as contested symbols, their meanings partially defined by the texts that construct them but also negotiated by the audiences who receive them.

Charivari in the Suburbs

Written and directed by John Hughes, *Uncle Buck* is essentially a vehicle for actor John Candy. Rather than the youth market that Hughes has cultivated, the movie was aimed at the Middle American tastes of Candy's primarily lower-middle-class and blue-collar audience. It was marketed as family entertainment, for adults and children alike.

The movie is set in the same elite Chicago suburbs that Hughes used in his 1986 blockbuster teen comedy, *Ferris Bueller's Day Off.* In both movies Hughes confronts us with the decline of parental authority, but it is inflected in different ways. What in *Ferris Bueller* provides an opportunity for youthful pleasure becomes a cause of adolescent angst in *Uncle Buck.* The establishing shots in the latter movie draw us into its conservative viewpoint. One by one, three sad-faced children come home to a silent, empty house. In what is apparently a two-career family, the dog is kept locked up in the dryer for lack of a caretaker, and Tia, the teenage daughter, alerts us to their other lack. When asked by her younger sister what men are needed for, Tia answers grimly: "We need men so they can grow up, get married, and turn into shadows."

Subsequent scenes swiftly fill out the picture of a typical New Class family, as it appears from the right. The mother, who has selfishly placed career over family, feeds them Chinese take-out and knows nothing about the kids' daily lives. Moreover, she is cold, stiff, and domineering, while the basically good-natured father is weak and ineffectual. Except for the emphasis on the mother's bitchiness, this is the same parental situation that Ferris Bueller exploited to his own advantage; Ferris's sister, however, was adversely influenced by parental neglect, and in *Uncle Buck* Hughes places the teenage girl at the center of his tale. Boys, these plots assure us, can handle freedom, but girls require both a nurturing female with whom they can identify and a male authority to set the limits that they really crave.[32]

Candy/Buck is clearly not a "shadow," but at first appearance he seems to be an odd choice for a patriarchal disciplinarian. Buck is quickly typed as an amiable wastrel, an avowed opponent of the work ethic who has successfully avoided adult responsibility in any form. He gambles for a living, and the abrupt summons to look after his brother's kids allows him to elude his girlfriend's attempts to stabilize him through marriage and a job in the tire company that she manages.

These character traits aside, there is the matter of his physical appearance and comportment. Candy/Buck is clearly intended to be an assault on the dominant tastes of the professional middle class, an assault that is literally embodied in his oversized, bulging carnivalesque physique. Contrasted to his stuffy, respectable relatives, Buck is transgressively low and open. He coughs noisily, rings the wrong doorbell in the middle of the night, chats with his tight-assed sister-in-law about his (lower) bodily functions, smashes china, and smokes cigars. His car (which also presided over the television show) is equally disrespectful of boundaries. As ungainly as its master, the car has all its orifices open. Its muffler is gone; it pollutes the environment with clouds of smoke from its exhaust; and when the car stops outside Tia's high school, it emits great explosive farts that bring the supercool teenage onlookers to the ground.

Buck's powers to make low the socially high are selectively deployed. Considering our hero's association with the carnivalesque, his visit might well usher in a festive period of licensed release. As an antistructural figure from the lower orders, he might exert an emancipatory influence, as Robin Williams does, for example, in *Dead Poet's Society*. In that movie, however, repressive, overcontrolling patriarchy is the problem, and the characters who need to be liberated are male, whereas Uncle Buck has come into an overpermissive household in which patriarchal controls need to be strengthened, not relaxed.

Yet the movie seems torn between its authoritarian project and the dominant emphasis on playful, nurturant paternalism. In Buck's and the movie's odd moments, he incarnates festive excess for the two younger children but always, as it seems, with a bad conscience. When the little girl wants him to sleep with her, he is visibly distressed; obliged to accede to her affectionate wish, he dozes fitfully at the edge of the bed, maintaining a fragile but unbroken boundary between them. For a birthday celebration he delights the children with his grotesquely oversized pancakes, a feast that brims over with fertility, and then he punches out a foulmouthed clown who arrives at the party drunk. He does defend the dreams of childhood against a sanctimonious school administrator, whom he attacks with the mocking, earthy spirit of the carnivalesque, but his tone is more resentful than playful ("I don't have a college degree," he mutters). And significantly, the authority that he subverts is not only petty (the office is that of assistant principal) but held by a woman to boot!

Displaced from authority per se onto authoritarian women, such mocking disrespect as Buck displays in the movie is complicit with the patriarchal order that he is asked to restore. According to a ritual logic of order and inversion that organizes the plot, when the world has been turned upside down, a particular category of carnival ritual is required to set it right. Known as the charivari (noisy procession), this was a popular form of social regulation that was traditionally directed against those who violated sexual norms, including cuckolds, adulterers, and "unruly" women (Stallybrass 1989: 49). In the movie, feasts, masks, and other festively transgressive rites of carnival are muted or avoided, and the charivari is the ritual model for Buck's action.

What the plot identifies as Buck's adversary is neither bourgeois respectability nor adult authority in any form but rather the sexual promiscuity of overprivileged, underregulated teenagers. Appearances notwithstanding, Buck is on the side of the tight, not the loose, and for Tia, his visit brings confinement rather than release. He describes himself as the children's "warden," and his overriding purpose, obsessively pursued throughout the movie, is to assure the continued chastity of his defiant teenage ward.

That turns out to be simpler than it at first appears. The movie affirms the neo-Victorian, right-wing construction of women as chaste by nature and men as predatory beasts. Consequently, it casts Buck as Tia's protector against her manipulative little creep of a boyfriend, whom the movie insists on naming "Bug." Buck defeats Bug by means of his superior phallic power. He first threatens him with an ax, and then in the climactic scene, he comes at him with a live power drill. Finally, when the kid continues to taunt him from a distance, Buck reaches for his golf clubs and starts bouncing balls off his enemy's skull in a display of what Mark Crispin Miller (1990: 218–219) calls the "promiscuous ridicule" that has become a prerogative of the star in 1980s movies.

Heavy-handed as the sadism may be, it is not entirely gratuitous. Having equated Buck and Bug as "naturally" irresponsible males, the movie must perform a rite of separation. Buck expels his own bad, adolescent self at the same time as he "protects" Tia against predatory male sexuality. Thus, he chooses his own future, which will be to submit to the disciplinary influences of work and marriage. In the process he imposes on Tia the discipline that she naturally desires, bringing her to renounce her "masculine" striving after sexual independence. Recalled to her true female self, Tia embraces her mother, who promises her that "it's going to be real different now." At these words, we can almost see Tia's shadowy father take on substance.

From Prison to Playground

Toward the end of *Uncle Buck,* a chastened Tia admits to Buck that he was right all along: "I don't want to talk about it," says the hero, not unkindly, "I just want to get you home." *Parenthood* is in sympathy with the latter sentiment, but its crew of earnest, upper-middle-class parents would overwhelmingly reject the first. Talk is essential to good parenting in the movie's liberal model. More a means of support than of control, talk ideally encourages self-direction in children and prepares them for the choices that they will be called on to make throughout their lives. Not coincidentally, however, all the choices that the movie approves of turn out to confirm a strict division of gender roles.

Unlike *Uncle Buck,* which most critics dismissed as slickly entertaining, *Parenthood* was critically acclaimed. It was directed by Ron Howard, one of Hollywood's most sensitive men, whose films tend to emphasize self-fulfillment over self-denial (his previous hit, *Cocoon,* was about old people who are rejuvenated and restored to their full sexual powers). *Parenthood* is a multicharacter movie with a relatively complex plot that uses crosscutting to construct a set of parallel stories about family life. It was superbly played by a fine ensemble cast of actors with upscale appeal, including Steve Martin, Mary Steenburgen, Dianne Wiest, Jason Robards, Rick Moranis, Tom Hulce, and Keanu Reeves.

Generically *Parenthood* is an admixture of 1940s maternal melodrama with the success-as-fulfillment story of the 1950s, in which the man chooses family over career advancement. *Parenthood*'s focus is on the problems that need solving at home, and the macro question posed in the movie is how to raise children or, in the terms used by Gil Buckman, how to make child raising into a playground rather than a prison.[33] It should come as no surprise that it takes a man to perform this feat.

Played by Steve Martin (who gets star billing), Gil is the movie's irresistibly playful domestic dad. He is the character who, confronted with the corporate-suburban choice, correctly sacrifices a partnership in his firm to devote himself to his emotionally troubled elder son. Although Gil performs his paternal role with impeccable sensitivity and consummate skill, parenting does not come naturally to him nor, for that matter, to any of the male characters. Fatherhood, in the movie's conception, is an acquired capacity. In Gil's case it requires strenuous effort and leaves him racked with anxieties that are amusingly dramatized in the movie.

Gil has an obsessional fear of replicating his own father's failure as a parent. Frank Buckman (Jason Robards) is one of several negative models of fatherhood presented in the movie. As the oldest male character (he is sixty-four), we might expect him to be an overauthoritarian patriarch, like the repressive father whose son commits suicide in *Dead Poet's Society,* or else a driven, inner-directed self-made businessman, like the boss whose model Tom Rath rejects in *The Man in the Gray Flannel Suit.* The movie, however, makes another selection. Although generated out of the same matrix of oppositions, Frank's overmasculinity is expressed in negligence rather than in excessive demands.

According to the movie, Frank is the old-fashioned, insensitive male, whose defensive fear of emotional contact has damaged his two sons in contrastive ways. Gil, the elder of the two, was a particularly needy child, much like his own son Kevin. Unfortunately for Gil, Frank was a product of the traditional family, which assigns emotional support to women and identifies maleness with the role of "good provider" (Bernard 1984). Consequently Frank lacked the emotional expressivity to respond to his son. Moreover, the movie implies, he experienced the boy's needs as a threat to his manhood from which he withdrew defensively, leaving Gil in want of what the movie would call a male role model.

Significantly the movie emphasizes Frank's leisure activities over his work life. He is supposed to have been a good provider who has made a comfortable living in plumbing supplies, and he may well have been a self-made man, for all that we know. Nevertheless, he derisively associates the disciplinary virtues of the traditional work ethic with his wife's family, accusing her and her mother of squirreling away their earnings, whereas he validates his masculinity in improvident hobbies such as gambling on sports and collecting antique cars.

Frank's younger son, Larry, has identified with the expansive side of his nature. Unlike Gil, who has hidden depths, Larry is a creature of surfaces and thus a more congenial companion for the father. Frank's mistake with Larry is overindulgence. He has spoiled the boy with dreams of rapid success without labor and has failed to instill in him any capacity for self-discipline. Larry's is a case of permanently arrested development. In his own eyes a high roller on the lookout for his big break, in the movie's therapeutic viewpoint Larry is an incurable Peter Pan, who will never accept adult responsibility in any form. All that we need to know about him is conveyed in his first scene, when we learn that his latest get-rich-quick scheme involves something called hydroponics, the science of growing plants without soil.

Only one character, Gil's brother-in-law Nathan, a believer in controlled environments, has any interest in this pseudoscience. Nathan, played by Rick Moranis, is an unemployed academic who cannot get grants and occupies himself in systematically managing the lives of his wife, Susan, and their daughter, Patti. He convinced Susan to pursue a career as a high school teacher, and he even supervises her diet, conscripting her into what he calls "power eating" (already a bad sign). But the education of little Patti is his overriding concern. Undoubtedly as compensation for his own failure, Nathan wants Patti to have a first-rate career, which, as he is earnestly explaining to the tiny girl at our first sight of them, requires that she give him "that extra effort." For his part, he is a tireless drillmaster, tutoring his pupil in everything from advanced mathematics to Oriental kick-boxing.

Patti adores her father, and Susan speaks gratefully if ambivalently about how Nathan took her life in hand, but the movie is never fooled for a moment. This professional Pygmalion is its symptomatic choice for the role of the overcontrolling, authoritarian patriarch, and it condemns him in no uncertain terms. The movie instructs us to contrast the playground that Gil has made for his children to the virtual prison in which Nathan confines the studious Patti. At Gil's home children frolic and cavort—behaving, in short, like children—whereas Patti has been subjected to an unnaturally demanding regime, which has crushed her childish spirit of play.

Perhaps, however, we need to be more precise. What Nathan violates is not childish nature but feminine nature, and what he stands accused of in the movie is encouraging masculine strivings in his wife and daughter. Consider his shameful treatment of Susan. Not only did he coerce her into a career, but—we learn midway through the movie—he has also forced her to control her procreative nature and practice family planning. Just how far rightward the movie has swung becomes apparent in a scene where Nathan lectures a sullenly defiant Susan for having punctured her diaphragm. It seems that while the couple used to take mutual pleasure in nonreproductive sex, Nathan's motives have become more austere. Sternly he reminds Susan of the importance of family planning if they are to avoid a drain on their resources that would adversely affect Patti.

Pro-choice activists might note that the movie's parody of their logic omits what most would call its central claim, which is that reproductive freedom is essential to women's achievement of full equality in the workplace. Implicit in that claim is the definition of motherhood as a choice rather than a natural role, and its omission from Nathan's speech is not accidental. The movie is attempting to execute a complex maneuver that will allow it to avoid the debate over motherhood while simultaneously resolving it in conservative terms. Its solution is to identify motherhood as the choice that women naturally make, the role that they inevitably choose unless, of course, they come under the influence of manipulative New Class men like Nathan.

Patti is caught in the same trap as her mother, only her will is too weak for resistance. Fixated on her father, she regards Susan as her rival, but her hostility is not a healthy, oedipal prelude to a stronger identification with the mother. For Nathan refuses to play his proper role in sex role socialization. He praises Patti only for intellectual achievements, never for girlish charm, encouraging her to strive to be like him rather than to possess him. It doesn't take Dr. Spock to see that he is systematically subverting her feminine development. An expert would simply pinpoint the problem, which is Nathan's prevention of the infantile wish to have a child that constitutes "normal" feminine identity. In defiance of the dominant model of gender-role formation adopted in the film, Nathan instructs Patti to accept no substitutes but to demand the phallus. No wonder the movie presents her as a neurotic mess.

A pattern in 1980s movie representations of father-daughter relationships is to punish fathers who encourage ambition in their daughters while requiring ambitious daughters to become more feminine in order to win attention from neglectful fathers.[34] *Parenthood* lets the overdemanding Nathan off with a relatively light sentence. When Susan finally rebels against him, he wins her back by acting silly, which tells her and us that Patti will also be liberated and get to be a normally silly little girl.

Meanwhile, over at Gil's, the movie's paradigmatic imp of fun is proceeding nicely with the oedipal socialization of his son Kevin. Both father and son have problems that the movie leaves unresolved, contributing to its widely praised reality effect. Nevertheless, the movie wants us to know that, despite Kevin's girlish hypersensitivity, his masculinity is secure. How could it not be? He not only has a dedicated dad who is both a pal and a good provider; he is also blessed with a truly feminine mother, a veritable angel of the house. Like Gerson's domestic women, Gil's wife, Karen (Mary Steenburgen), has embraced motherhood as her vocation and finds it more fulfilling than the unidentified job that she used to have. Moreover, the couple respect expert opinion and, good liberals that they are, submit dutifully to therapeutic authority. When school officials advise them of Kevin's problems, they promptly pack him off to a psychiatrist, and their efforts at home would win approval from the leading experts in progressive child raising.

How could Kevin not be okay? Gil steps firmly into the father's instrumental role in socialization. He escorts Kevin into the all-male world of Little League with its important lessons in cooperation, competition, and endurance, its opportunities for building self-confidence through effort and achievement. Always supportive and never demanding, Gil takes pains to let Kevin know that he will be loved no matter how he performs. Above all, Gil infuses the father-son relationship with excitement and pleasure. When a professional entertainer fails to appear at Kevin's birthday party, Gil performs in his place and is a smashing success, which boosts Kevin's standing with his peers.

The movie asks us to attend to Gil's sensitivity to Kevin's needs and to his irrepressible spirit of fun. What it never asks us to contemplate is the rigidly divided world to which Kevin needs adjustment. All his playmates are boys, and Gil himself adheres strictly to the neomasculine role. Not only is he the breadwinner, but he is never shown performing any conventionally feminine household tasks. *Parenthood* includes several scenes of women in the kitchen preparing, serving, or cleaning up after meals, but not one man so much as lifts a dish throughout the movie. Gil's sole encounter with the nitty-gritty of nurturance is when his daughter throws up on him, a mishap that leaves him in a state of helpless confusion. It is also his first and last one-on-one dealing with his daughter in the movie. Combined with Nathan's clearly abnormal attention to Patti, Gil's apparently normal neglect of his daughter implicitly suggests that girls do not require a way into the world.

Immersed in a world of clearly defined gender roles, Kevin is well on the way to internalizing its principles of division. He has learned to equate activity with the father who models it so engagingly and with the productive sphere outside the home where, he tells Gil, he would like them to work together when he grows up. No sooner has he identified with his father as breadwinner (thereby avoiding Larry's mistake) than he separates himself from the female sphere and cutely objectifies it by trying out on his mother his father's lessons in how to ogle girls.

How could Kevin not be okay? A crosscut contrasts his situation to that of his cousin Gary, "a kid who really has problems," according to Gil and the movie. Divorce has left adolescent Gary and his older sister Julie in the dreaded "father absent" situation. Their mother, Gil's other sister, Helen, is a successful executive at a bank, struggling to be breadwinner as well as caretaker. A first-rate performance by Dianne Wiest gives the character dignity as well as appeal, nor is the movie without sympathy for its only independent woman. The movie expects us to be critical of her negligent ex-husband, a remarried dentist who shirks his responsibilities to his first family. Nevertheless, the movie also understands that, however justifiable Helen's rage toward him may be, its uncontrolled, castrating energies can only impact her children adversely.

Helen's masculinized nature is heavily marked in the movie. She is the breadwinner, of course, and the movie more than hints at an unresolved case of penis envy. She keeps a vibrator in the bedroom for her sexual pleasure, wishes that her ex would drop his drill down his pants, and recalls how at Woodstock she once urinated in a field. Her underlying strategy in child raising is to eliminate any need for the father, an attempt that is clearly doomed from the start. By overprotecting Gary and urging him to repudiate his "lousy father," she has endangered his masculinity and forced him into a defensive withdrawal. With Julie she makes the same mistake as Nathan and encourages masculine strivings, although of a somewhat more moderate kind. Helen simply wants Julie to be independent, which means avoiding romantic entanglements and pursuing her academic career. Unfortunately the daughter has identified less with her mother's ambition than with her castrating anger toward men. She has fallen in love with and married a class inferior, an amiable lumpen type named Tod, whom she seems destined to dominate so long as their relationship lasts.

Tod, played by Keanu Reeves, is the movie's closest thing to a natural father, and the source of his ability is easy to locate. Poor, uneducated, and intellectually underendowed, he has one powerful advantage over Helen, which endears him equally to Julie and to Gary.[35] A scene in which Tod traces Gary's mysterious moodiness to adolescent masturbation rather pointedly informs us that what Tod has and Helen lacks is nothing other than a penis.

Before the movie is over, it has enlisted Gary's biology teacher to drive the lesson home and recall Helen to her true destiny. The final scene discovers Helen in a delivery room, giving birth to the biology teacher's baby, while outside in the waiting room every female character of reproductive age turns out to be either a recent or an expectant mother. What this means in narrative terms is that every woman has been brought closer to Karen's model, while every man who needed transformation has become a little more like Gil. A seemingly interminable montage of happy children, glowing parents, and female bodies framed as reproductive vessels resolves into the final image, the ideal couple locked in an embrace.

Yet the insistence on a single model is as symptomatically excessive as the reproductive frenzy, and what was intended to provide a sense of narrative closure threatens instead to undermine it. The logic of narrative and the law of patriarchy have been made to converge too closely, to the point where the one is as likely to weaken as to reinforce the other. The movie is in danger of sabotaging its own subject positions by provoking actual spectators, and female spectators in particular, into refusing its patriarchal constructions. Female spectators, as Christine Gledhill (1984) reminds us, bring to their viewing experiences extracinematic definitions of women that mediate what they view. *Parenthood,* I would argue, blunts its own ideological force by fixating on a nostalgic vision of family life while appealing to middle- and upper-middle-class audiences who hold less rigid views on gender and who are experimenting with diverse family strategies. Indeed, the movie's narrative structure undermines its own family ideal. It is never clear why Gil and Karen's kids are as messed up as they are if their parents are the ideal model the film wants them to be, the one couple who need no transformation but merely continue as they are. In trying to shore up a residual model of family and gender roles, the movie invites us to imagine another.

Something Besides a Breadwinner

An irony of the 1980s is that a movie that can be taken as affirming the personhood of the fetus envisions a family free from gender hierarchy. *Look Who's Talking* was written and directed by Amy Heckerling, one of the relatively few women directors currently working in the Hollywood cinema and one of even fewer with a box-office smash to her credit.[36] Heckerling demonstrated her skill at playing with generic formulas in her first movie, *Fast Times at Ridgemont High,* which as Robin Wood (1986: 215–221) observes, cleverly undercuts the conventional sexism of the high school coming-of-age cycle. *Look Who's Talking,* a romantic comedy about child raising, is equally skillful at subverting the genre to which it belongs.

The child alluded to in the movie's title is Mikey, the illegitimate son of a single working mother. Thanks to a voice supplied by Bruce Willis, Mikey is able to comment on and guide the narrative action, which revolves around his mother's quest to find him a good father. Willis's voice starts up even before the womb, rising over the chatter of a pack of happy sperm on their way to penetrate an unsuspecting, silent egg. From any feminist perspective, this is not an auspicious beginning, and how spectators handle the device of Mikey's prefetal and fetal voice is likely to influence their perceptions of the movie as a whole.

Neoformalist film analysis is helpful at this juncture for its close attention to the interaction between textual structures and viewing activities. According to David Bordwell (1985) and Kristin Thompson (1988), understanding a narrative film is an active process in which spectators draw on prior experience to respond to assorted cues given in a particular work. One type of cue is what neoformalists call "motivation." This refers to the procedures by which spectators are encouraged to justify the inclusion of any given textual element or device, how they are asked to account for its presence in the film. Devices can be motivated in different ways, and while a film suggests what type of motivation is relevant for a particular device, how spectators actually respond to these cues is mediated by what Thompson (1988: 21) calls "background norms," the prior experiences that form the larger context for any viewing.

To return to *Look Who's Talking*, it seems to me that when the sperm frolic to the Beach Boys' "I Get Around," while the egg is accompanied by a plaintive female love song, the soundtrack is rather pointedly instructing us *not* to assign a realistic motivation to the procreative imagery. A film like *The Silent Scream* asks the spectator to appeal to beliefs about the real world in justifying its humanized fetus, and the spectator implicitly understands that the purpose of the device is rhetorical persuasion. But the equivalent device in *Look Who's Talking* is more readily justified compositionally in terms of its relevance to the story and perhaps transtextually as a playful allusion to the solemnity of textbook accounts of reproduction. Spectators, however, do not necessarily notice the cues a film provides, as feminist critic Kathi Maio proves in denouncing what she calls "the most outrageous piece of 'Right-to-Life' propaganda you are likely to see on your neighborhood screen" (1991: 152). Given the saliency of the abortion debate in popular consciousness, other viewers may have shared this response and gone on to evaluate the movie according to their own positions on abortion. I suspect, however, that most viewers are more attuned to comic convention than Maio seems to be and are able to discriminate playful humor from propaganda.[37]

Even if the movie's representation of reproduction is not viewed as "pronatalist" propaganda, the assignment of subjectivity to the sperm alone warrants critical attention. In the article cited previously, Lynne Joyrich's (1991) hostility to *Look Who's Talking* is based on what she sees as its one-sided affirmation of the male role in reproduction and family life. Joyrich astutely identifies a transtextual association carried by the voice of Bruce Willis, who played a fetus in an episode of *Moonlighting* entitled "A Womb with a View," and her critique of this episode is convincing. Less convincing, to my mind, and weakly substantiated by her analysis is her assimilation of *Look Who's Talking* to the ideology of the purely fathered family. As the movie unfolds, I will argue, the device of the active, talking sperm, on which Joyrich founds her case, is reinterpreted ironically and made to contrast with the more egalitarian gender relations that are affirmed in the narrative.[38]

Molly, the mother-to-be, is played by Kirstie Alley, an actress associated with spunky female roles. In the movie she is a white-collar working girl, a CPA who has followed in the professional footsteps of her mother and father. Although she is having an affair with a married man (the source of the above-mentioned sperm), Molly is not the swinger she at first appears. On the contrary, she clings to what the movie regards as an outmoded attitude toward marriage and spends the better part of the narrative in pursuit of a traditional breadwinner male. What initially attracts her to her lover Albert (George Segal) is the image he projects of a "happy family man," notwithstanding that "it's somebody else's family" as her girlfriend observes. Even after Albert has two-timed her as well as his wife, Molly continues to see in him a mature, responsible man whose masculinity is defined by his ability to support a family.

Although Albert has been a good provider, his wife, Beth, is a neurotic upper-middle-class housewife, who suffers from the problem that once had no name. Bored, frustrated, and unhappy, she wastes her energies in managing her bulimia and driving her children nuts with New Age fads. Beth, whom we never actually meet, is constructed as Molly's opposite—frivolous, mystical, and literally regressive (she has her children's past lives read), where Molly is practical, rational, and progressive (she has a will drawn up on learning that she is pregnant). Beth is also overcultivated and overcontrolled. She keeps her weight down by jogging throughout her pregnancies and is religious about Lamaze, whereas the more relaxed and natural Molly eats voraciously, accepts her weight gain with equanimity, and (an ambiguous signifier, to which I return) drops her Lamaze class.

The film contrasts the elite dependent wife to the independent working girl much as eighteenth-century conduct books contrasted the idle aristocrat to the industrious mistress of the bourgeois home (Armstrong 1987: 69–75). In each case, the qualities of the desirable woman are redefined and used to attack the perceived excesses of the upper classes. *Working Girl* also pitted its title character against elite women, as we saw in Chapter 4, but in the process it fused feminine decadence with feminine ambition. *Look Who's Talking* studiously avoids this fusion by selecting only the idle wife, not the overambitious career woman, as its negative model of womanhood.

Eventually Molly realizes that she is as antagonistic to Albert as to Beth. Her first lesson (and she has to learn it twice) is that he is not the responsible breadwinner of her dreams. Albert belongs to that new type of man or that type of new man that has emerged in the 1980s, both as a mass-mediated ideal and in the way that some men choose to live. "These men," writes Barbara Ehrenreich, "have been, in a word, feminized, but without necessarily becoming feminist" (1990: 122). For such men, sensitivity is a critical marker of class status, equivalent to and expressed in upscale consumer tastes in clothes, food, furniture, sports—a disposition of what Pierre Bourdieu (1984) would call the habitus of the professional middle class.

Albert is a parody of this new masculinity. Although still a breadwinner when we meet him, he no longer identifies himself with the role but is more concerned about the class status asserted through his New Age office decor. When Molly tells him of her pregnancy, he is studiously enthusiastic and supportive of her choice to become a single mother. They go shopping for her maternity clothes, and he anticipates "little Armani diapers" for the baby. Soon enough, however, his hostility to commitment is revealed. Discovered by Molly with yet another other woman, Albert invokes the pop psychology that derived from the Human Potential movement and earnestly defends growth over maturity, mobility over stasis, healthy narcissism over perverse self-sacrifice.

Although Molly twice dumps Albert for his self-nurturing narcissism, she continues to hunt for what she thinks her child needs—a mature, responsible breadwinner, on the order of *Parenthood*'s Gil Buckman. But the audience, the movie, and Mikey all know better. Mikey's true father is the man who has participated in his life since his birth, the taxi driver who rushed his mother to the hospital, wound up in the delivery room, and stayed around to be the baby-sitter.

James, played by John Travolta in a comeback role, is an interesting type. He has more in common with the sensitive outsider heroes of left-wing 1950s movies than with more recent Hollywood working-class characters. A dominant tendency from the late 1970s through the 1980s has been to use the blue-collar working-class community as a metaphor for traditional masculinity, which is either celebrated or attacked, according to the ideological orientation of a given narrative.[39] The twist in *Look Who's Talking* is a neat one. The working-class world imagined in the movie is not an enclave for patriarchal discipline or cocky male comraderie but is coded instead as a woman's domain, a place where the nurturant ties of kinship and community are supreme.

By attacking a narcissistic, materialistic society from the perspective of culturally female values, the movie can potentially appeal to conservative viewers, especially to those outside the New Right, for whom nurturance, self-sacrifice, and devotion to dependents are oppositional ideals. As the narrative unfolds, however, defenders of the traditional family may find the positions constructed for them to be less than comfortable. Nurturance is celebrated in the movie and pitted against elite selfishness, but in place of the traditional division of family roles, the movie imagines a couple who share the caring. Both Molly and James are presented as competent, nurturant caretakers. She is slightly overprotective, but largely because she is inexperienced and consequently tends to overrely on medical authorities.[40] James is more relaxed about child care than Molly and less deferential to the expert advisers. Through Mikey the film supports James's position, which is to return to parents the control that was expropriated from them by the experts over what Ehrenreich and English (1979) call "the century of the child." James's advantage is attributed to his greater practical experience, having all but raised his sister's kids. The movie makes no attempt to charge the sister with negligence; it simply notes that she, like Molly, is a working mother who had to forge an alternative to full-time domesticity. James has also assumed another responsibility usually assigned to women, and a subplot has him arranging his grandfather's admission to a good nursing home.[41]

At first glance James's easy bonding with Mikey is reminiscent of Tod, the "natural" working-class father in *Parenthood,* whose abilities derived from his physical endowment. However, *Look Who's Talking* seems determined to put James's genital equipment in its proper place, which is to give sexual pleasure, and it playfully detaches the man and his activities from the organ. Thus, when Molly's mother, about to enter her daughter's apartment, hears Molly exclaim from within: "I never had such a big one inside me before!" she draws the obvious conclusions. We, however, know that James has just maternally removed a splinter from Molly's finger, which she got when she hit him with a broom in one of her many fits of temper.

When Molly belittles James, he and the movie gently rebuke her, but the movie is not preoccupied with proving his manhood to her or to us. It does have him aspire to a hypermasculine career as an airline pilot, and the idea that he is trying to accumulate airtime by moonlighting as a flight instructor links him to the traditional disciplinary virtues. That link, however, remains a weak one, for the movie stresses his skill as a small-time scam artist over any commitment to the old ethic of work and reward. Moreover, his career goals remain unachieved in the plot. His aviator identity is enacted only once, when he takes Molly up in a plane and teasingly invites her to "hold my stick," which she does with visible pleasure and mounting pride. Had the movie wanted to resolve the question of James's professional progress, he could easily have donned a uniform for the epilogue. That he remains instead in his ordinary attire suggests that Molly has kept hold of the stick, that is, within the terms of the gender polarity that the narrative is trying to undermine.

By the epilogue, of course, James and Molly are married, and she has learned that good providing is not the essence of good fathering. Indeed, the image of fatherhood presented in the movie stubbornly resists essentialist definitions. The movie breaks the chain of correspondences that align the male/female difference with other differences, with authority/nurturance, absence/presence, autonomy/dependence, separation/connectedness, public sphere/private sphere and all the other polarities that are institutionalized along the path to oedipal socialization.

Just how far the movie has gone toward collapsing the oedipal polarities becomes apparent in a confrontation between James and Albert over who is Mikey's father. Travolta/James manages, with some difficulty, to throw the slighter, weaker Segal/Albert out of Molly's apartment, but it is not machismo that wins the contest. By way of challenging Albert's claim to paternity, James assaults him with questions about the child's daily needs and wishes; his favorite breakfast cereal, stuffed animal, and rock star; or the number of diapers that he goes through in a day. When Albert can only stammer impatiently, James sums up his case by exclaiming: "Don't you think that a father should know some of these things!" Perhaps so, but only once fatherhood has been redefined in terms of the pure, nurturing presence and emotional connectedness conventionally assigned to the mother.[42]

Under James's influence the image of male individuality undergoes a striking transformation. At first it seems as if he is needed to provide a conventional male role model for Mikey by detaching him from his somewhat overprotective mother and instilling in him a properly masculine taste for mobility and adventure. But James's lessons to Mikey about planes and cars are not what the movie foregrounds. Their most memorable and intimate scene together comes midway through the movie, when James is baby-sitting while Molly is out on a particularly unpleasant date. At home the boys are having a great time. James turns up the stereo, forgets all about the "hot date" he had planned for later on, and works off his Saturday night fever with Mikey in a spectacular display of erotic masculinity that brings them mutual delight.

In Hollywood movies of the 1980s, masculinity as spectacle has been a problem, driven by the dynamics of homoerotic desire and homophobic repression. Steve Neale (1983: 6) has suggested that for the male body to appear as the object of the male gaze in films, any erotic component of the gaze must be repressed. What is repressed may then return in distorted form, for example, Neale argues, as the sadomasochism that has become a ubiquitous feature of action films.[43]

Look Who's Talking has devised a less repressive way to authorize the gaze between males by sublimating desire into paternal affection. Moreover, when we recall that the baby on whom Travolta looks with such devotion speaks in the voice of Bruce Willis, it is easy to take the scene as a symbolic enactment of homoerotic love. In the next scene James is repositioned and watches from the doorway as Molly dances for Mikey. But before she can be fixed as the object of the male gaze, he joins her, and they dance as a couple for the child, composing a libidinal triangle of unobstructed desire.

In romantic comedies, as Steve Neale and Frank Krutnik (1990: 139–140) explain, such scenes confirm to the audience the specialness of the couple as a couple, a quality that sanctions their eventual union. Progress toward that union is typically retarded by delays (see Thompson 1988: 36–38), in the form of various obstacles that function to keep the couple apart. The general problem to be resolved in romantic comedies is the couple's failure to recognize their compatibility, and the responsibility for this failure tends to be unequally distributed. If the courtship involves the transformation of those desires that have been constructed as obstacles to marital union, there is also a tendency in the genre to mark the woman's desires as the major obstruction. Hence, Neale and Krutnik observe, the woman and her desires are "the principal object of comic transformation."

Look Who's Talking is entirely conventional in its romantic resolution and in its identification of Molly's desires as the central narrative problem that needs to be resolved. What is important, however, is the specific content of Molly's conversion, the nature of the wish that she must learn to renounce. Whereas a characteristic wish of the "screwball" heroine is for wealth and luxury, Molly's desires are less self-seeking and have transgeneric associations. She is not a gold digger intent on marrying up but a self-sacrificing mother who, like the heroines of romantic melodramas, struggles with a conflict between her heterosexual love for James and her maternal duty to Mikey. In maternal melodramas romantic fulfillment is typically blocked, and the female protagonist sacrifices herself to her child. This is the course that Molly sets out to follow. Unlike the negligent and rejecting unwed mothers of other romantic comedies, from *Bachelor Mother* (1939) to *Three Men and a Baby,* Molly is prepared to sacrifice her sexual subjectivity to maternal duty, as she (mis)understands it, by marrying a man who will be a good provider for her child.

The wrongful marriage is a conventional device in romantic comedy, used to underscore the "rightness" of the main protagonists for each other (Neale and Krutnik 1990: 140–141). What is foregrounded in

Look Who's Talking is the loveless character of Molly's intended match, which violates the ideology of love affirmed in the genre as a whole. But the "true love" that the genre celebrates has also been predominantly associated with the woman's rejection of her economic independence (disguised, perhaps, as her renunciation of her gold-digger fantasy) and her acceptance of dependence on the "right" man. Indeed, according to Neale and Krutnik (1990: 154), the romantic comedies of the 1930s "tend to hinge upon the dangers to patriarchal order posed by the (potential) economic and social independence of women," and we have seen how contemporary genres, comic and dramatic, represent the independence achieved by female characters as a threat to be overcome.

From the perspective of the genre to which it belongs and the historical moment in which it appeared, *Look Who's Talking* seems to me exceptional for its validation of the independent woman. Molly's "mistake," in the movie's terms, is not only her attempted denial of her sexuality but also her adherence to what the movie presents as the outmoded breadwinner family and the oedipal model of socialization that has accompanied it. Thus, neither she nor Mikey need what she thinks they need. She does not need a man to support her economically, and the man whom we know to be right for her and Mikey is conspicuously lacking in the traditional signs of masculine authority that Molly falsely believes are essential to her son's development.

Molly's more conventional lesson in the connection between good sex and good parenting is also divested of its potentially oppressive implications. In the 1950s, as Ehrenreich and English (1979: 243–244) observe, the experts' acknowledgement of female sexuality all too easily lost its emancipatory potential and became an injunction on women to define themselves as sexual objects. By contrast, *Look Who's Talking* never suggests that Molly's sexuality exhausts her identity, and conversely, as we have seen, the movie allows the male as well as the female to be displayed for erotic contemplation. In this movie the ideal of self-sacrificing motherhood that *Parenthood* revives is firmly projected into the past. Not only can a woman be "something else besides a mother," to recall Stella Dallas's famous complaint, she is a better mother for being something else besides, not only a sexually fulfilled wife but also an active, independent working woman. If the heroine's "conversion" is a standard device of romantic comedy that has tended to entail her subordination to a man, what Molly is converted to in *Look Who's Talking* is a project of reconstructing gender difference in a more egalitarian way.

Although James and Molly unite against the narcissistic "permissiveness" of the film's upper middle class, they look toward the future and not toward the past. The critique of elite self-indulgence is made in the name of an expansive ideal of self-development and freedom that has little to do with the nostalgic conservative culture of self-denial. What speaks through James to Mikey, to Molly, and to us is the optimistic voice of what Warren Susman (1984: ix–xx) calls the "culture of abundance," a complex, multifaceted phenomenon that encompasses the culture of consumer goods, therapeutic culture, and the mass media of entertainment. If all of these have been powerful forces of repression, as Susman concedes, he nevertheless holds, as do I, that in their common promise that all things may be transformed, they also offer utopian possibilities.

Look Who's Talking puts definite limits on the transformation it envisions. By identifying its heroine as a white-collar worker in a midlevel position, the movie avoids rather than unmasks the imaginary threat of female ambition. Molly's independence is asserted in relation to James, but within the workplace she and her female co-workers are clearly subordinated to male authority, a situation that the movie seems to view as inevitable. Although the movie refrains from punishing an aggressive, upper-level career woman, which is refreshing, the implicit suggestion is that only moderate aspirations are acceptable in women. There is also the matter of Molly's resistance to Lamaze. Initially this device marks her superiority to the elite and faddish housewife, but Molly's resistance is revalued when James echoes Albert's support of Lamaze. Their interclass alliance is contracted against a woman's right to control her own body, in this case, to choose drugs over the experience of natural childbirth. When Molly continues to assert her independence in this register by compelling a reluctant doctor to give her a painkiller, a shot of the baby stoned inside the womb projects a negative image of female resistance to male authority.[44]

In other words, the figure of the independent woman is contested within the movie itself, as this figure has been throughout its production under patriarchy. Such contestation creates an opening for viewers with competing frames of reference to negotiate the movie in different ways, perceiving and evaluating it in terms of their socially constructed definitions of women (Gledhill 1988). Romantic comedy as a genre celebrates the heterosexual couple, and its revival, Neale and Krutnik argue (1990: 172), appeals to widespread anxiety over the instability and insecurity of contemporary marital relationships. This nostalgic generic appeal may command recognition from defenders of the traditional family, among others, while the strong affirmation of nurturant values in *Look Who's Talking* would enhance its capacity to give pleasure to domestic women. However, as I have argued, the movie deploys the established conventions of romantic comedy to validate a union of a nontraditional type. If Molly's delight in motherhood is able to endear her to women whose identities are invested in that role, she is represented in the narrative as a self-reliant New Woman who combines motherhood with a career. That representation seems more attuned to the aspirations of Ruth Sidel's (1990) New American Dreamers, young women determined to make it on their own, if need be, but also hoping to find a partner willing to share the caring.

Indeed, I would argue that all mass-cultural representations of the nurturing father include an element of recognition of longings felt by men as well as women for more democratic forms of family life. In most cases, however, the utopian wish is short-circuited by plots that construct the positively nurturing man as a replacement for the negatively independent woman. In fictions of this latter type, in which women are excluded from the imagined familial space, we should indeed be wary of what Joyrich calls "an aggressive male appropriation of the maternal realm" (1991: 182).

Look Who's Talking seems to me to deserve more credit than it has received from feminist critics for depicting genuinely shared parenting rather than single male mothering and for its playful subversion of its own generic antecedents. Interpretations vary, of course, but there may be something more at stake here than a disagreement over a cinematic text. Were the movie as unambiguously and insidiously patriarchal as Joyrich finds it or as blatantly "pronatalist" as Maio believes it to be, then its tremendous and quite unexpected popularity would be a disturbing index of widespread and unadulterated resistance to change on the part of women and men alike.

This seems to me to be a serious misreading of the current state of gender relations and one that is all too common among contemporary cultural feminists. Against the pessimism that overtook that strand of feminist thought in the late 1970s, I would stress the contradictory and conflictual character of any process of social change. Thus, while right-wing antifeminism indeed became a powerful social force during the 1980s, it represents the residual ideology of a declining minority. Despite the political gains that the "pro-family" movement has achieved, it remains a backlash movement, an attempt to repress newer, unequally distributed possibilities and to return to an idealized past. If studies from the early 1990s are to be believed, the majority of women and men in America do not anticipate any such return. In all social classes, albeit with unequal resources, women and men have been remaking family life—sometimes alone, sometimes together—without any single pattern becoming culturally dominant as yet. "Instead," Judith Stacey observes, "Americans today have crafted a multiplicity of family and household arrangements that we inhabit uneasily and reconstitute frequently in response to changing personal and occupational circumstances" (1990: 17).

This is not to say that there has been a feminist family revolution. The breadwinner family may be waning, but women continue to do the bulk of the caring, nor does such increase in male involvement in child care as has taken place automatically undermine men's power. On the contrary, "Change is itself contradictory," Lynne Segal notes concerning the new images and practices of fatherhood: "It may be seen as primarily a way of modernising certain types of contemporary masculinity, allowing men to experience some of the pleasures more traditionally connected to women's lives and 'feminine' pursuits, while nevertheless retaining privileges and power over women more generally, even if undesired" (1990: 290). But changing masculinities, as Segal repeatedly reminds us, also need to be seen as part of the interconnected struggles for less polarized gender identities and for more equal relations between women and men. These struggles will not be won simply because some men are now willing and able to share the caring more equally with women, yet they cannot be won until such willingness becomes second nature, and that cannot happen without massive changes outside the family as well as inside it. In the long run, the abolition of gender inequality presupposes a society in which the existing boundaries between the public and the private are broken down, and caring is defined as a collective as well as an individual responsibility.

The main problem with *Look Who's Talking,* in my view, is neither antifeminism nor neopatriarchal tendencies, but its unabashed romantic individualism. Like its generic antecedents and, indeed, like the vast majority of the products of the culture industries, the movie consistently privatizes social issues, representing the egalitarian couple as a sufficient solution to the problem of caring for dependents. Obscured in this individualistic viewpoint are the class restrictions on the new domestic ideal. The happiness that seems to flow solely from Molly's and James's "rightness" for each other is implicitly underwritten in the movie by flexible work schedules and paid child care—in short, by privileges of the professional middle class. That only a sweeping reorganization of the workplace, as well as the family, would make the ideal attainable by all is not a suggestion that the movie entertains.

Look Who's Talking may look no further than the family, but the transformation in parenting that it envisions has emancipatory potential. Against the increasingly shrill attacks on women's independence and the clamorous calls for the return of the father, the film imagines a family system free of gender domination. In a system where women and men alike can be nurturing as well as independent, we no longer need the father to free us from the mother, because she no longer appears as the antithesis of freedom and autonomy. Although there has been progress toward this goal, it remains today a utopian vision. "But at least we are in a position," writes Jessica Benjamin, "to begin thinking about reunifying aspects of life that have been split, preserved as antagonisms in the gender system" (1981: 220). For all its flaws, *Look Who's Talking* offers a vision of that reunification.

Conclusion

To discover patriarchal tendencies in the Hollywood cinema is hardly surprising, but what I have foregrounded in this chapter are the competing versions of and the resistance to patriarchy embodied in Hollywood movies during the 1980s. Patriarchy, it needs emphasis, is not a monolithic system. It is a set of practices of domination that vary along lines of class, race, and ethnicity; and while patriarchal fictions are centrally produced in the culture industries, they are received by diverse social audiences. Female-oriented movie genres such as those that I have examined in this chapter are not made by Men for Women, as much of psychoanalytic feminist film criticism implies. They are made by members of the professional middle class, who are overwhelmingly white and male, for primarily white audiences who are divided by class as well as gender. What needs appreciation, then, is how particular gender fantasies appeal to women and men who occupy particular social positions. It is not precisely a matter of combining a gender approach to film with a class approach, as Jackie Byars (1991: 259–260) suggests in a work for which I have considerable sympathy. Rather, in this chapter I have tried to show how certain class variations in responses to female independence have been treated in the movies.

The chapters in this volume have detected the fictional threat of female power in diverse movie genres. Hollywood movies in the 1980s have dwelt upon the dangers posed by the independence of women, and the restoration of a disrupted sexual order is a ubiquitous component of their narrative resolutions. What is restored, however, varies in socially significant ways. Thus, on the one hand, there have been movies such as *Fatal Attraction, Cocktail,* or *Uncle Buck,* which attack female independence in terms strongly reminiscent of conservative "pro-family" ideology. Personified by the economically and/or sexually independent woman, change is constructed in these movies as an essentially negative phenomenon, a deviation from proper order that must be definitively reversed. Such movies appeal primarily, I have suggested, to the anxieties of downwardly mobile middle- and lower-middle-class men and women and to members of the blue-collar working class who have also suffered disproportionately during the last decades. From these class positions the advances made by some middle- and upper-middle-class white women and minorities are all too visible and can become the focus of bitter resentment. If the New Right has sought to tap that resentment for political gain, Hollywood moviemakers tap it for commercial profit with fantasies that represent elite women as forces of chaos who must be controlled.

But the authoritarian fantasy of recovering a traditional familial order has not dominated the movies of the 1980s. The professional middle class is a critically important movie audience, as well as the class to which moviemakers themselves belong, and its sensibilities are overrepresented in mass-cultural fictions. Movies aimed at this audience are subtler in their antifeminism; typically, they endorse change in gender relations but seek to limit or confine it. Thus while it is increasingly permissible in the movies for women to be independent and men to be nurturant, the levels of independence acceptable in women and of nurturance acceptable in men are rather strictly circumscribed. Alternately, when men are represented as primary caregivers rather than as supportive fathers or sensitive lovers, their nurturing capacity is frequently converted into a new signifier of masculine self-sufficiency.

What these movies appeal to, I suggest, are the suppressed resentments and anxieties of men and women enmeshed in the real and imaginary difficulties of change, individuals who have consciously repudiated traditional gender roles and attitudes but still confront gender polarity at institutional and psychic levels. I do not mean to suggest that change in gender relations today is confined to the professional middle class. Nevertheless, a "progressive" social style is a badge of membership in this class, and its men and women are expected to move more freely between the traditionally separate spheres. In practice, however, the new intercourse remains fraught with ambivalence and uncertainty. If breadwinning and motherhood no longer validate masculinity and femininity respectively, men and women are under continual pressure to reinvent gender identities appropriate to their class situation.

Inasmuch as the movies provide imaginative resources for such reinventions, there is reason for concern. Hollywood in the 1980s has done more to retard than to advance the dissolution of gender polarity. Indeed, it is as if the movies have been engaged in reconstructing the cultural dualism out of less polarized images of masculinity and femininity. They have attacked the independent woman in diverse ways, even making her potential ally, the domestic man, into a weapon to be used against her. Although women are no longer exclusively defined in the movies as wives and mothers, the warning conveyed to female spectators in more or less explicit terms is that only moderate ambition is compatible with femininity. But if the dominant tendency in the movies has been to reconstruct gender difference along hierarchical lines, the struggle to imagine a world free of gender polarity continues and leaves its traces on the texts. The ideological forces that repress new possibilities will continue to be contested in the movies themselves and by the audiences who negotiate their meanings.

Notes

Introduction

1. On the entertainment status of mass market movies as one source of the reluctance to analyze their ideological messages, see Noël Carroll (1988: 158).

2. According to Peter Biskind (1990: 120), the explicit cultural program of the Lucas and Spielberg movies was to infantilize movie audiences, just as the heroes are compelled in the narratives to repudiate adulthood and return to childlike "innocence." Biskind argues further that an unintended effect of infantilization was the rise of a new patriarchy intratextually and a heightened receptiveness to patriarchal figures in political life. Thus strong but nonauthoritarian, avuncular figures, from Obi Wan and Yoda to Henry Jones, authorize in the movies the reversion of the heroes to childhood. The political implications of this program, which Biskind stresses were not conscious to the moviemakers, were realized in Ronald Reagan, "the ideal president for the Age of *Star Wars*." Like the acceptable authorities in the movies, Reagan's public style was "a blend of adult and child" (1990: 142).

3. On the interplay of dominant and subordinate narratives in films and the sociohistorical conditions of their asymmetry, see Dana Polan (1986).

4. As an instance of the putative power of "relevance" over "textual structure," Fiske (1991) cites the adoption of Rambo by Australian aboriginals as a popular hero. He goes on to explain that what these viewers saw as the major conflict in the movie was not between Western democracy and Communist totalitarianism but rather a conflict relevant to their own social situation between a hero coded as a racial subordinate and his bureaucratic white superiors. To me, this suggests that Fiske has a very weak notion of textual structure. It is hard to see how any serious textual analysis of *Rambo* could fail to observe that what structures the plot is not the Democratic Us/Communist Them opposition but the opposition between the passionate hero and the bureaucratic system. In short, this would seem to be a case where audiences from very different cultures perceived roughly the same narrative structure and related it to their particular social situations.

5. On the practical mastery of cultural systems that participants acquire through experience and cannot necessarily objectify, see Pierre Bourdieu (1977).

6. Elsewhere Carroll (1990) points out that many of the effects that Lacanian film theorists attribute to the "gaze," suggesting that they result from camera

positioning, are actually produced by practices of blocking, pacing, and staging relative to the camera.

7. Carroll's critique of the Althusserian-Lacanian model is considerably more elaborate and is set out in detail in *Mystifying Movies*. The points noted relate specifically to his refutation of the claim that classic realist film (a category that, he contends, is incoherently defined) is inherently ideological. For a critical assessment of the appropriation of Benveniste's linguistic categories by film theorists, see David Bordwell (1985: 21–26). On the baring of the device as a case of artistic motivation, see Kristin Thompson (1988).

8. Other studies in this sociohistorical mode, which looks for connections between representations of women in film and changes in women's social position, include Marjorie Rosen (1973), Brandon French (1978), and Andrea Walsh (1984).

9. As Noël Carroll (1990) observes, the turn itself is unargued. Mulvey does not consider whether there are rival theoretical frameworks that might offer competing accounts of visual pleasure. When Lacanian feminists do attempt to justify the relevance of psychoanalysis to cinema, they rely on an analogy between the experiences of film viewing and dreaming, the claim being that both are regressive activities that recreate the world of the imaginary (E. Ann Kaplan 1983). Of course, the analogy fails to address the substantial differences between dreaming, an individual activity involving a private code, and film viewing, a social activity that presupposes a public code. That cultural symbolism has properties of its own, irreducible to individual psychological processes, is a fundamental tenet of modern cultural anthropology, from Durkheim and Mauss to Levi-Strauss.

10. Mulvey is a feminist filmmaker, and her 1975 essay was motivated by her politico-aesthetic project. The problem, which feminists soon recognized, is that inasmuch as avant-garde works have so far proved unable to attract anything resembling a mass audience, their effectiveness as instruments of resistance is limited.

11. Chodorow (1978) herself also tends to emphasize the positive aspects of female socialization. Such emphasis is part of a general effort to redeem aspects of feminine experience denied by the dominant psychoanalytic theories of subject formation, which equate individuation with separation. There is, however, a temptation inherent in this strategy to succumb to what Jessica Benjamin calls a "reactive idealization of the feminine . . . a simple reversal that leaves the terms of the sexual polarity intact" (1988: 91). Benjamin also rejects the opposite position represented within feminist film theory by Mary Ann Doane (1982), who views the mother-daughter relationship as a negative phenomenon, the source of women's inability to differentiate themselves as individuals. Instead, Benjamin argues that a feminist theory of subject formation needs to transcend the polarity that makes maternal connectedness and paternal separation appear as opposites.

In Williams's case, I wonder if inattention to the distinction between identification and object love does not contribute to a tendency to idealize female socialization. Thus at points she seems to suggest that the girl adds an identification with the father to her early maternal identification: "We might recall . . . Nancy Chodorow's theory that female identity is formed through a process of double identification. The girl identifies with her primary love object—her mother—and then, without ever dropping the first identification, with her father" (1978: 316). But a major point in the feminist critique of oedipal socialization is that while the girl is supposed to take the oedipal father as a love object, she is not encouraged to establish an identification with him, that is, to model her identity on the masculine representative of the outside world.

12. For a summary of the Kaplan/Williams interchange that unfolded in *Cinema Journal* between 1984 and 1986, see Jackie Byars (1991: 166–171).

13. That sociologically oriented criticism cannot comprehend "how meaning is produced in film" is implied in E. Ann Kaplan's (1983: 15) distinction between semiology and sociology, which would surely have startled Swiss linguist Ferdinand de Saussure. Kaplan accuses sociologists of "linking screen image and lived experience too simplistically" (1983: 20). While this accusation is not entirely unfounded, reflectionism is not inherent in a sociological orientation, as Kaplan would have it. Her own analyses, moreover, effectively bypass the social, to connect images directly with their putative psychosexual sources. When she does allude to historically located, socially conditioned anxieties, in an analysis of cinematic representations of motherhood (1989), for instance, her analysis slants sharply away from the socially particular to the psychically universal, the unconscious anxieties that are supposedly aroused and given expression in the films.

14. See, for example, *The Female Gaze* (1989), a recent collection of essays on female spectatorship edited by Lorraine Gamman and Margaret Marshment. Although not all contributors concur, the editors apparently believe that psychoanalytic theory (by which they seem to intend the Lacanian version) and cultural analysis are inherently antithetical and that any attempt to apply the first to the second results inevitably in reductionism (1989: 5–7). In *Breaking the Glass Armor* (1988), film critic Kristin Thompson also rejects the possibility of synthesizing neoformalist poetics with psychoanalytic interpretation. Thompson's position, as I understand it, relies on a cognitive psychological model that in effect denies the existence of a dynamic (repressed, libidinal) unconscious. Film viewing, according to this model, is a goal-oriented process, composed of nonconscious, preconscious, and conscious activities, untroubled by any disturbed or disturbing libidinal forces. From a psychoanalytic perspective, however, any conscious process, including film viewing, also has unconscious dimensions.

15. Williams (1988) draws explicitly on a model of history and textuality formulated by Frederic Jameson in *The Political Unconscious,* which partly accounts for the resemblance to cultural studies. She takes the concept of textual "management" from Jameson's essay "Reification and Utopia in Mass Culture," which, as previously noted, marked a critical moment in the mass culture debate. I should point out that Williams herself does not contrast the *Mildred Pierce*

analysis to her earlier analysis of *Stella Dallas* but rather presents both as dedicated to "the most important task of feminist film criticism [which] now seems to be that of locating the variety of different subject positions constructed by the text of the woman's film" (1988: 28). Nevertheless, if there is not a break, there appears to be a shift in inflection, a heightened interest in the actual social contexts in which "historical viewers" take up textually constructed positions.

16. "Symbolic power," as Lynne Segal reminds us in a comparable critique of Lacanian feminism, "does not operate in splendid isolation from other social forces" (1990: 91). On the tendency of psychoanalytic film criticism to focus on sexual difference to the exclusion of racial and class differences, see also Jane Gaines, "White Privilege and Looking Relations," originally published in 1986.

17. Byars overlooks the parallel distinctions between competing masculinities that are also signified by class differences. For example, in her discussion of *Giant* (1956), she suggests that the hero's nonmacho son, who wants to be a doctor rather than a cattle rancher like his father, expresses what she calls "pre-emergent ideologies" (1991: 228). According to Peter Biskind (1983), however, the contrast between the overly masculine, authoritarian father and his more sensitive, nurturant, professional son in *Giant* is one instance of a struggle to define the dominant masculine style. In liberal films such as *Giant,* old-fashioned, rugged masculinity is represented as an outmoded style, destined to pass away.

18. On American success mythology, see, among others, C. Wright Mills (1953), John Cawelti (1965), Richard Weiss (1969), Daniel Rodgers (1978), Alan Trachtenberg (1982), Loren Baritz (1982), Elizabeth Long (1985), and Ruth Sidel (1990).

19. Just how seriously these latter usages were intended is a matter of debate. Reagan often gave a postmodern accent to his denunciations of foreign "savagery," as if to alert his audience to attend to the manly style of his discourse rather than to its content.

20. The idea of structural scheme employed here derives from Marshall Sahlins (1985), who emphasizes what he calls the "internal diachrony" or narrative dimensions of cultural structures. Sahlins's point is that cultural categories are not conceived of by their users as static correspondences but as a set of unfolding relations or generative schemes that may be objectified in mythological narratives. Analytical models, he argues, ought to be guided by these usages and view cultural categories "from the standpoint of a diachronic structure" (xvi).

21. On the "new class" in New Right rhetoric, see Barbara Ehrenreich (1989). I discuss this rhetoric at some length in the final chapter in this volume.

22. Slotkin (1986: 139–140) describes an alternative use of gender categories in the early industrial period to distinguish "the active (male) white citizen of the Frontier Myth and the passive (female) nonwhite laborer of the Metropolis." With intensifying proletarianization, Slotkin argues, this classification was challenged from within by white urban workingmen as well as by blacks and women. Since their "rediscovery" by the mass media in the late 1960s, the

white working class have been stereotypically associated with the "traditional" masculinity that is celebrated in conservative discourse.

23. See also George Mosse, *Nationalism and Sexuality* (1985).

24. On the importance of image manipulation in bureaucratic organizations, see C. Wright Mills (1953), Joseph Bensman and Arthur Vidich (1971), and Robert Jackall (1988).

25. On how structural changes in the industry may have affected the movies, see Miller's introduction to his collection *Seeing Through Movies*. For an insider's account of movie production under the new corporate system, see *Final Cut* by Steven Bach.

26. Movies from the 1970s that attacked bureaucratic power from a liberal viewpoint include *The Candidate* (1972), *The Parallax View* (1974), *Three Days of the Condor* (1975), and *Coma* (1978).

27. See Michael Moffatt (1990).

Chapter 2

1. This article was first conceived of in the course of discussions with my Wesleyan colleagues Noël Carroll, David Konstan, and Khachig Tölölyan and with Carl Freedman, Neil Lazarus, and Moishe Postone. An earlier draft was delivered at the Wesleyan Center for the Humanities, and I have incorporated many of the suggestions made at that time into the present version. I am particularly grateful to Richard Slotkin for his extensive comments, and to Tony Pippolo for his sound editorial advice.

2. That claim was later amended in terms that a speech act theorist would appreciate. Thus we learned that while the Syrians may have *thought* there was a deal, they were under a misunderstanding.

3. Greenwald's argument is contained in an unpublished paper delivered at the Wesleyan Center for the Humanities in May 1985.

4. In approaching genre development as the product of a conflict, an unconscious effort on the part of a text to contain ideological contradictions, I am adapting a model set forth by Pierre Macherey (1978), among others.

5. I have borrowed the concept of "recognition scene" from Noël Carroll (personal communication).

6. See Slotkin (1986: 33–47).

7. Richard Slotkin (personal communication) helped me to appreciate the significance of Rambo's implicit horror film ancestry. The point is developed further in reference to *Rambo: First Blood, Part Two*.

8. According to Carl Freedman (personal communication), the nationalism of the Reagan era, which encouraged "feeling good" about America, was compatible with but not constituted by anticommunism.

9. See Slotkin (1973: 440–445).

10. For contrast, consider *Indiana Jones and the Temple of Doom,* in which a fantasy of dangerous femininity is overtly projected onto the cultural alien.

11. This line of argument was developed in the context of discussions with Moishe Postone and through a close reading of his article, "Anti-Semitism and National Socialism" (1980).

12. As if implicitly aware of speech act theory, the films present deeds as like words inasmuch as they convey meaning, while words, when invested with institutional authority, are shown to have the force of deeds.

13. I do not mean to disregard the specificity of the generic antecedents of the films in question. Rather, I am suggesting that at this historical and cultural moment, it makes sense to treat the descendants of earlier platoon movies and swashbuckling romances as members of a new, emergent subgenre of Vietnam films. What links the MIA films is more than an historical referent. As this analysis seeks to demonstrate, the question of American POWs was incorporated into a discernible plot structure, the dynamics of which are the objective of the analysis.

14. See also the film's handling of the conventional character type of the Rookie. This particular Rookie is an overbureaucratic West Point type who keeps aloof from the playful activities of the proven professionals. His overbearing attitude precipitates a confrontation, which is only resolved when Jason discloses the young man's motives for participating in the mission. His own father is said to be an MIA, and while this detail does not contribute to the subsequent action, it effectively restates the thematic contrast between personal ties and abstract relationships. The moral value of the mission derives from the content of the rallying ideal. It is precisely because the men are motivated by personal loyalties, and not by commitment to an abstraction such as the nation, that their actions can redeem the country.

15. This effect is reinforced by the comparative realism of the representations of combat. While the premise of the film is fantastic (in the sense that there is no obvious historical referent for such a mission), the enactment of the desired event is constructed to generate the effect of the real. I would also note that the battle scenes are intensely suspenseful, in part owing to a convention of the platoon genre that some members of the team must die.

16. See Richard Slotkin (1981).

17. This model of the conditions for the effect of suspense derives from Noël Carroll, "Toward a Theory of Film Suspense" (1984).

18. Carl Freedman (personal communication) first drew the religious connotations of this line to my attention.

19. See Sigmund Freud, "On the Mechanism of Paranoia," in *General Psychological Theory* (1963).

20. See Mary L. Bellhouse and Laurence Litchfield, "Vietnam and Loss of Innocence: An Analysis of the Political Implications of the Popular Literature of the Vietnam War" (1982: 165–167).

21. As it turned out, of course, the next "just war" was in the Gulf, and the mobilization effort drew on many of the themes articulated in the action movies of the 1980s.

Chapter 3

1. A draft of this paper was presented at the Little Three Conference on "Work and Play," held at Wesleyan University's Center for the Humanities

(CFH), January 14–16, 1988. I am grateful to the conference organizers, especially Richard Vann and the CFH staff, and to the participants; in particular, I thank Jan Dizard for his thoughtful commentary.

2. Mark Crispin Miller (1986) also discusses the ideological implications of this general character type in an essay that has many points in common with this one, although I was well into the analysis when I read it. Foster Johnson, a student in my seminar on mass culture, first called the character type to my attention and speculated on the social sources of its popularity. In retrospect, I think his comments were a point of departure for this essay. I hope he will feel they have been put to good use.

3. I have in mind Paul Willis's (1981) ethnography of working-class youths. Willis's primary concern in this important study is with the creativity of working-class culture and, specifically, with everyday forms of resistance to dominant values. Yet the resemblances between the narrative he elicits from the lads' discourse on work bears such strong resemblances to the romantic adventurism of mass media fictions that the connection warrants analytical attention.

4. Since this essay was written, the myth of the self-made man played a central role in the legitimation of Judge Clarence Thomas's nomination to the Supreme Court.

5. The term "service class" is also used to refer to this class fraction (Lash and Urry 1987), as is "professional middle class."

6. The larger phenomenon of consumption culture has roots in therapeutic culture, which is now one of its several strands. On therapeutic culture, see Philip Rieff (1966) and T.J. Jackson Lears (1981, 1983).

7. Thanks to Michael Moffatt (1990) for pointing out that I had incorrectly referred to this character as a school principal.

8. The hero of *War Games,* also played by Matthew Broderick, performs a similar prank, only to suffer pangs of remorse. Ferris's casual rule-breaking indicates how far advanced he is along the path away from the older selfhood.

9. See, for example, *Back to the Future* (1985) and *Adventures in Baby-Sitting* (1987) for other instances of the motif. Retrospectively, I would accept Michael Moffatt's argument that the parade scene in *Ferris Bueller* also provides a glimpse of what Moffatt calls "communitas." What I would stress, however, is that, even in comparison to *The Secret of My Success,* the vision of interclass alliance that is projected in *Ferris Bueller* is highly distorted and, to use Fred Pfeil's (1985: 292) terms, "vaingloriously delusive."

10. Daniel Rodgers (1978: 140–142) also detects the split in children's literature within Alger's stories. Thus even the self-avowed defender of the Protestant Ethic included elements that undercut the old morality by making his heroes' success depend on luck as well as on industry. In a recurrent pattern, the Alger heroes perform impulsive acts of kindness or courage for strangers, who turn out to be rich and powerful and subsequently become their benefactors.

11. The term "remissive" derives from Rieff's concept of an ethic of release. It is used by John Carroll (1987) in a critique of the psychological type promoted

by the consumption ethic. The last sentence in the paragraph was added and reflects my increasing emphasis on the professional middle-class work orientation.

Chapter 4

1. C. Wright Mills's 1953 classic *White Collar* is a key text for my approach to bureaucratization. Subsequent studies that extend Mills's analysis of the culture of corporate bureaucracies include Joseph Bensman and Arthur Vidich (1971), Rosabeth Kanter (1977), and Robert Jackall (1988). On the psychological dimensions of corporate life see Michael Maccoby (1976), Christopher Lasch (1979), and Loren Baritz (1982).

2. The quasi-narcissistic type that Michael Maccoby (1976) identifies as the "corporate gamesman" would seem to represent an extreme form of a general tendency.

3. The best known statements of this position are David Riesman (1950) and William Whyte (1956).

4. I am grateful to Bruce Greenwald (personal communication) for calling my attention to the ways in which these films may miseducate their audiences.

5. From this perspective, the image evokes the history of attempts to adapt the ethic of success embedded in the Frontier Myth to new socioeconomic conditions. Abraham Lincoln, for example, sought to adjust the myth to reality through the theory of free labor. According to Lincoln, free labor was "the just and generous, and prosperous system, which opens the way for all—gives hope to all, and energy, and progress, and improvement of condition to all. If any continue through life in the condition of the hired laborer, it is not the fault of the system, but because of either a dependent nature which prefers it, or improvidence, folly, or singular misfortune" (cited in Slotkin 1986: 218). In corporate society, success may be signified by rising to a middle-management position rather than by becoming an employer, but the ideological necessity is still to represent the system as capable of rewarding industrious citizens.

6. Suggestions from Fred Pfeil and from Arjun Appadurai are incorporated into the conclusion to this section.

7. On the dialectical relationship between New Right ideology and the consumer culture, see Barbara Ehrenreich (1987). As the objective source of the "permissiveness" that the New Right condemns, the consumer culture is a major obstacle to the envisioned restoration of traditional values. But much of the appeal of New Right ideology, Ehrenreich suggests, derives from its ability to deflect the diffuse anxiety aroused by consumer dependency onto peripheral targets such as the "new class" proponents of the welfare state and its beneficiaries among the poor.

Chapter 5

1. Kathleen Gerson (1985: 138–157) argues that many nondomestic women who decide to remain childless share with domestic women the belief that child care is primarily a woman's responsibility. For these women, the possible costs

of motherhood appear unacceptably high. Reasoning in the terms of the traditional ideology of motherhood, they conclude that were they to take on the maternal role, their personal development would be limited and their children would also suffer.

2. On shared-parenting families and other experiments in family life in the Unites States, see Hood (1983), Hertz (1986), Ehrensaft (1987), and Stacey (1990). For an analysis of Australian experiments in shared parenting see Russell (1983). Commenting on shared and role-reversed parenting in Sweden and in the United States, Lynne Segal (1990: 312–319) emphasizes that fathers who assume major child care responsibilities are primarily from the professional middle class.

3. See also R. W. Connell (1987) whose theory of the multiple, interacting structures that underlie gender domination is drawn on by Segal. Both theorists are particularly concerned with establishing the links between the psychic and the social while preserving the autonomy of these spheres.

4. According to Judith Stacey (1990: 262–266), many working-class women in the United States today who explicitly reject feminist ideology have also implicitly incorporated feminist principles into their expectations and practices.

5. See Hood (1983) and Ehrensaft (1987). Stacey (1990) argues that while middle-class women may appear to be in the vanguard of family change, working-class women, African-American and white, have been quietly devising alternatives to full-time domesticity and are "the genuine postmodern family pioneers" (252). Although this may be so from the viewpoint of practice, the changes championed by middle-class women have a disproportionate ideological effect, in part because these are the changes recognized (which is also to say misrecognized) by the culture industries.

6. It is important to keep in mind the distinction between jobs and careers. Many of the domestic women in Gerson's study continued to work part-time, and most were generally positive about their work experience. Despite the acknowledged costs of full-time domesticity, however, none of these women expressed a desire for a full-time career that, as they saw it, would have meant adding work responsibilities to their roles as wives and mothers (1985: 130). In other words, as Rosanna Hertz (1986: 85–87) also argues, the woman with a job as opposed to a career does not ordinarily get the increased leverage in the household that enables her to insist on a more egalitarian division of household labor. Instead, she carries a "double burden," as in the pattern that Lillian Rubin (1976) found among working-class families. But Rubin's working-class women also took great satisfaction in their work outside the home, and in many cases the experience gave them an increased sense of independence, which some husbands apparently resented. Judith Stacey (1990) argues that working-class women do indeed translate the enhanced sense of autonomy they derive from work into a more equal sharing of household labor.

7. Hertz (1986), for example, notes that having a self-actualized career woman as a wife is status enhancing for many middle-class men.

8. Jessica Benjamin's version of the object relations model seems to me to anticipate Gerson's criticism of the psychoanalytic approach. Thus, Benjamin

does not assume that female mothering means that all women identify inevitably or unambiguously with the mother. Instead, what she stresses is that within the oedipal model, it is the father who represents the outside world, which means that the route to autonomy for girls is especially difficult, and even if taken, the father or some other culturally masculine figure serves as their guide. As Benjamin (1988: 134) notes, although the idea that girls need a "pathway to the wider world" is beginning to find acceptance, "man's occupation of this world remains a given; and few imagine that the mother may be capable of leading the way into it." Like Segal (1990) and Connell (1987), Benjamin seeks to account for the "intractibility" of gender polarity while also identifying changes in actual practices that may contribute to structural transformation but do not automatically produce it. For all three, the theoretical challenge is to link the psychic and the social in a nonreductive way, whereas Gerson seems to assume that any appeal to psychic causality is necessarily exclusive.

9. A closer inquiry into the class variations in the dream would doubtless be productive.

10. Sidel (1990) assumes that the identification figures or media role models for young women are the rich, successful career women depicted in popular television shows and movies. I suspect, however, that the young women she studied may also have been trying to identify with the male heroes who typically realize the unrestricted fantasy of success in 1980s fictions. Freedom is increasingly an option for women, but what changes more slowly is its association with the male principle.

11. Faye Ginsburg (1989: 217–218) ignores the distinction between capacities and qualities when she argues, unconvincingly, that since conservative women say that nurturance must be developed, they do not understand it as natural. Yet a woman who does not develop her nurturing capacities is perceived as masculine, which to my mind confirms the perceived "naturalness" of her maternal counterpart. The problem, I think, is that Ginsburg mistakenly equates the ideological concept of the "natural" with biological determinism. But in popular discourse, "nature" is a moral category with roots in the old metaphor of fertile ground, which is either improved through cultivation or allowed to run wild. On women's natural mothering capacity, see Cott (1977) and Smith-Rosenberg (1985).

12. On Victorian sexual ideology, see Cott (1977), Smith-Rosenberg (1985), and Stearns (1990).

13. On the narrative dimensions of dualistic schemes, see Sahlins (1985) and Traube (1989).

14. Stacey (1990: 267) also found a growing ambivalence about the breadwinner role among contemporary working-class men.

15. Since the late 1970s, one strand of contemporary feminism has pursued a similar strategy of reversal and now celebrates the supposedly natural superiority of women. For a beautifully articulated critique of cultural feminism and its fundamentally pessimistic outlook on gender, see Lynne Segal (1987). To my mind, Ginsburg's (1989) emphasis on the moral reform movement's resem-

blance to feminism is seriously in need of qualification. There is a resemblance between the oppositional stance of antiabortion activists and the cultural feminist reduction of patriarchy to masculine "nature," but both of these models are rejected by other feminists who see gender polarity as a culturally and psychically constructed problem, not as a solution.

16. On the appeal of this symbol, see also Conover and Gray (1983).

17. Although many members of the mainstream antiabortion movement may be personally unsympathetic to New Right antiwelfarism, they are at least potentially susceptible to this ideological construction that defines welfare as an instance of the more widely deplored "permissiveness."

18. Petchesky seems to view nurturant motherhood as an ideological fiction that was imposed on women by men in the nineteenth century and is now being revived, again in the interests of middle-class men. By contrast, from Ginsburg's ethnographic perspective, nurturant motherhood appears as an element of a genuine culture of resistance, an inherited resource for the construction of an oppositional identity. In part, these different emphases reflect the authors' focuses on the New Right and the "right-to-life" movement, respectively. To my mind, however, both positions are overdrawn and fail to account for the dialectical interactions between ideological forces and subjectively intended meanings. If Petchesky is relatively insensitive to the ways in which women can use the ideology of the spheres to contest male domination, Ginsburg consistently ignores or deemphasizes the ideological forces that limit and distort the "cultural critique" that she has identified.

19. See Christopher Lasch (1977, 1979) for a version of this defense of oedipality. Lasch has modified his position somewhat in *The Minimal Self* (1984), partly in response to feminist criticism. Nevertheless, he fails to understand the main point of that criticism, which is that the psychoanalytic categories he uses are not neutral but implicitly gendered and that he himself consistently privileges male-valued states and processes.

20. The decade's toughest heroes were not fully empowered, paternal lawmen but boyish vigilante cops, descendants of the renegade lawman popularized by Clint Eastwood in the 1970s. The 1980s renegades were a more domesticated breed. One widely repeated plot device identified by Miller paired the loose cannon with a "tighter," by-the-book partner, whose stabilizing influence is inscribed in the underlying narrative structure.

21. I am grateful to Bruce Greenwald for providing a lucid and precise formulation of this pattern at a faculty seminar.

22. On bureaucratization as a threat to middle-class identity, see C. Wright Mills (1953) and William Whyte (1956). David Riesman (1950) provided one of the first sociological analyses of a shift in middle-class cultural values, but he did not link the shift to bureaucratization, nor for that matter did he clearly mark its class specificity. Riesman's "other directed" man was introduced as a new type of American rather than a new middle-class personality.

23. On men's preference for the pleasurable aspects of child raising see Oakley (1974), Hunt (1980), Ehrensaft (1987), Hertz (1986), and Segal

(1990). As the recent dates suggest, this pattern persists and continues to characterize the relatively egalitarian families that are emerging.

24. In the Parsonian language that many experts adopted, the father's "instrumental" function in socialization was opposed to and valued over the "expressive" function performed by the mother. In this scheme, the father, thanks to his superior rationality, was expected to play the primary role in transmitting gender identities to children of both sexes.

25. See Dana Polan (1986) for a similar model of the tensions contained within any dominant narrative ideology.

26. Lynne Segal also describes the popular culture of the 1950s as characterized by "high levels of confusion and conflict over male identity" (1990: 22).

27. Succession narratives, such as *Executive Suite* (1954) or *Written on the Wind* (1957), mourned the passing of the patriarch and posed as their macro question the location of his true heir among a weaker, laxer generation. Alternately, the patriarch himself might be required to restore discipline within his overindulged family, as in *The Desperate Hours* (1955), which was remade only to flop at the box office this fall.

28. Examples from the 1970s include *Coming Home* and *Alice's Restaurant*.

29. Although shared parenting remains unrepresented in the movie, it is constructed as the final resolution, and the sequel, *Three Men and a Little Lady* (1990) provides an extended look at a highly unconventional, communal parenting arrangement. The sequel opened to generally favorable reviews, but it was nowhere near as popular as the original. Opening at Christmas, *Three Men and a Little Lady* was also in competition with *Home Alone,* the sleeper hit of 1990, in which a negligent mother manages to leave her youngest child behind when the family goes off on a vacation. Such differences in commercial success suggest to me that, when packaged properly for particular target audiences, antifeminist themes have considerable box-office appeal.

30. On men's involvement in child care, see Russell (1983), Ehrensaft (1987), Segal (1990), and Stacey (1990).

31. Television sitcoms based on all three films went on the air between fall 1990 and spring 1991. With the exception of *Uncle Buck,* which had a modest popularity despite negative reviews, none of these shows were on long enough to find an audience in their first year. A movie sequel to *Look Who's Talking* opened for the Christmas season in 1990 to poor reviews and moderate business.

32. By far the most successful Hughes fantasy of masculine self-reliance was the 1990 blockbuster, *Home Alone.* In this movie, which grossed over $200 million, the resourceful boy hero turns abandonment by his family into a learning experience. The popularity of this fantasy, I suggest, derives from its ability to arouse and allay widely shared anxieties over the effects of maternal absence. Thus, that the hero survives maternal absence may reassure working mothers who are obliged to leave their children; at the same time, the movie makes it very clear that the mother is the family member to blame for the boy's abandonment, and its relatively subtle critique of bad mothering would also appeal to domestic women as a confirmation of their own choices.

33. On "macro questions" and what he calls the "erotetic" movie narrative, see Noël Carroll (1988: 170–181).

34. For example, in *Say Anything* the father who wants his daughter to go to Oxford winds up in prison for embezzlement, whereas in *Dirty Dancing* the intelligent daughter who wants to join the Peace Corps wins her father's attention only when she gets up on stage and cavorts with a man who is her intellectual and class inferior.

35. Tod belongs to the same general type as the male leads in *Say Anything* and *Dirty Dancing* (see note 34), the sweet but none-too-bright youth whom the movies represent as an appropriate match for intelligent and ambitious young women.

36. Penny Marshall's *Big* (1988) was also a smash hit.

37. Many women with whom I discussed the movie reported the same experience that I had. That is, on the basis of the publicity for the movie, they went to see it reluctantly, expecting it to reinforce pronatalist politics, and were then surprised to find themselves in sympathy with the movie's overall treatment of its theme.

38. Given the weight Joyrich placed on the device of the talking sperm, I was interested to see what would happen in the sequel, *Look Who's Talking Too,* which was to introduce Mikey's sister. Sure enough, the sequel "corrects" the original and provides a voice (Alley's) for the egg as well as for the sperm (now Travolta) and then gives a new voice (Roseanne Barr's) to the fertilized egg. And yet, while the sequel thus avoids the "error" of overvaluing the male role in procreation, it goes on to mute or revoke most of what was emancipatory in the original. To my mind, this supports my argument that the gender politics of the original were not consistent with the assignment of subjectivity to the sperm.

39. In the *Rocky* cycle, *Cocktail,* and *Uncle Buck,* for example, the patriarchal values assigned to the working class are positively represented, whereas the protagonists in *Saturday Night Fever* and *Working Girl* are required to transcend old-fashioned patriarchy along with their blue-collar origins. In effect, in *Look Who's Talking* Travolta plays Tony Manero, his *Saturday Night Fever* character, after the latter acquired sensitivity. But James, unlike Tony, does not depend on an upwardly mobile woman to tutor him in elite manhood. His sensitive, caring, feminine nature is understood as a product of his working-class environment.

40. Molly is particularly defensive of Dr. Spock, whom she reveres as much for his antiwar protests as for his child care advice. Although James is bemused at her passion for "an emotionless Vulcan," he and the film refrain from attacking this particular hero, the very figure who bore the brunt of the conservative attack on "permissiveness" in the 1960s and 1970s.

41. That the grandfather cannot be cared for at home by his family could be construed as a sign of a crisis of nurturance. However, the film suggests no such crisis, and it represents the nursing home as an ideal place for the grandfather.

42. According to Joyrich (1991: 194–195), the movie "naturalizes" James's replacement of Mikey's biological father by having him present in the delivery

room and using other devices. This, however, is less than fair. The important and socially relevant distinction in the movie is not between inheriting and choosing a father (the distinction that Joyrich sees the text as confounding) but between two principles for determining paternal rights. What the movie asserts with clarity and force is that it is not biology that determines fatherhood but rather the actual shouldering of responsibilities. In championing the caring father against the biological father, the movie neatly resists the conservative appropriation of the new fatherhood.

43. For a particularly vivid instance, see *Tango and Cash* (1989) starring Sylvester Stallone and Kurt Russell.

44. However, Mikey is unharmed by his prenatal drug experience, which he seems to have found pleasurable at the time.

References

Armstrong, Nancy
  1987 *Desire and Domestic Fiction.* Chicago: University of Chicago Press.
Bach, Steven
  1985 *Final Cut.* New York: New American Library.
Baritz, Loren
  1982 *The Good Life: The Meaning of Success for the American Middle Class.*
         New York: Harper and Row.
Bauman, Zygmunt
  1987 *Legislators and Interpreters.* Ithaca, N.Y.: Cornell University Press.
Bell, Daniel
  1976 *The Cultural Contradictions of Capitalism.* New York: Basic Books.
Bellhouse, Mary, and Laurence Litchfield
  1982 Vietnam and Loss of Innocence: An Analysis of the Political Impli-
         cations of the Popular Literature of the Vietnam War. *Journal of
         Popular Culture* 16: 165–167.
Benjamin, Jessica
  1981 *The Oedipal Riddle: Authority, Autonomy, and the New Narcissism.* In
         The Problem of Authority in America, ed. John P. Diggins and Mark
         E. Kahn, 195–224. Philadelphia: Temple University Press.
  1988 *The Bonds of Love: Psychoanalysis, Feminism, and the Problem of Domi-
         nation.* New York: Pantheon Books.
Bensman, Joseph
  1983 *Dollars and Sense: Ethics and the Meaning of Work in Profit and
         Nonprofit Organizations.* New York: Schocken Books.
Bensman, Joseph, and Arthur Vidich
  1971 *The New American Society.* Chicago: Quadrangle Books.
Benveniste, Emile
  1971 *Problems in General Linguistics,* trans. Elizabeth Meek. Coral Gables,
         Fla.: University of Miami Press.
Bernard, Jesse
  1984 The Good Provider Role: Its Rise and Fall. In *Work and Family:
         Changing Roles of Men and Women,* ed. Patricia Voydanoff, 43–60.
         Palo Alto: Mayfield Publishing.

Biskind, Peter
   1983   *Seeing Is Believing: How Hollywood Taught Us to Stop Worrying and Love the Fifties.* New York: Pantheon Books.
   1990   Blockbuster: The Last Crusade. In *Seeing through Movies,* ed. Mark Crispin Miller, 112–149. New York: Pantheon Books.
Biskind, Peter, and Barbara Ehrenreich
   1987   Machismo and Hollywood's Working Class. In *American Media and Mass Culture,* ed. Donald Lazere, 201–215. Berkeley: University of California Press.
Blau, Peter, and Marshall Meyer
   1971   *Bureaucracy in Modern Society.* New York: Random House.
Bordwell, David
   1985   *Narration in the Fiction Film.* Madison: University of Wisconsin Press.
Bordwell, David, Janet Staiger, and Kristin Thompson
   1985   *The Classical Hollywood Cinema: Film Style and Mode of Production to 1960.* New York: Columbia University Press.
Bourdieu, Pierre
   1977   *Outline of a Theory of Practice,* trans. Richard Nice. Cambridge: Cambridge University Press.
   1984   *Distinction: A Social Critique of the Judgement of Taste,* trans. Richard Nice. Cambridge, Mass.: Harvard University Press.
Braverman, Harry
   1974   *Labor and Monopoly Capitalism.* New York: Monthly Review Press.
Byars, Jackie
   1991   *All That Hollywood Allows: Re-Reading Gender in 1950s Melodrama.* Chapel Hill: University of North Carolina Press.
Carroll, John
   1987   *Puritan, Paranoid, Remissive: A Sociology of Modern Culture.* London: Routledge and Kegan Paul.
Carroll, Noël
   1984   Toward a Theory of Film Suspense. *Persistence of Vision* 1: 65–89.
   1988   *Mystifying Movies: Fads and Fallacies in Contemporary Film Theory.* New York: Columbia University Press.
   1989   Back to Basics. In *American Media,* ed. Philip Cook, Douglas Gomery, and Lawrence Lichty, 111–125. Washington, D.C.: Wilson Center Press.
   1990   The Image of Women in Film: A Defense of a Paradigm. *Journal of Aesthetic and Art Criticism* 48 (4): 349–360.
Cawelti, John
   1965   *Apostles of the Self-Made Man: Changing Concepts of Success in America.* Chicago: University of Chicago Press.
Certeau, Michel de
   1984   *The Practice of Everyday Life,* trans. Steven Rendall. Berkeley: University of California Press.

Chodorow, Nancy
　1978　*The Reproduction of Mothering: Psychoanalysis and the Sociology of Gender.* Berkeley: University of California Press.
Connell, R. W.
　1987　*Gender and Power: Society, the Person and Sexual Politics.* Stanford: Stanford University Press.
Conover, Pamela Johnston, and Virginia Gray
　1983　*Feminism and the New Right: Conflict over the American Family.* New York: Praeger.
Cott, Nancy F.
　1977　*The Bonds of Womanhood: "Woman's Sphere" in New England, 1780–1835.* New Haven, Conn.: Yale University Press.
Davidoff, Leonore, and Catherine Hall
　1987　*Family Fortunes: Men and Women of the English Middle Class, 1780–1850.* Chicago: University of Chicago Press.
de Lauretis, Teresa
　1984　*Alice Doesn't: Feminism, Semiotics, Cinema.* Bloomington: Indiana University Press.
Denning, Michael
　1987　*Mechanic Accents: Dime Novels and Working-Class Culture in America.* London: Verso.
　1990　The End of Mass Culture. *International Labor and Working-Class History* 37 (Spring): 4–18.
Doane, Mary Ann
　1982　Film and the Masquerade: Theorising the Female Spectator. *Screen* 23 (3-4): 74–87.
Edwards, Richard
　1979　*Contested Terrain: The Transformation of the Work Place in the Twentieth Century.* New York: Basic Books.
Ehrenreich, Barbara
　1983　*The Hearts of Men: American Dreams and the Flight from Commitment.* Garden City, N.Y.: Anchor Press/Doubleday.
　1987　The New Right Attack on Social Welfare. In *The Mean Season,* by Fred Block, Richard Howard, Barbara Ehrenreich, and Frances Fox Piven, 161–195. New York: Pantheon Books.
　1989　*Fear of Falling: The Inner Life of the Middle Class.* New York: Pantheon Books.
　1990　*The Worst Years of Our Lives: Irreverent Notes from a Decade of Greed.* New York: Pantheon Books.
Ehrenreich, Barbara, and John Ehrenreich
　1977　The Professional-Managerial Class. *Radical America.* Pt. 1, March-April; pt. 2, May-June.
Ehrenreich, Barbara, and Deirdre English
　1979　*For Her Own Good: 150 Years of the Experts' Advice to Women.* New York: Anchor Books.

Ehrensaft, Diane
   1987   *Parenting Together: Men and Women Sharing the Care of Their Children.* New York: Free Press.
Ellis, John
   1981   *Visible Fictions.* London: Routledge and Kegan Paul.
Epstein, Barbara
   1981   *The Politics of Domesticity: Women, Evangelism and Temperance in Nineteenth Century America.* Middletown, Conn.: Wesleyan University Press.
Fiedler, Leslie
   1962   *Love and Death in the American Novel.* Cleveland: Meridian Books.
Fiske, John
   1991   Popular Discrimination. In *Modernity and Mass Culture,* ed. James Naremore and Patrick Brantlinger, 103–116. Bloomington: Indiana University Press.
French, Brandon
   1978   *On the Verge of Revolt: Women in American Films of the Fifties.* New York: Frederick Ungar Publishing Co.
Freud, Sigmund
   1963   On the Mechanism of Paranoia. *General Psychological Theory,* 29–48. New York: Macmillan.
Friedan, Betty
   1963   *The Feminine Mystique.* New York: W. W. Norton.
Gaines, Jane
   1986   White Privilege and Looking Relations. *Cultural Critique* 4: 59–79.
Gamman, Lorraine, and Margaret Marshment, eds.
   1989   *The Female Gaze: Women as Viewers of Popular Culture.* Seattle: Real Comet Press.
Gans, Herbert
   1974   *Popular Culture and High Culture: An Analysis and Evaluation of Taste.* New York: Basic Books.
Gerson, Kathleen
   1985   *Hard Choices: How Women Decide About Work, Career, and Motherhood.* Berkeley: University of California Press.
Gilder, George
   1975   *Sexual Suicide.* New York: Bantam Books.
Ginsburg, Faye
   1989   *Contested Lives: The Abortion Debate in an American Community.* Berkeley: University of California Press.
Gitlin, Todd
   1983   *Inside Prime Time.* New York: Pantheon Books.
   1986   We Build Excitement. In *Watching Television,* ed. Todd Gitlin, 136–161. New York: Pantheon Books.

Gledhill, Christine
    1984   Developments in Feminist Film Criticism. In *Re-Vision: Essays in Feminist Film Criticism,* ed. Mary Ann Doane, Patricia Mellencamp, and Linda Williams, 18–48. Frederick, Md.: University Publications of America.
    1987   ed., *Home Is Where the Heart Is: Studies in Melodrama and the Woman's Film.* London: British Film Institute.
    1988   Pleasurable Negotiations. In *Female Spectators: Looking at Film and Television,* ed. E. Deirdre Pribram, 64–89. London: Verso.

Gramsci, Antonio
    1973   *Letters from Prison.* New York: Harper and Row.
    1985   *Selections from Cultural Writings: 1929–1935.* Cambridge: Harvard University Press.

Hall, Stuart
    1981   Notes on Deconstructing "the Popular." In *People's History and Socialist Theory,* ed. Raphael Samuel, 227–240. London: Routledge and Kegan Paul.
    1982   The Rediscovery of "Ideology": Return of the Repressed in Media Studies. In *Culture, Society and the Media,* ed. Michael Gurevitch et al., 56–90. London: Methuen.

Halle, David
    1984   *America's Working Man.* Chicago: University of Chicago Press.

Harding, Susan
    1981   Family Reform Movements: Recent Feminism and its Opposition. *Feminist Studies* 7 (1): 57–75.

Haskell, Molly
    1987   *From Reverence to Rape: The Treatment of Women in the Movies.* 2d ed. Chicago: University of Chicago Press.

Heath, Stephen
    1981   *Questions of Cinema.* Bloomington: Indiana University Press.

Hertz, Rosanna
    1986   *More Equal than Others: Women and Men in Dual-Career Marriages.* Berkeley: University of California Press.

Himmelstein, Jerome
    1983   The New Right. In *The New Christian Right: Mobilization and Legitimation,* ed. Robert Liebman and Robert Wuthnow, 13–30. New York: Aldine.

Hoffstadter, Richard
    1962   *Anti-Intellectualism in American Life.* New York: Vintage Books.

Hood, Jane
    1983   *Becoming a Two-Job Family.* New York: Praeger.

Horkheimer, Max, and Theodor Adorno
    1972   *The Dialectic of Enlightenment.* New York: Herder and Herder.

Hunt, Pauline
    1980   *Gender and Class Consciousness.* New York: Holmes and Meier.

Jackall, Robert
   1983   Moral Mazes: Bureaucracy and Managerial Work. *Harvard Business Review* 16 (5): 118–130.
   1988   *Moral Mazes: The World of Corporate Managers.* New York: Oxford University Press.
Jameson, Frederic
   1979   Reification and Utopia in Mass Culture. *Social Text* 1: 130–148.
   1981   *The Political Unconscious: Narrative as a Socially Symbolic Act.* Ithaca, N.Y.: Cornell University Press.
Jarvie, I. C.
   1970   *Movies and Society.* New York: Basic Books.
Jeffords, Susan
   1989   *The Remasculinization of America: Gender and the Vietnam War.* Bloomington: Indiana University Press.
Johnson, Richard
   1986–1987   What Is Cultural Studies Anyway? *Social Text* 16: 38–80.
Joyrich, Lynne
   1991   Tube Tied: Reproductive Politics and *Moonlighting.* In *Modernity and Mass Culture,* ed. James Naremore and Patrick Brantlinger, 176–202. Bloomington: Indiana University Press.
Kael, Pauline
   1989   Review of *Working Girl. New Yorker,* 9 January: 80–81.
Kanter, Rosabeth Moss
   1977   *Men and Women of the Corporation.* New York: Basic Books.
Kaplan, E. Ann
   1983   *Women and Film: Both Sides of the Camera.* New York: Methuen.
   1989   Motherhood and Representation: From Postwar Freudian Figurations to Postmodernism. In *Psychoanalysis and Cinema,* ed. E. Ann Kaplan, 128–142. New York: Routledge.
Kohn, Melvin
   1977 [1969]   *Class and Conformity: A Study in Values.* Chicago: University of Chicago Press.
Lasch, Christopher
   1977   *Haven in a Heartless World.* New York: Basic Books.
   1979   *The Culture of Narcissism.* New York: Norton.
   1984   *The Minimal Self: Psychic Survival in Troubled Times.* New York: Norton.
Lash, Scott, and John Urry
   1987   *The End of Organized Capitalism.* Madison: University of Wisconsin Press.
Lears, T.J. Jackson
   1981   *No Place of Grace: Antimodernism and the Transformation of American Culture.* New York: Pantheon Books.
   1983   From Salvation to Self-Realization: Advertising and the Therapeutic Roots of the Consumer Culture. In *The Culture of Consumption,* ed. Richard Fox and T.J. Jackson Lears, 2–38. New York: Pantheon Books.

Levitan, Sar A., and Richard S. Belous
    1981   *What's Happening to the American Family?* Baltimore: Johns Hopkins University Press.

Long, Elizabeth
    1985   *The American Dream and the Popular Novel.* Boston: Routledge and Kegan Paul.

Luker, Kristin
    1984   *Abortion and the Politics of Motherhood.* Berkeley: University of California Press.

Maccoby, Michael
    1976   *The Gamesman: The New Corporate Leaders.* New York: Simon and Schuster.

Macherey, Pierre
    1978   *A Theory of Literary Production,* trans. Geoffrey Wall. London: Routledge and Kegan Paul.

Maio, Kathi
    1991   *Popcorn and Sexual Politics.* Freedom, Calif.: Crossing Press.

Marchand, Roland
    1985   *Advertising the American Dream.* Berkeley: University of California Press.

Maslin, Janet
    1988   Review of *Working Girl. New York Times,* December 21.

Metz, Christian
    1982   *The Imaginary Signifier: Psychoanalysis and the Cinema,* trans. Celia Britton, Annwyl Williams, Ben Brewster, and Alfred Guzzetti. Bloomington: Indiana University Press.

Meyer, Donald
    1987   *Sex and Power: The Rise of Women in America, Russia, Sweden, and Italy.* Middletown, Conn.: Wesleyan University Press.

Meyers, Marvin
    1960   *The Jacksonian Persuasion.* Stanford: Stanford University Press.

Miller, Mark Crispin
    1986   Deride and Conquer. In *Watching Television,* ed. Todd Gitlin, 183–228. New York: Pantheon Books.
    1990   Introduction; End of Story. In *Seeing Through Movies,* ed. Mark Crispin Miller, 7–13; 186–246. New York: Pantheon Books.

Mills, C. Wright
    1950   *The Power Elite.* New York: Oxford University Press.
    1953   *White Collar.* New York: Oxford University Press.

Modleski, Tania
    1984   *Loving with a Vengeance: Mass-produced Fantasies for Women.* New York: Methuen.
    1988a *The Women Who Knew Too Much: Hitchcock and Feminist Theory.* New York: Methuen.
    1988b Three Men and Baby M. *Camera Obscura* 17: 69–81.

Moffatt, Michael
  1990 Do We Really Need "Postmodernism" to Understand *Ferris Bueller's Day Off*? A Comment on Traube. *Cultural Anthropology* 5 (4): 363–373.
Mosse, George
  1985 *Nationalism and Sexuality: Middle-class Morality and Sexual Norms in Modern Europe.* Madison: University of Wisconsin Press.
Mulvey, Laura
  1975 Visual Pleasure and Narrative Cinema. *Screen* 16 (3): 6–18.
  1977 Notes on Sirk and Melodrama. *Movie* 25: 53–56.
  1981 Afterthoughts on "Visual Pleasure and Narrative Cinema" Inspired by *Duel in the Sun* (King Vidor, 1946). *Framework* 15-16-17: 12–15.
  1989 *Visual and Other Pleasures.* Bloomington: Indiana University Press.
Neale, Steve
  1983 Masculinity as Spectacle: Reflections on Men and Mainstream Cinema. *Screen* 24 (6).
Neale, Steve, and Frank Krutnik
  1990 *Popular Film and Television Comedy.* London: Routledge.
Oakley, Ann
  1974 *The Sociology of Housework.* New York: Pantheon Books.
Ohmann, Richard
  1981 Where Did Mass Culture Come From? The Case of Magazines. *Berkshire Review* 16: 85–101.
  1991 History and Literary History: The Case of Mass Culture. In *Modernity and Mass Culture,* ed. James Naremore and Patrick Brantlinger, 24–41. Bloomington: Indiana University Press.
Petchesky, Rosalind Pollack
  1981 Antiabortion, Antifeminism, and the Rise of the New Right. *Feminist Studies* 7 (2): 206–245.
Pfeil, Fred
  1985 Makin' Flippy-Floppy: Postmodernism and the Baby Boom PMC. In *The Year Left,* ed. Mike Davis, 263–295. London: Verso.
Polan, Dana
  1986 *Power and Paranoia: History, Narrative, and the American Cinema, 1940–1950.* New York: Columbia University Press.
Postone, Moishe
  1980 Anti-Semitism and National Socialism. *New German Critique* 19: 97–115.
Radway, Janice
  1984 *Reading the Romance: Women, Patriarchy, and Popular Literature.* Chapel Hill: University of North Carolina Press.
Rieff, Philip
  1966 *The Triumph of the Therapeutic: Uses of Faith After Freud.* New York: Harper and Row.

Riesman, David
  1950 *The Lonely Crowd: A Study of the Changing American Character.* New Haven: Yale University Press.
Rodgers, Daniel
  1978 *The Work Ethic in Industrial America.* Chicago: University of Chicago Press.
Rogin, Michael
  1987 *Ronald Reagan, the Movie and Other Episodes in Political Demonology.* Berkeley: University of California Press.
Rosen, Marjorie
  1973 *Popcorn Venus: Women, Movies and the American Dream.* New York: Coward, McCann and Geoghegan.
Rubey, Dan
  1978 *Star Wars:* Not so Far Away. *Jump Cut* 18: 9–13.
Rubin, Lillian
  1976 *Worlds of Pain: Life in the Working Class Family.* New York: Basic Books.
Russell, Graeme
  1983 *The Changing Role of Fathers.* London: University of Queensland Press.
Ryan, Michael, and Douglas Kellner
  1988 *Camera Politica: The Politics and Ideology of Contemporary Hollywood Film.* Bloomington: Indiana University Press.
Sahlins, Marshall
  1981 *Historical Metaphors and Mythical Realities: Structure in the Early History of the Sandwich Island Kingdom.* Ann Arbor: University of Michigan Press.
  1985 *Islands of History.* Chicago: University of Chicago Press.
Schlafly, Phyllis
  1978 *The Power of the Positive Woman.* New York: Jove.
Segal, Lynne
  1987 *Is the Future Female? Troubled Thoughts on Contemporary Feminism.* New York: Peter Bedrick Books.
  1990 *Slow Motion: Changing Masculinities, Changing Men.* New Brunswick, N.J.: Rutgers University Press.
Sidel, Ruth
  1990 *On Her Own: Growing Up in the Shadow of the American Dream.* New York: Penguin Books.
Sklar, Robert
  1975 *Movie-Made America.* New York: Vintage Books.
Slotkin, Richard
  1973 *Regeneration Through Violence: The Mythology of the American Frontier, 1600–1860.* Middletown, Conn.: Wesleyan University Press.
  1981 Nostalgia and Progress: Theodore Roosevelt's Myth of the Frontier. *American Quarterly* 33: 608–637.

1984 Prologue to a Study of Myth and Genre in American Movies. *Prospects* 9: 407–432.

1986 *The Fatal Environment: The Myth of the Frontier in the Age of Industrialization.* Middletown, Conn.: Wesleyan University Press.

Smith, Paul

1989 Pedagogy and the Popular-Cultural-Commodity-Text. In *Popular Culture: Schooling and Everyday Life,* ed. Henry A. Giroux, Roger I. Simon, et al., 31–46. New York: Bergin and Garvey.

Smith-Rosenberg, Carroll

1985 *Disorderly Conduct: Visions of Gender in Victorian America.* New York: Oxford University Press.

Stacey, Judith

1990 *Brave New Families: Stories of Domestic Upheaval in Late Twentieth Century America.* New York: Basic Books.

Stallybrass, Peter

1989 "Drunk with the Cup of Liberty": Robin Hood, the Carnivalesque, and the Rhetoric of Violence in Early Modern England. In *The Violence of Representation: Literature and the History of Violence,* ed. Nancy Armstrong and Leonard Tennenhouse, 45–76. London: Routledge.

Stearns, Peter

1990 *Be a Man! Males in Modern Society.* New York: Holmes and Meier.

Susman, Warren

1984 [1974] *Culture as History: The Transformation of American Society in the Twentieth Century.* New York: Pantheon Books.

Thompson, Kristin

1988 *Breaking the Glass Armor: Neoformalist Film Analysis.* Princeton, N.J.: Princeton University Press.

Tilly, Louise, and Joan Scott

1978 *Women, Work, and Family.* New York: Holt, Rinehart and Winston.

Trachtenberg, Alan

1982 *The Incorporation of America: Culture and Society in the Gilded Age.* New York: Hill and Wang.

Traube, Elizabeth

1989 Obligations to the Source: Complementarity and Hierarchy in an Eastern Indonesian Society. In *The Attraction of Opposites: Thought and Society in the Dualistic Mode,* ed. David Maybury Lewis and Uri Almagor, 321–344. Ann Arbor: University of Michigan Press.

Walsh, Andrea

1984 *Women's Film and Female Experience, 1940 to 1950.* New York: Praeger.

Weiss, Richard

1969 *The American Myth of Success: From Horatio Alger to Norman Vincent Peale.* New York: Basic Books.

Weitzman, Lenore

1985 *The Divorce Revolution.* New York: Free Press.

Whyte, William
  1956   *The Organization Man.* New York: Simon and Schuster.
Williams, Linda
  1987 [1984]   "Something Else Besides a Mother": *Stella Dallas* and the
        Maternal Melodrama. In *Home Is Where the Heart Is,* ed. C. Gledhill,
        299–325. London: British Film Institute.
  1988   Feminist Film Theory: *Mildren Pierce* and the Second World War. In
        Female Spectators, ed. E. Deirdre Pribram, 12–30. London: Verso.
Willis, Paul
  1981 [1977]   *Learning to Labor: How Working Class Kids Get Working Class
        Jobs.* New York: Columbia University Press.
Wolfe, Alan
  1989   *Whose Keeper? Social Science and Moral Obligation.* Berkeley: Univer-
        sity of California Press.
Wood, Robin
  1986   *Hollywood from Vietnam to Reagan.* New York: Columbia University
        Press.
Wyllie, Irvin
  1954   *The Self-Made Man in America.* New Brunswick: Rutgers University
        Press.

About the Book and Author

IN THIS BOOK Elizabeth Traube argues that over the course of the 1980s, Hollywood participated in a wider move by mainstream political and social forces that attempted to absorb and contain critical cultural currents by rehabilitating images of masculine authority. At the movies we saw parallel constructions of wild, antibureaucratic warrior-heroes and smooth, seemingly rebellious tricksters adapted to the corporate order. We saw the demonization of the independent woman and the complementary formation of the nurturing father as her adversary. The author relates these representations to two cultural narratives of long duration—the American frontier myth and the myth of success, or the American dream, both of which also figured prominently in the rhetorical themes of Reagan-era politics.

Utilizing structuralism, Marxism, feminist object relations psychoanalysis, and neoformalist film criticism, Traube emphasizes specific aspects of cinematic representations of gender and authority to explore the relationships between culture and politics. Unlike other feminist critics of "patriarchal Hollywood," she stresses the multiple, competing versions of masculinity and femininity constructed in Hollywood movies and the different class positions of their primary, intended audiences. Attention to particular forms that cultural narratives assume in changing circumstances gives Traube's film analyses a unique sociohistorical dimension, while her focus on narratives used by political elites as well as by moviemakers reveals significant variations in ideology production in different sites.

Elizabeth G. Traube is professor of anthropology at Wesleyan University. She is the author of *Cosmology and Social Life* (1986).

Index